LAKE CHELAN

JOHN FAHEY

LAKE CHELAN

THE GREATEST LAKE IN THE WORLD

JOHN FAHEY

GRAY DOG PRESS
SPOKANE, WA

Gray Dog Press
Spokane, Washington
www.graydogpress.com
facebook.com/graydogpress
@gdpeditor on twitter

Front Cover Photo: Andy Simonds, used with permission
Back Cover Photo: Danyul B, under Creative Commons License
Cover & Interior Design: Andrew Marcus Corder
Illustration: Alyssa Parkinson

ISBN: 978-1-936178-46-9

Printed in the United States of America

For Amy

And the end of all our exploring will be to arrive where we started
and know the place for the first time.

T.S. Eliot

Preface

Many years ago, never mind how many, I took to the notion that Lake Chelan was the greatest lake in the world. It was a bold theory. The hypothesis proved to be the catalyst for a long series of trips around the planet to prove it.

This book is about those adventures. It is about all lakes in the world, and it is about Lake Chelan in particular. Everyone who has come to love Lake Chelan has their own story about why. This is mine.

Be warned, the tales in this book are equal parts funny, tragic, fascinating, and irreverent. They are not for the faint of heart. The opinions expressed are mine. If they offend anyone, which they undoubtedly will, I apologize in advance.

LAKE CHELAN

JOHN FAHEY

Lake Chelan, the Greatest Lake in the World

"It's the color of the water," I think to myself, "that's what really makes this lake extraordinary."

This seems like a strange thought to have considering I'm about to die. In a few seconds, my short and somewhat frivolous life will reach a dramatic conclusion, right on the glassy smooth water of Lake Chelan. It's not going to be a pretty death either. It's going to be spectacularly gruesome.

I imagine at my funeral they will say, "He died doing something he loved, out water-skiing on his favorite lake."

Actually, my death will be the result of being dragged by a speedboat eighteen inches behind the swim step and getting hacked up by the engine. Getting chopped up by a stainless steel propeller is not an activity that I love.

My older brother is piloting the boat. He is unaware that I'm wrapped up in the ski rope and clinging with one hand to a small cleat. Most of my body is extended out over the water, my face inches from the churning outboard motor.

I'm hollering with great enthusiasm, but no one can hear me over the engine. I can't hold back the force of the ski rope that is stretched out into the lake and pulling me with hundreds of pounds of force. The near end of the rope is tied to the boat, so when my hand slips off, I will fall into the water, spin around, and be dragged right on top of the motor, the blades of which I can actually see.

In the midst of this, I can't help noticing how blue the water is. Between the frothing prop wash and the side spray of the boat, the hull is carving out deep glassy troughs in the lake, and it looks as if we're moving across a glowing backlit sapphire. It seems odd to me that my last thought on this earth is going to be about how beautiful the water is in Lake Chelan.

Maybe that's not such a strange last thought. It might even be a fitting last thought. I have always loved lakes, lakes of every kind. I've enjoyed swimming in them, boating across them, gazing at them, fishing in them, watching storms come up over them. For my entire life, I've been enchanted by lakes and swept up in their romance. Of all those that I have visited, I have loved Lake Chelan the most. I will probably miss this particular lake quite a bit after the speedboat has chopped me into mulch.

I am hardly alone in being so enamored with Lake Chelan. Upon those of us who have been lucky enough to spend some time in the Chelan Valley, the lake has readily cast her alluring spell. She is an incredible ribbon of beautiful glacier melt water that slices fjord-like through the eastern front of the Cascade Mountains in Washington state.

She is a multifaceted gem. In the lower foothills near the lake's end, the shores are framed by orchards and vineyards, a patchwork of green and gold and red that climbs the gentle slopes of the valley. On warm summer days, the lake shimmering, the skies blue, the orchards and vineyards drooping with fruit, the lower Chelan Valley is the very definition of the word bucolic.

Moving northwest up the lake, the shores grow more precipitous. Sheer granite cliffs drop right to the water's edge. At the head of the lake, 9,000-foot pinnacles tower above the evergreens and glaciers loom in the distance, remnants of the same glaciers that formed the lake. These are the glaciers that still feed the lake and, in many ways, define it. They nestle in the jagged spires of the North Cascade Mountains, high rock ramparts so stunning that they are often called the Alps of America.

Lake Chelan sits in a deep glacial-cut valley. The lake is approximately 55 miles long. It is very narrow, just over a mile and a half across at its widest point and less than a half mile at its narrowest point. The surface of the lake, when it is at full pond, is at an elevation of 1,098 feet above sea level. The deepest part of the lake extends a remarkable 388 feet below sea level, making the lake 1,486 feet deep. In the United States, only Crater Lake in Oregon and Lake Tahoe on the border of California and Nevada are deeper.

After making its long run through a narrow valley that is, at times, over 8,000 feet deep, the lake ends as dramatically as it began.

At the town of Chelan, a river exits the basin and then drops some 390 feet in under three miles. When the river is left unchecked, it thunders downward. An average of 13.5 billion gallons of water flows out of the lake each year. Over thousands of years, this torrent has carved a dramatic chasm of near-vertical walls known as the Chelan Gorge. This deep gash in the earth would be a standalone tourist attraction of its own merit if the lake that feeds it didn't garner so much attention.

When held in check by the dam and harnessed for energy, the river supplies a two-mile underground penstock with enough hydraulic power to generate an average of 356,000 megawatt hours of electricity per year. The Chelan River is the culmination of billions of gallons of water siphoned into the atmosphere from the Pacific Ocean each year and then dissipated across an enormous drainage area of 924 square miles.

This tract of wilderness encompasses some of the most scenic territory in the world, and over 92 percent of it is untouched. Dry sage and grasslands nestle around ancient rocks. Deep evergreen forests sweep up rugged hillsides. Mountains tower into the skies. Glaciers groan and creak. Avalanches thunder downward. Rivers roar. Wildfires rage. All of this plays out year after year across a dynamic landscape. Through the heart of this splendor, the lake weaves a long and graceful course. Its regal, blue, coruscating waters capture it all and reflect it back from every angle in never-ending still-life postcards of nature at its best.

I didn't die on that warm July day out on Lake Chelan. A towel saved my life. From the bow of the boat, it got caught by the wind. Everyone turned to watch as it flew backward and then got wrapped around my legs, which were sticking straight up in the air behind the inboard engine case. My brother quickly throttled back the boat. He came to a slow troll just seconds before my last two fingers peeled off the cleat. After catching my breath, I took a few moments to offer him a little constructive criticism with regard to his boat piloting safety skills. Decorum prevents me from quoting that conversation, but suffice it to say that some new and truly distasteful words and phrases were invented that day.

I have spent many happy years since then exploring the Chelan Valley. My love for the lake has continued to grow. At times she has entertained me, vexed me, frustrated me, intrigued me, mystified me, comforted me, romanced me, and twice again attempted to claim my life. To me, she is the sultry, alluring, bohemian maiden of the North Cascades. What I could not have known on that warm, sunny, near-death day on the lake was the extent to which she would eventually affect my life.

Welcome to the Lake

I first heard of Lake Chelan long before I saw it. I was in grade school at the time. The internet was not yet standard in every home, so you couldn't just browse a thousand pictures of any place in the world on demand. Also, not every twelve year old had a camera built into his portable phone. That didn't happen until two years later. As such, we frequently had to rely on the rickety old tool of imagination to visualize a place we'd never seen before.

As more and more friends returned to the suburbs of Seattle with tales of their camping trips at Lake Chelan, I constructed an imaginary photo album. It was filled with pictures of a giant alpine lake, beyond the mythical Cascade Mountains. Sandy beaches were blanketed with bikini-clad girls, all of them my exact age and inexplicably interested in me. Towering pine trees nestled between untamed mountains in a vast wilderness. The woods were teeming with grizzly bears that came to the water's edge every night to drink from the trout-infested waters.

I was already a certified lover of lakes. Growing up, I spent a month of every summer with my great aunt and uncle at a place called Wallace Lake north of Winnipeg in Manitoba, Canada. They made the trip up from Langdon, North Dakota every May and stayed at this lake until September, in a cabin they referred to as "rustic." Rustic meant that we were 70 miles from the nearest paved road, living in a one-bedroom cabin with no electricity, no running water, and no toilets.

If you headed north from Wallace Lake, you would find 2,500 miles of empty tundra, swamps, lakes, and wetlands, all the way to the Arctic Circle. This was smack in the middle of the North American Boreal Forest, where bears carpeted the local dump, and swarms of saber tooth mosquitoes often blacked out the sun.

What we did at Wallace Lake, every day, all day, was play in the lake. We water-skied, fished, swam, skied again, and fished some more. Then we slept, got up, and repeated the routine. It was a young kid's dream, and it was there that I became hooked on lake living.

My aunt and uncle's neighbors had a sign beside their front door that said, "Welcome to the lake." That sign always struck me. No one ever puts a sign up next to their door that says, "Welcome to the suburbs," or "Welcome to the cul-de-sac." "Welcome to the lake," however, is almost motif de rigueur in lake houses. This speaks to me now, as it did when I was a kid. It's a subtle statement that says, You're here now, by a lake, and things are different. It means you can slough off the stress of the working man's world, relax, take a breath and enjoy yourself. It means you're on lake time now, and lake time is fun time.

I loved seeing that sign as a child. I loved Wallace Lake as a child. I never had a dull moment there. My only pangs of homesickness came when I was in the biffy. "Biffy" is a Canadian word for an outhouse that reeks in an abominable way. On some days, it emitted a foul stench that smelled like a dead musk ox rotting in the sun, but usually it smelled much worse.

Nailed to the wall above the toilet paper roll in the biffy was an old postcard of Lake Louise in Banff. The glacier-blue water framed by the snowcapped peaks of the Canadian Rockies reminded me of my own beloved Cascade Mountains. In those fleeting moments, I yearned to leave the forested flatlands of midwestern Canada for the rugged highlands of my home state. I also yearned for indoor plumbing.

When I was thirteen years old, my sister and I concluded our yearly month-long stay at Wallace Lake and flew from Winnipeg to Vancouver, British Columbia. I didn't know it at the time, but this was to be my last summer sojourn to Manitoba. When my mom met us at the airport, she announced a surprise that would change my life. We weren't going home to Seattle. We were going someplace else. She wouldn't say where.

We headed south across the border into Washington state and then turned east onto the North Cascades Highway. We drove past the milky blue-green waters of Diablo Lake and above the crystal blue waters of Ross Lake. We drove through the North Cascades National Park below towering summits with deliciously scary names like Forbidden Peak, Desolation Mountain, Mount Formidable, Mount Challenger, and Mount Torment.

We drove down the eastern front of the mountains, where the sun dropped below the horizon, and the daylight faded.

"Where are we going?"

"If you guess, I'll tell you," my mom said.

Spokane, Montana, Idaho, Sun River—we made a litany of guesses, until we turned south along the Columbia River.

"Are we going to Lake Chelan?"

"Yes," she said. "We've bought a condominium at Lake Chelan."

My imaginary photo album ripped open. Pictures of mountain goats, water-skiing, and girls in bikinis all swam through my head. I couldn't wait to see the lake, but it was dark as we climbed the hill up from the Columbia River Valley and entered the town of Chelan. As we headed up State Route 150 along the north shore toward the town of Manson, all I could see were the slight silhouettes of low mountainsides against a star-filled sky, and the wavy reflection of lights on the black surface of the lake. We pulled into Wapato Point, a resort community, sometime around 11 p.m. After eighteen hours of travel, I fell asleep on an air mattress in the living room of a two-bedroom condo, dreaming about what the lake would look like in the morning.

The Extraordinary Lake Chelan

Lake Chelan is a formidable geological structure. It is the third deepest lake in the United States. It resides in a precipitous depression that, from top to bottom, is almost 4,000 vertical feet deeper than the Grand Canyon.

The lake holds a significant, though not very well known, distinction. About 200 miles away, on the border between Idaho and Oregon, is the gorge of the Snake River known as Hells Canyon. This canyon has long been touted, and is widely recognized, as the deepest gorge in North America. The designation was calculated by using the river bed as the bottom of the gorge and the nearby high peaks of the Seven Devils Mountains in Idaho to arrive at the depth of 7,993 feet.

Hells Canyon is actually not the deepest gorge in North America. This is because Lake Chelan reaches a depth of 388 feet below sea level. Contrast this to the many 8,000-foot peaks that lay in close proximity to her shores and you have a clear argument that the gorge which encumbers Lake Chelan is much deeper. That a good portion of it is full of water should not rob the gorge of this significant title.

It is significant because at the heart of the Chelan Valley, at the essence of the lake, is the fact that, during the course of history, on this narrow swath of land, an extraordinary thing happened: An awesome force of nature and a confluence of events combined to create one of North America's most amazing natural wonders. It is from this collision that the lake came into existence, and the impact on the landscape, the geology, the geography, and even the weather has been profound.

The lake, simply because it is there, has spawned myths and legends and has been the impetus of countless true stories of human existence. Some of these are exquisite and exciting tales of drama. Others are rather banal, but all have converged to alter the course of people's lives just as the glaciers and the lake so dramatically altered the surface of the earth over thousands of years.

My own love affair with the lake began early on that July morning when I awoke and sprang from my sleeping bag to go have a look. Lake Chelan was all I had hoped it would be. The clear blue waters danced in the early morning rays. A blazing red sunrise painted the plateau on the other side of the Columbia River. The peaks of Stormy Mountain, still holding a late-season snowcap, radiated with a soft pink glow.

For a young kid, Wapato Point was a dream come true, with endless lawns and long sandy beaches. I jumped in the water at six in the morning and only came out of it hours later, when my dad took us on a boat cruise. Moving up the lake, my eyes grew wider in amazement with each passing mile.

I didn't know it at the time, but this was the first day of what would become, for me, an obsession. Over the years, I tried to explore every corner of the lake. I plunged deep into the mountains where the lake begins, among the many glaciers high in the North Cascades. I climbed to the summits of the massive peaks that tower above it. I explored its terminus where the Chelan River exits the deep gorge to blend with the tea colored waters of the Columbia River as it makes its way to the ocean. I wandered up tributaries and climbed along ridge tops. I soared on the winds above the lake, and waded through the deep snow that feeds her.

I probed, further still, into the hills that embrace the valley, and I began to get the sense that there was something epic about this particular little point on the map. I became so curious that I started asking questions and doing research about the many facets of the lake. I talked to anyone who knew anything and was willing to share his or her time with me.

At first, my curiosity centered on the geology of the region, but it soon began to drift into the flora, the fauna, and the human history of the lake as well. I began scribbling notes and collecting articles and clippings.

My parents traded in their condominium at Wapato Point for a waterfront home on the north shore in the Mill Bay area. When they started accumulating grandchildren at an alarming rate, they bought an adjacent old farmhouse with a barn on an acre of land to accommodate the spillover. Suddenly, I had a place to stay in Chelan whenever I could find the time. I was increasingly finding the time.

I went away to college. After a few years there, I met a clever, witty woman named Amy. She had long dark hair and beautiful, green, cartoonishly big eyes that had earned her the title of "Most Provocative Peepers" in her high school yearbook. I liked her immediately.

We dated and eventually returned from college together. After a few years, we got married. Fortunately, she shared my enthusiasm for "all things Chelan." We lived in Seattle, but we were spending so much time over at the lake that eventually we decided to buy a piece of property there. Three years later, we had purchased seven pieces of property and owned five homes on the lake. My notes are unclear as to exactly how that happened. We began operating a vacation rental business in Chelan. The lake had become a very big part of our lives.

Throughout this process of crazy acquisitions and home building, we ended up driving back and forth from Seattle to Chelan dozens of times, year round. We often lived there for months at a time. My appetite for knowledge about the lake and its history only grew stronger.

I talked to people all over the valley. I spoke with locals and transplants. I spoke with apple farmers, winery owners, small business owners, contractors, migrant farm workers, and developers. I spoke with geologists, hydrologists, and glaciologists. I spoke with a cultural anthropologist. I spoke with local bartenders, state wildlife agents, local politicians, mountain guides, and park rangers. I spoke with mountain goat experts, grizzly bear experts, and an expert on bats. I sent emails to one person who claimed to be a cryptozoologist, but actually turned out to be just a raving nut job.

I'm not sure what I was hoping to find out. I didn't know why it was consuming me so much, or where it would lead me. I just knew I was perpetually interested, and everything I learned made the lake seem more fascinating.

I had one particular notebook that was full of fascinating tidbits about the lake. I started to carry it around religiously like some kind of sacred text. One day, I looked at it, and the thought occurred to me, "I should write a book."

I didn't want to write a history book. It seemed there were plenty of those. I didn't want to write a guidebook either. Instead I wanted to examine the lake from top to bottom. I wanted to somehow encapsulate exactly what the lake is and how it came to be. I wanted to tell the stories of the people who had lived at the lake over the ages and of those who still live there today. I wanted to delve into the hidden corners of the valley and learn the lake's secrets. I wanted to reflect on how the area came to affect me so much and explore why a multitude of other people, like me, were so totally enthralled by Lake Chelan.

I also wanted to give the impression that there was a legitimate reason for carrying around the notebook and asking everybody questions. My friends and family were starting to look at me like I was some kind of weirdo. Writing a book seemed like the perfect reason.

Most of all, I hoped to somehow put the lake into a context of other lakes around the globe and see if I would find what I was already starting to believe. I wanted to confirm my suspicion that this long, thin, freshwater fjord, buried in the wild and remote mountains of north central Washington state, might be one of the most extraordinary places on the planet. I wanted to prove that Lake Chelan was, in fact, The Greatest Lake in the World.

I looked at my precious notebook, and I thought about what such a book would be like. I even thought about calling the book *The Notebook*, but it turns out that title was already taken. I wasn't too disappointed, because I really wanted a name that would better communicate the idea that Lake Chelan was the greatest lake in the world. To that end, I was drawing a blank. I hoped at some time in the future I would find some inspiration and eventually concoct a title that would convey the notion.

I knew that in order to be successful in my endeavor, I would have to do four things. First, I would have to establish a list of criteria that would determine what constituted the greatest lake in the world. Second, I would have to come up with a list of lakes that seemed to embody these criteria. Third, I would have to narrow that list down to the top 10 or 12 contenders. Finally, I would have to go out and visit those lakes and see how they measured up against each other and ultimately against Lake Chelan.

I turned to a blank page in my notebook, and I wrote down this four-step process. It was at that moment that my adventure truly began. I made a little note in the margin that said, "Lake Project/Day One." I was now officially a little less weird or a little more weird, depending on how you looked at it.

Lake Project

Day 1

I announced my intention to Amy. I have to credit her with the incredible poker face she maintained. I imagine her mind was swimming with images of the fame and wealth that would come from writing a book with such obvious mass-market appeal. She was likely entertaining visions of walking down the red carpet in Hollywood at the premiere of the blockbuster movie that was sure to arise from this book. Still she managed to maintain an almost unreadable blank stare. It was as if I had just told her I was going to build a 100-foot-tall pyramid out of tuna fish salad. She shook her head slightly. Perhaps there was the slightest, almost imperceptible smirk on her face as she left the room without a word. It may have just been a shadow.

I should mention that I don't have the best track record when it comes to projects. On the scrap heap of my past endeavors are: three full-length unpublished novels, a failed line of sports clothing, a pet accessory called the Pooper Trooper, two board games, and three incomplete internet companies. I could write a book about the projects I have started and failed to complete, except I would probably never finish that book.

Despite a lukewarm reception by Amy, I began to write, hoping to capture what I felt were the high points and the subtle nuances that make Lake Chelan such a fascinating place. I had no idea of the extent of effort involved in what I was about to undertake. As it turned out, my research would lead me through swamps, up mountains, deep into canyons, over deserts, through third world countries and across four continents. I would come face to face with bears, fight off a nasty tropical waterborne illness, and confront one of the most horrific trials that any man could ever be forced to undergo (hint:

it involved leeches). Still I proceeded, undaunted, and driven ever forward by the powerful and significant fact that...well...I really didn't have anything else to do.

Finally, in the most hair-raising part of this entire strange (and some might say pointless) journey, I took my wealth of knowledge (some might say pointless knowledge) to the very top of the lake (by "some," I'm referring to Amy). I traveled to the farthest reaches of the entire Chelan drainage system along the crown of the mighty Cascade Range.

Only after all of that did I feel it was finished. Only then could I render with authority the answer to the central question that had motivated all of my efforts: Was Lake Chelan the greatest lake in the world?

When I was finally done, I submitted the book. Then I sat back and waited for Hollywood to contact me.

They would call.

Any minute.

I was sure of it.

What Makes a Lake Great?

Although the majority of my projects end in a quick and obscure death, each of them starts with a tremendous amount of effort and enthusiasm. That's why, within a few days, I had accumulated a vast amount of information about the lakes of the world. I had put together a long list of potential contenders for the title of The Greatest Lake. I had been able to eliminate a few but not many. It was obvious I would never be able to visit every lake on my list, and I would need some clever approach to facilitate reaching a conclusion. It was time to get serious and start whittling down the list. The first step was the creation of some ground rules.

If one were searching for the greatest lake in the world, a natural place to start might be in the Great Lakes. This collective chain of veritable freshwater oceans is a celebrated landmark of North America. The lakes are beloved by Americans and Canadians across the continent, even those who don't live anywhere near them.

The Great Lakes are full of romance. Gordon Lightfoot captured the spirit of the lakes with his song, "The Wreck of the Edmund Fitzgerald." He sang:

> *Lake Huron Rolls, Superior sings*
> *In the rooms of her ice-water mansion.*
> *Old Michigan steams like a young man's dreams;*
> *The islands and bays are for sportsmen.*

These lyrics always played through my mind growing up. They seemed to be the perfect poetry for encapsulating the romance of the Great Lakes. The lakes were, to me, extraordinary and somewhat mythic bodies of water. I finally got to see them when I took a hiatus from college and moved to Chicago. I remember standing on the shores of Lake Michigan for the first time and watching the waves roll in. I was spellbound by the immensity of the water.

Might the Great Lakes contain the greatest lake in the world? If so, which one? Does having a beautiful city like Chicago—brimming with culture, fun, professional sports teams, and nightlife—on the shores of a lake add to the potential greatness of the lake itself? If so, would I have to consider all the other metropolitan centers on each of the Great Lakes in both the United States and Canada? What about the Great Lakes from a working man's perspective? Should the massive flow of commerce that ships through these waters be a consideration?

What about Lake Champlain, or the Finger Lakes in New York? There was a time when a push was made to include Lake Champlain as one of the Great Lakes. Champlain is a huge narrow lake, 110 miles long. Situated largely in Adirondack Park, it has miles of undeveloped shoreline, and a backdrop of the Adirondack High Peaks and the Green Mountains of Vermont. These gorgeous mountains, many over 4,000 feet high, certainly add some cachet to the lake, particularly when the fabled fall leaves of new England are painting the Vermont hillsides.

The Finger Lakes, to the west, are thought by many to be the most enchanting in the world. According to the official New York state tourist website, "The Finger Lakes Region has miles of unspoiled forests snuggled along steep, grapevine-covered hillsides. Cold streams race through deep gorges bursting into sunshine at thundering waterfalls."

What about Squam Lake in New Hampshire? This became famous because it was the site for the filming of the movie *On Golden Pond*. To many, this lake, with its smooth rock islands, inlets, and deep-forested hillsides, was the epitome of the traditional American country lake.

These were just some of the lakes in North America. There were six other continents to consider. After reading, researching, and asking a lot of questions, I made a preliminary list of lakes. The list was huge, but I felt the project was off to a good start.

A Brief History of Lake Chelan

At the end of the nineteenth century, settlers were heading to the Chelan Valley en masse. One of the first women of European decent to live in the valley was Mrs. Ben F Smith. She described her experience of coming to the valley at a banquet in 1905:

> My first view of Lake Chelan was on one July evening in 1888 from the top of the hill across the Columbia River, opposite what is now called Chelan Landing. We had driven overland in a covered wagon from Ritzville, the nearest railroad town, a distance of 126 miles, crossing a dreary waste of sage-brush country. But here at the top of the hill we had a fine camping ground, and as I looked across to this side and beheld this beautiful lake surrounded by hills and valleys, it looked like an oasis in the desert, and I was eager for a nearer view.[1]

What she saw nestled into the eastern front of the Cascades is as glorious a sight today as it was back then. When the mountains behind are covered in snow, the vista gains an added measure of pure spectacle. It is an image worthy of being framed and displayed. What makes the picture more compelling is that it represents only a fraction of the lake, and, to most observers, perhaps not even the most scenic part of the lake.

People have marveled at the lake since prehistoric times. The Native Americans are known to have lived, at least during winter camps, for thousands of years near the outlet of the lake and along the north shore. They used the lake as a trade route, paddling all the way uplake and then crossing the mountains to reach the tribes on the western side of the mountains.

The name Chelan comes from a word in the Inland Salish Native American dialect and means "deep water." Fur trader Alexander Ross first recorded this in his journal, using the spelling "Tsillian" and referring to the natives of the area as the Tsill-anes.[2]

Ross was very likely the first non-native to hear of the lake. He passed through the area in 1811 and met the indigenous people of the region who he described as "friendly, intelligent, and communicative." Although he didn't go up and see the lake, he traveled by the mouth of the Chelan River and was told by the Native Americans about a large body of water that gave rise to the river just a short way up into the mountains. His journal represents the first European record of Lake Chelan.

Some of the first Europeans to settle near the lake were William Sanders and Henry Domke. They encountered the lake in 1886, while coming over the mountains from the Methow Valley to the north. Their first visit was an epic adventure.

When they arrived at the water's edge, they found the rugged steep shoreline impassable. The terrain was so hard to navigate that the journey met with tragedy above a small creek, where their packhorse stumbled and fell to his death. (The horse was named Prince, and the creek now bears that name as well.)

Without a packhorse, Sanders and Domke were forced to improvise in order to get home. At another creek, they found a cedar log and, using a hatchet, they constructed a makeshift canoe. (This second creek was given the name Canoe Creek). They used the impromptu vessel to navigate all the way down to the end of the lake.

The valley so captivated them that they decided to move there and thus became the two original homesteaders. Other settlers arrived soon after with names like Navarre, Knapp, Woodin, and Nichols, names lent to local streets, mountains, hills, coulees and roads in the area.

During the late 1880s, word spread about the beauty of Lake Chelan, and enterprising emigrants began moving up and into the lake valley. The influx of people in Chelan and the surrounding region created some friction and hostility with the original inhabitants. Throughout Washington state, and particularly in the Columbia Plateau, several military engagements and all-out battles took place as the Native Americans sought to protect their lands against an onslaught of settlers from the east.

In an effort to ease the hostilities, the tribes of the inland Columbia region, under the accepted leadership of Chief Moses, negotiated for, and received claim to, a reservation that stretched from the north shore of Lake Chelan all the way to the Canadian border. Pressure from settlers at the end of the nineteenth century induced the government to abrogate the treaties that established this reservation and, instead, grant the Native Americans 640-acre homesteads if they filed claims to land. Many did along the north shore of the lake. They were not at first allowed to sell this land, but further pressure from the homesteaders coerced the revocation of that law. Consequently, all of the land around the lower lake became available to the incoming pioneers.

In 1892, the first train from the east arrived in Wenatchee, notably increasing the inflow of people to the region. In the late 1800s, even tourism had become an ongoing and viable business on the lake. Just after the turn of the century, steam ships were taking visitors deep into the Cascade Mountains, and grand hotels were accommodating them. The secret of Lake Chelan was out, and the years after the turn of the century would see dramatic settlement accompanied by timber, mining, and agricultural pursuits throughout the valley.

To increase tourism, the bureau of statistics and immigration for the state produced a book called *The Beauties of the State of Washington.* Then-Deputy Commissioner Harry F. Giles wrote a guide to the scenic wonders of the state in prose that seems relinquished to a bygone age. His descriptions ring just as true today as they did decades ago.

> Chelan, 'Beautiful Water,' is the name of one of the grandest sheets of fresh water reposing upon the bosom of the American continent. It is one of a number of beautiful lakes found throughout the highlands in the vicinity of the upper Columbia, but on account of its thrilling beauty and easy approach has become one of the favorite resorts for the entire northwest.
>
> Surpassing the canyons of the Yosemite, the Yellowstone, the Columbia, and the Colorado, the total depth of the Chelan canyon reaches in places nearly 8,000 feet, while its waters occasionally cover a bottom 1,700 feet [sic] below the surface. Throughout the 55 mile ride from Chelan to Stehekin, views are

> observed that for immensity, sublimity and color blending are unexcelled. Right into the heart of the Cascades the traveler is drawn, while the solemnity and general impressiveness of the whole increases, as he is gradually brought in closer intimacy with divine nature.[3]

Vast improvements in the regional transportation infrastructure began to arise as well. In 1900, the first Cascade tunnel was completed, allowing railroads to move year round through Stevens Pass. By 1922, Blewett Pass was built, connecting Wenatchee to Snoqualmie pass. The final section of Highway 2 was completed in 1931 between Everett and Cashmere over Stevens Pass. Highway 10 over Snoqualmie Pass was paved in 1934, and the new Interstate 90 opened to replace it in 1969.

During the post-war boom, cars became commonplace in American households. This, combined with a host of new roads, made Lake Chelan a destination for travelers from the more densely populated western side of the state. Resorts flourished along the shoreline. Summer homes were built. Campgrounds were crowded. A love and appreciation for the lake was taking strong root throughout the Pacific Northwest.

Lake Project

Day 12

My notebook was clogged up with a crushing amount of lakes, all with their various charms and claims to fame; it seemed that establishing the criteria would be a difficult and somewhat delicate task. In the end, I had to revert to the root of the project. In defining the greatest lake in the world, I needed to assess what it was, exactly, that I was trying to encapsulate when I began this project. I had to think back to my earliest experiences with lakes.

I harkened back to my days in Wallace Lake, in the wilderness of midwestern Canada. Manitoba, Canada is similar to Minnesota in its topography but differs from Minnesota in that it is almost three times as large and stretches all the way north to the polar bear covered shores of Hudson Bay. Where Minnesota is said to be the land of 10,000 lakes, Manitoba has over 110,000 lakes. Almost 16 percent of Manitoba is covered by freshwater lakes. One of these is Lake Winnipeg, which is the tenth largest lake in the world by surface area.

Wallace Lake, the lake of my childhood summers, was a small lake by Manitoba standards, but for me it was the perfect playground. I couldn't wait to go back each summer. There was an incredible sense of "lake community" in this remote spot.

My aunt and uncle had a small floating dock with an outboard motor on it. They called it "The Merry Maker." They let me and the other kids take it around the lake by ourselves. On one such outing, I took Shelly Sorrell out, ostensibly to go fishing. She was two years older than me. The fishing was a ruse. I was going to kiss my first girl.

We smuggled two sleeping bags onto the boat. We then drove it to a remote hidden bay. We anchored the dock and zipped the two sleeping bags together, and climbed inside.

I can't say that I had practiced kissing melons, or anything like that, but I had given a tremendous amount of thought to what would be my first kiss, and now that moment was upon me. Shelly had already consented. It was our reason for piloting the dock out to the bay. I was intent on making it a memorable performance. Since we were lying down, I was thinking something along the lines of Burt Lancaster kissing Deborah Kerr on the beach in *From Here to Eternity*. Shelly would likely dedicate pages of her diary to this first kiss. Perhaps she would tell stories about it to her grandchildren.

The lake was smooth, with just the slightest ripples blurring the otherwise unblemished reflection of evergreens on the water. There was a pair of loons swimming near the shore. It was romance at its finest. Inside the sleeping bags, I licked my lips, lowered the lids of my eyes halfway, and in a swift but smooth motion, I rolled over to kiss Shelly, just like Burt Lancaster. Her eyes were now just six inches from mine, and I'll never forget the look of intensity and excitement in them.

They were intense and excited because, as I rolled over to kiss her, I sort of kept on rolling. I had made a critical miscalculation—my right leg had landed slightly over the edge of the dock. Inertia and gravity were not to be my friends on that day.

I ended up dangling completely over the edge of the dock, as if I was in a hammock. My body was halfway in the lake. The motion paused for a second, and I was suspended in a strange Newtonian battle as the properties of physics played against each other: Shelly's weight and the friction of the sleeping bag fabric on the dock against my mass and momentum.

I let out a quick silent prayer to the fates and the stars and everything that was holy to not drag Shelly into the lake with me. Apparently the fates and the stars and everything that was holy were all gathered in a room watching this unfold on the big screen TV and having themselves a good old laugh. We both entered the water with a tremendous splash.

If this sounds like an amusing tale, I can assure you that, at the time, it was not. Two people, who had moments before shared the tender feeling of genuine young romance, were now locked in an epic life-or-death struggle to free themselves from a waterlogged sleeping bag that was sinking. I can honestly say that I was battling mostly with the sleeping bag, but Shelly was rending flesh and hair from my body. Houdini might have made some incredible escapes from confinements while underwater, but I would submit that he never attempted that feat while affixed to a hysterical drowning fourteen-year-old girl. The fact that I'm alive today is a triumph of the human will to survive.

To our great fortune, we were only in about three and a half feet of water. Once we had a little leverage from the sandy bottom, we were able to extract ourselves and explode to the surface gasping for air.

I was now pretty sure Shelly would be telling her grandkids about this kiss, but not in the manner I had originally contemplated. We pulled ourselves from the lake and sat there on the dock for a full 10 minutes, catching our breath. I got back in the lake and rescued the two sleeping bags that now weighed about 40 pounds each. I started the engine, and we drove back home in near silence.

Lakes are powerful things. When kids grow up around lakes, those experiences affect their lives forever, for better or worse. As it turns out, my encounter with Shelly would pretty much set the stage for most of my attempts at being suave and debonair in the ensuing years. Although the majority of my efforts didn't end in life-threatening struggles or injury, on more times than I care to recall they seemed to come to an overwhelmingly comic conclusion.

Once, back when I was a starving student working in Chicago, I met a beautiful young lady in a bar near the shores of Lake Michigan. She had just stepped in for a beer, following an afternoon of shopping on the Magnificent Mile. I beguiled her for an hour with a charming array of outright lies and deceptions, and she finally consented to give me her phone number. I grabbed a felt-tip pen from the nearby darts scoreboard and tried to write her number on my arm, but the pen had gone dry.

Ever the quick thinker, I touched the tip of the pen to my tongue to dampen it, whereupon a half teaspoon of bitter tasting black ink exploded into my mouth. I turned to a garbage bag sitting by the wall and spit out the ink.

At this point, time went into slow motion. As the ink fell downward, I realized it wasn't a garbage bag, but the shopping bag of the girl I was pursuing. On top of the pile of new clothes inside the bag was a white cashmere sweater that probably cost more than my two-week paycheck. When the ink splashed down, the sweater owner, my would-be date, actually screamed. In an instant, her formerly perfect white sweater had transformed into what looked like the black and white hide of a Holstein cow.

I looked up slowly and gave her a weak smile, my lips black, my teeth covered in ink.

"I'm so sorry," I said.

She grabbed the bag and stormed out of the bar without a word. In the commotion, she even forgot to give me her phone number.

This was one of many similar events that defined my romantic travails. Despite years of concerted effort, I fear I never developed into what one might consider a smooth operator. I trace it all back to that first mishap in a remote bay in Wallace Lake.

I did get around to kissing Shelly Sorrel, three days after our near fatal drowning. My kissing skills were nothing shy of pure genius, if I do say so myself. I kissed her the following day, and the day after that too. My aunt and uncle must have thought we were terrible at fishing, since we were constantly returning without any fish.

As I sat at my desk with my notebook open, reminiscing about the lake of my youth, I realized that this was what I was after. This was some of the romance I was trying to quantify when considering the quintessential lake. The perfect lake had to be a place where kids could play in the woods, wander through the orchards, splash in the shallow water near the shore, catch creel after creel of fish, and sneak away to steal a first kiss. The lake had to be about lemonade and s'mores, hot dogs and water-skiing, ghost stories and all the things that make summer so fun for kids.

The lake also had to be about grand sweeping vistas, gathering storms and incredible sunsets, skinny dipping and cruising in a boat with a cooler full of beer, and all of the things that make summer so fun for adults. It's hard to define this kind of outdoor being-by-the-water feeling that a great summer lake can engender, but all of us know what it is on an almost instinctual level. It's as if our ancestors have always taken a break from the hot, dirty, exhausting toils of hunting and gathering to cool down, relax, and enjoy the fruits of their efforts at the nearest lake. It is an ancient and time-honored tradition.

I began scribbling notes to try and define the ultimate lake experience. I focused on a small but significant detail. Seared in my memory was the postcard of Lake Louise in the Canadian Rockies that was nailed to the wall in the biffy at Wallace Lake. This tiny little trinket was important because, even though I loved Wallace Lake, and as beautiful as the area was, I would always be reminded of the fact that it was, for me, missing a critical component. It was not a mountain lake. A lake without mountains is a wonderful entrée; but a lake with stately mountains, rushing rivers and waterfalls is like a fantastic meal with a delicious dessert thrown in for free.

The mountains are there to complement the lake. Their reflections are the fancy clothes that the lake wears. They allow the person sitting on the dock to gaze up and dream of alpine adventures right on the horizon, waiting to be undertaken. There is also nothing more heavenly than returning from an epic journey into the mountains to collapse into the cool waters of a lake. It's not uncommon to sit on the lakeshore and look up at the mountains dreaming of being up there. It's also a frequent occurrence to stand up in the mountains, looking below at the lake, and dream of being down there. An alpine lake, and the mountains that surround it, are like the yin and yang, a perfect complement to each other.

There are extraordinary lakes all throughout the midwest of Canada and the United States, but without the backdrop of a mountain range to frame them, I knew I would have to eliminate them from the contest. This was difficult to do, but someone had to make these tough choices, and it had fallen to me.

Other choices were far more sweeping and yet far easier to make. I felt in the core of my being that a lake could not be the greatest lake in the world if it had any of the following:

Crocodiles
Alligators
Deadly, venomous water snakes

Nothing can screw up a relaxing day at the lake as quickly or as thoroughly as being bitten by:

Crocodiles
Alligators
Deadly, venomous water snakes

This is not to say that having any of these reptiles in the vicinity destroys a lake. On the contrary, there are tons of beautiful and fun lakes that have these critters in residence. Generally, they don't bother anyone. I could best sum up my thoughts on this matter by using the following analogy: A beautiful woman can still be a beautiful woman if she has bad teeth. She just probably won't win the Miss Universe Contest. She might still be voted Miss Scotland, and that's pretty good.

To the list of disqualifiers, I also added leeches and any abundance of freshwater eels. I'm sure both are a valuable part of the ecosystems in which they dwell, but they lend a creepiness factor to any body of water that cannot be overlooked. A fun, slightly risqué late night of skinny dipping with a pretty girl can take a crucial turn for the worse when a disgusting slimy eel suddenly decides to have a territorial battle with your nether regions. Suffice it to say, the romance is rather abruptly lost.

These delimiters proved very helpful, because they removed from the contest two entire continents. Australia is not home to very many year-round lakes, mostly due to a lack of historical glacier activity there. Since it is also home to the highest amount of deadly snakes in the world and copious amounts of crocodiles, it was out. Africa, also teaming with snakes and crocodiles, was out. Antarctica, although devoid of snakes and crocodiles, was also out. It was now down to North America, South America, Europe, and Asia (also, I hadn't yet ruled out New Zealand). What's more, my search was limited to the mountainous regions of the continents. Now I was making progress.

There were some other characteristics that a valid contender lake would have to have. The greatest lake in the world needed to have relatively clear water. It would also, during the summer, have to be warm enough for swimming, water-skiing and general aquatic frolicking and merriment.

Finally, the lake would have to be beautiful. It didn't have to be the most beautiful lake in the world—that was not the title I was trying to bestow. Being beautiful was just one of many criteria, albeit an important one. Since no lake that wasn't extremely beautiful would be considered by anyone to be the greatest lake in the world, it seemed like a good category to start with when attempting to further define the playing field. I started asking for opinions from people and doing research about what were the most beautiful lakes in the world.

From these inquiries I received a wealth of valuable information. I was beginning to refine my list of competitors. At this point, the list was still two pages long. I realized that I would have to set up additional criteria as my research progressed.

I knew of one lake that was not going to get filtered off the list. Everyone who had visited there seemed to love it. This was a lake that was very similar to Lake Chelan, but it was an ocean away. It seemed like as good a place as any to start my exploration. I decided our first trip would be to Italy to visit Lake Como.

Chelan Falls

3 miles east of the lake

When I first met Amy in college, I quickly found out she was a package deal. She had recently adopted a golden Labrador puppy. His name was Otis.

He was our constant companion as we wandered around the mountains and rivers of Washington, Idaho, and Montana. Otis fancied himself as a wild mountain dog. He could scale steep cliffs, and, on occasion, even trees. Although Labradors take to the water like ducks, Otis had a traumatic experience falling into a creek as a puppy. The result was that he was briefly afraid of water.

It was only through rigorous occupational therapy, conducted by me in a muddy backwater of the Snake River, that I was able to teach him how to swim. This involved many days of picking him up, wading him out into the water and then letting him swim, assisted at first, back to the shore where he would receive a treat. After a week, he had been rehabilitated to full-fledged water dog. He couldn't get enough of lakes, rivers, and streams.

If this makes Otis sound like a bit of a wimp, I can vouch that he was not. He once saved us, unassisted, from a pair of hostile moose in the Idaho panhandle. If you've never seen a moose up close, you might be surprised. They look bigger than the average horse. Also they're mean and aggressive. In Alaska, more people are injured by moose attacks than by bears. I was not pleased when we stumbled across two of them on the trail. They were not planning to give way and appeared ready to charge.

Otis was a superhero. Sixty-five pounds of blurry blond fur and snarling teeth flashed into action, tearing the leash from my hands, and charging the moose, yapping with the sound of a fierce wolf pack. Both moose had an immediate change of heart and trotted off into the woods. I'm not advocating that dogs should ever harass wildlife, but in this incident, I was grateful that he was there. Taking on 4,000 combined pounds of stubborn moose without hesitation was one of the many things about Otis that impressed me. He may very well have saved us from serious injury that day.

Whether hiking through mountains, swimming in lakes, or jumping in rivers, Otis was never happier than when he was out in the wilderness. One of the wild places he was most fond of was Lake Chelan. He was born in Lewiston, Idaho and raised in the rolling hills of the Palouse country. I think the dry grasslands of the lower Chelan Valley always spoke to him. After college, when we would drive across the state from our home in Seattle, he would slowly get more excited as we crossed through the Cascades and headed up the Columbia River toward Chelan. He was literally whining and howling when the lake came into sight. It was as endearing as it was annoying.

Throughout all of the Chelan area, the place Otis loved the most was the park in Chelan Falls at the confluence of the Chelan and Columbia Rivers. This large public utility district park is a dog's paradise. Amy and I would head down there with coffee in hand almost every morning and give Otis free rein. He was ecstatic, dashing into the river, disappearing into the tall grass, throwing sticks with his own mouth and then chasing after them. During our frequent trips, we came to love this park as well. This is where Lake Chelan comes to its end. This is where water that has pooled in the lake basin for an average of ten years completes its final fantastic run 390 feet down into the Columbia Valley. This is where billions of gallons of water a year joins up with the Columbia River and continues its journey back to the Pacific Ocean. The confluence of the two rivers is an extraordinary place.

Only in this last stretch of brilliant blue water can you experience the full measure of the Chelan River year round. For the last quarter mile, all of the water has exited the penstock, moved through the turbines of the power generator, and blended with any water escaping over the dam. The lower Chelan River is a beautiful sweep of undulating current. Watching the tendrils of glacier blue runoff mix into the more turbid water of the Columbia River is mesmerizing.

The Columbia River, which takes in all of this water, is an amazing force of nature. With an average of 4,700 cubic meters per second of flowing water, it is, by volume, the largest river flowing into the Pacific Ocean from North America. On the continent, the Mississippi River is the largest, but on rare years, the water volume flowing down the Columbia River can actually exceed that of the Mississippi.

From its start to the Pacific Ocean, the Columbia River flows 1,232 miles, and drains 258,000 square miles. This is an area roughly the size of France. It produces more hydroelectric power than any other river in North America. If you include its tributaries, it produces more hydroelectric power than any other single drainage system in the world. Because of the unique topography in the area that it drains, the Columbia is the largest river in the world that has no delta.

By the time it reaches the ocean, the water mixed in the Columbia River has traveled from some of the most impressive places on the continent. Some of that water has boiled near the magma chambers beneath the huge caldera of Yellowstone National Park and flung upward as scalding geysers. Some of it has tumbled down the mighty flanks of the Rocky Mountains in places like Mt. Robson and Glacier National Park. It has rested in the vast waters of Flathead Lake in Montana, the largest freshwater lake west of the Mississippi. It has seeped down off the flanks of numerous active volcanoes, one of them the highest volcano in the lower 48 states, another the deadliest volcano in all of North America.

It has melted down from world-class ski areas like Sun Valley and Jackson Hole. It has tumbled over the second highest free-falling waterfall in the United States and flowed through the two deepest gorges in North America. It has gouged its way through one of the largest flood basalt structures ever to appear on the planet. From British Columbia, Montana, Wyoming, Idaho, Utah, Nevada, Oregon, and Washington, all of this water has used the Columbia River as a superhighway on its return to the Pacific.

A significant portion of this water, of course, has also rested in the third deepest lake in the United States. From there, it flows out to enter the Columbia River at Chelan Falls.

In the summer, boats congregate at the mouth of the Chelan River as sand and gravel bars appear and disappear. The water is warmed by the sun as it sits in Lake Chelan and stays warm as it flows into the Columbia River. There aren't that many places in the world where a glacier-melt river is warm enough for swimming. This is one of those places. Kids splash around in the water. Footballs fly. Beer cans crack and hiss. Simply put, this is a good old-fashioned swimming hole. It frequently feels like a party, an appropriate celebration for this unique spot and the incredible natural wonder that spawned it.

That natural wonder is the 952 square miles of mountainous terrain high above the confluence that is drained by the Chelan River. It is the towering mountains of the North Cascades, which stand as a wall in front of the never-ending onrush of moisture-packed air that flows in from the Pacific Ocean. As the mountains force the air upward, the moisture is released and is channeled down into the lake which inundates the valley. Throughout the lake's 55-mile length, many more treasures abound.

Lake Project

Day 60: Lake Como

Amy may have been skeptical of my project and my research efforts, but to her great credit, she did not complain at all when I booked our first trip to go see one of the world's great lakes.

"Once we get our initial trip under our belt," I told her, "I'll practically be done with the project."

"I was thinking the same thing," she said.

After a lengthy combination of plane trips and train rides, we arrived safely on the shores of the jewel of the Italian Lake District.

Lake Como resides in the Lombardy region of Northern Italy. It is a thin freshwater fjord that slices down from the Alps and then splits into two arms so that it appears on a map as an upside down *Y*. It is almost thirty miles long. The lake bed plunges 656 feet below sea level, and with 1,358 vertical feet of water in its basin, it is nearly as deep as Lake Chelan. Lake Como and its neighbors were formed at the same time and in the exact same way as Lake Chelan.

Our first stop was Villa del Balbianello, on the western shore of the lake. Built in 1787, the house is famous for its elaborate terraced gardens. It has been the location for the filming of many prominent Hollywood movies, such as the location in *Star Wars Episode II: Attack of the Clones*, where Padmé and Anakin Skywalker are married. It was also the location in *Casino Royale* where James Bond went to convalesce after having his crotch pulverized by a rope-wielding terrorist financier. Additionally, it was the principle setting for another movie called *A Month by the Lake*, in which strange characters acted really weird for about an hour and a half while failing to develop any kind of plot or occurrence of interest. Amy once remarked that this particular movie seemed very similar to my book. I assume she meant because they were both about lakes.

At one time a church, Villa Balbianello was later deconsecrated and became a private residence. The manor house and grounds still play host to a mausoleum, a giant map room, and secret passageways within the house, from a time when secret passageways might have been helpful for trying to avoid the marauding armies of the French, the Austro-Hungarians, the Nazis, or Mussolini's fascists.

Perhaps the most interesting, and most recent, private owner of the villa was Count Guido Monzino. He was the last of the noble counts in Italy, as the Italian government chose to cease the practice of bestowing nobility.

Count Monzino was a twentieth century Italian mountain climber and explorer who led the first Italian expedition to climb Mount Everest. He made a total of 21 expeditions to, among other places: Africa, the North Pole, Greenland, Patagonia, and various additional mountains in the Himalayas.

The map room was the staging area for his many travels. The villa now has a museum upstairs with paraphernalia of his extraordinary trips around the globe. While touring the place, I started to feel that the count was becoming a bit of a personal hero. This was a man who lived on one of the most beautiful lakes in Europe, in a home fit for the filming of epic movies. He embarked on incredible voyages to the most exciting and remote places on the planet. He was wealthy, and known to be both an intellectual and a bit of a playboy. In many ways, he reminded me of myself, except for the beautiful lake villa, the incredible voyages, the wealth, the intellect, and the playboy lifestyle.

One of the things that struck me about the count was that, throughout his house located on the shores of Lake Como, almost all of the paintings and sketches he had on the walls were depictions of various locations on the lake. Despite all of the places in the world he had traveled, it was Lake Como in Italy that he loved the best, and it was pictures of Lake Como that he chose for his decor.

This spoke to me on many levels. If you have visited Lake Como and Lake Chelan, it is impossible not to draw comparisons between the two. Both lakes have the remarkably brilliant blue water. Both are narrow, glacier-cut freshwater fjords lined on either side by towering mountains. Lake Como spills out of the high Alps; many of the peaks that frame the basin at the upper lake end are actually in Switzerland.

Lake Chelan spills out of the North Cascades, the aforementioned "Alps of America."

For one of the websites that I used to market our vacation rental houses, I wanted a picture of people having fun at Lake Chelan to spice up the home page. Having spent so much time there, I figured I would have a photograph of my friends and family that would be perfect. After browsing through them all, nothing quite seemed to work.

I'm embarrassed to admit that the picture I finally used was of me, my wife, and four of our friends having a drink at sunset with the lake and the silhouette of the mountains behind us. I'm embarrassed because the picture was actually taken in the town of Varenna at Lake Como with the Italian Alps in the background. In the daylight, my subterfuge might have been a bit more obvious, but because the picture was taken at sunset, the fraud has never been uncovered by any of our customers.

Like Count Monzino, my own house, located in Lake Chelan, is covered with pictures of Lake Chelan. Were he alive today, we would probably argue back and forth about whose lake was more extraordinary, his with its stately old towns and villas and rich history, or Chelan with its pristine waters and undisturbed wilderness. We would both agree, however, that there is something sublime about these deep glacier-cut lakes set in the midst of inspiring mountains. It is this love that, I think, so many people truly feel when they think about Lake Chelan.

Lake Como is frequently cited as being the most beautiful lake in the world. Referring to Lake Como, in 1818 Percy Bysshe Shelley wrote to Thomas Love Peacock: "This lake exceeds anything I ever beheld in beauty, with the exception of the Arbutus Islands of Killarney. It is long and narrow, and has the appearance of a mighty river winding among the mountains and the forests."

I read this in a pamphlet while Amy and I were lying in the hot sun on the lakefront promenade in front of our hotel. I lifted my head and said, "Amy, we have to go to the Arbutus Islands."

She lifted onto her elbow and reached for an ice-cold peach bellini on the table next to her.

"Where are the Arbutus Islands?"

"Somewhere in Ireland."

She took a sip from her cocktail, glanced out at Lake Como, and then laid back down in her lounge chair without a word about Ireland. How she masks her enthusiasm is a mystery I may never unravel.

I may have been setting my expectations too high, but over the next few days, as we toured more of Lake Como, I didn't in any way feel that my own personal favorite lake should somehow take a back seat. Taking in the view from Mount San Primo looking uplake toward Switzerland, you could almost believe you were at Lake Chelan, standing on top of Domke Mountain looking up toward Stehekin.

It was on my trip to Lake Como that I realized I was officially holding Chelan as the standard by which all other locations in the world should be judged. I went to Lake Como in the first place because it was, basically, the Italian version of Lake Chelan. This is not to say that Lake Como was a disappointment. There are many incredible things to see throughout the valley, and the centuries-old towns that dot the lakeshore are right out of a storybook.

There are things about Lake Como that Lake Chelan simply cannot match. Likewise, however, there are many things about Lake Chelan that Lake Como cannot match. If someone were to take the time to do a head-to-head, in-depth comparison of the pros and cons of each, certainly one of the two could be declared the winner. The task, I realized, was going to have to fall to me for a variety of reasons, but most notably because I was probably the only person in the entire world who actually cared.

Sitting on the balcony of our hotel in Bellagio (the town on Lake Como, not the casino in Las Vegas), I started to feel a slight anticipatory thrill. Stunning, gorgeous, romantic, historic Lake Como was laid out below me. At the head of the lake, Switzerland formed a wall of mountains that vaulted up into the sky. It was a beautiful sight, to be sure, but was it more beautiful than Lake Chelan? I couldn't say yes, but neither could I say no. This was going to be a hard-fought contest.

This marked a small turning point for me. Prior to that trip, I knew that Lake Chelan was a spectacular place. I had made the assertion that it might be the greatest lake in the world, but I had not been such a Pollyanna as to believe that the odds were in favor of that conclusion. I suspected that my personal favorite lake would likely be unseated at some point. It was just a matter of finding, and visiting, the lake that would do it.

As our trip progressed, I began to firmly believe that Lake Chelan and Lake Como were of relatively equal stature. Continuing along that train of thought, if Chelan was on par with Lake Como, and Lake Como was thought by many to be the greatest lake in the world, then might not Lake Chelan actually be the greatest lake in the world?

Of course, calling Lake Como the greatest lake in the world was presumptuous as well. I had a whole list of other incredible lakes in the world. I would also have to be careful that I wasn't just looking for another lake exactly like Chelan only a little better. In the end, the greatest lake in the world could be entirely different from the narrow freshwater fjord with which I was enamored.

The trip was a wonderful first foray. When we left Italy, I definitely couldn't say that I had eliminated Lake Como as a contender. I certainly hadn't eliminated Lake Chelan. I had learned that the criteria for greatest lake was something that I was going to have to consider and reconsider as I visited more lakes. Lake Como was so spectacular that I suspected, once I had a better understanding of what I was looking for, we would probably have to come back. As I looked across the beautiful Italian lake, I couldn't say I was dreading it.

Lake Project

Day 80: A home on the lake

When you take a moment to review your life, it is often possible to find distinct moments that are significant. They are not always significant in the sense that something dramatic happened. They are more significant in that they signal a turning point. Frequently, they pass by almost unnoticed. Only in retrospect do they stand out from the unending treadmill of happenstance.

I had such an occurrence 40 miles south of Chelan on the sandy shore of the Wenatchee River, just below the Bavarian-themed mountain town of Leavenworth. It was early summer. Amy and I and our friends Mark and Meggan found a perfect sandbar. It sat next to a deep swimming hole surrounded by tall evergreens.

My friend Meggan has a magnetic personality and an infectious laugh. Her face is framed by long, thick, shampoo-commercial hair. She is thin, with a runner's physique, despite the fact that in 20 years of knowing her the only time I've ever seen her run was when she wandered within kissing distance of a bear behind our barn in Chelan. To her credit, when confronted by a carnivore she is extremely fleet of foot.

She is married to Mark, who is an introspective, easy-going, kinetic guy with short sandy blond hair. His face wouldn't look out of place on a baseball card or on the poster of a Scandinavian bobsled team. He and I are old college buddies who have spent the last decade trying to figure out a way that we could become full-time ski bums.

Our dog Otis and their dog Levi were tearing around the beach, in and out of the water. Meanwhile, the four of us were busy laughing, occasionally swimming, and drinking beer.

Mark observed that there was nothing better than lying in the sun, drinking beer by the water. A small debate ensued. The four of us tried to decide what might be better. Many ideas were postulated, including fresh powder skiing, traveling, puppies, world peace, slurpees, sex, skydiving, dark chocolate, sex while skydiving, space travel, surfing, and caramel apples. The debate raged throughout the day, but between points and counterpoints we would sit back on the warm sand, drink our beer, and watch the river go by. Nobody felt like skiing or trying to create world peace.

So it was decided that nothing is better than lying in the sun drinking beer next to the water. We also came to the conclusion that, henceforth, we would make a concerted effort toward maximizing our time doing just that. At some point in the warmth of the late evening, on the sandy beach in the woods, we agreed we would pool our resources and buy a cabin together somewhere sunny, next to the water. With my aforementioned bias, I declared that the somewhere should be at Lake Chelan.

This was a significant moment. Although it was disguised as four intoxicated people babbling on about nonsense on the side of the river, it was actually a decision that would change all of our lives. Even Otis and Levi, two soaking wet Labrador retrievers, now exhausted and curled up in the sand, would be swept up in what resulted from this seminal moment. We were on the path toward having a place at Lake Chelan.

There were a couple of missteps. I found a cabin up the north shore of the lake in a place called Emerson Acres. When I say up the north shore, I mean actually as far up the north shore as it is possible to drive and five miles past the extinction of such not-so-trivial things as pavement, electricity, and cell phone coverage. This cabin was off the grid.

The road in to it could only be described as harrowing. Not in the sense of a harrowing adventure across a rough ocean, but more in the vein of a harrowing encounter with an axe murderer deep in the woods. This was a scary drive.

I went and did the reconnaissance mission with my trusty dog Otis as my sole appraiser. I was impressed. The cabin was perched high on a 200-foot cliff above the water with a magnificent view uplake. The cliff was perfect for rock climbing. This was a very positive attribute, since Mark and I are avid rock climbers. By avid, I mean we have all the gear and we talk about rock climbing often. On the rarest of rare occasions, when we've exhausted every excuse for avoiding it, we have even been known to actually go rock climbing. Having a cliff on the property that looked like a formidable climbing challenge was a definite bonus.

The staircase over the cliff and down to the dock was a triumph of engineering. When I got to the bottom and examined the shoreline, I could easily picture spending countless hours there drinking beer in the sun, as was our mission statement. I couldn't help noticing on the way back up the stairs that getting back to the top of this triumph of engineering was also a triumph of fitness. At one point, halfway up the cliff, Otis stopped and stared at me, ears low, eyes squinting. The message was obvious.

"Are you kidding me with this staircase?" he was saying.

"You have to get high up off the lake to get the good views," I told him.

He appeared unconvinced as he turned and continued loping endlessly upward.

The pros to this cabin were abundant. The views were astounding. The cliff was perfect for rock climbing or, at the very least, for talking about climbing. There were rocks for jumping off into the lake. There was also a large family of fat furry marmots that were constantly frolicking all over the rock face.

I love marmots. Marmots mean that you're in the mountains. Marmots were a definite pro. Also, the price of the cabin was right: roughly $20,000 per marmot.

Not to be blinded by my enthusiasm for the place, I had to admit there were some drawbacks. There was the treacherous access road. There was the extreme remoteness. There was the Tibetan-style trek down to the lake.

I drove into town and conference-called Amy, Mark, and Meggan, who were back in Seattle. I gave them my assessment. I focused heavily on the marmots. They gave me the marching orders. "Just buy it."

"I really think you ought to come out here and take a look first," I said.

"The price is right. Just buy it."

I drove back to take one more look. I loved the place. It was rustic and quaint. The marmots were clearly very happy there. I just kept having a nagging feeling about the road. In addition, Otis, now an avid water dog who would jump through fire to swim in a lake, suddenly seemed less than inclined to head back down the stairs to go swimming.

I have, on occasion, been accused of getting overly excited about things and maybe even acting a bit impulsively. I was worried that perhaps, in my lust for owning my very own cabin at Lake Chelan, I had oversold the place.

I drove back into town and conference called again.

"You guys really need to come see the place first. I don't think we can buy until you've looked at it."

Two days later, we left the pavement and started along the road toward the cabin. We went through a small gate just off of lower Joe Creek Road and headed through Elysian Fields of green grass bejeweled with an explosion of brilliant yellow balsamroot flowers. The car curved around a beautiful escarpment of smooth granite. Above us, the pine studded hillside drifted up toward the vast tracts of lightly timbered mountains.

The site visit was going well. The property was selling itself, and we hadn't even arrived yet. There were four excited would-be cabin owners, and two excited would-be lake dogs. The dogs could sense we were heading toward the lake and their anticipation was evident.

Then we came to the steep part of the trip. The lake spread out 600 near-vertical feet below us. The narrowness of the road necessitated that the car tires roll just a few inches from this precipitous drop. With the water now clearly in view, there was a cacophony of loud howling and whining from the back of the car. This noise was not made by the dogs. In fact, this noise seemed to really upset the dogs, who had immediately crouched quietly down on the floor, trembling in terror. This noise came from the passengers, now staring horror stricken over the edge and into the abyss. I suspect many of the sounds made by Meggan, in particular, were so high-pitched that only the dogs could hear them.

I had been to the cabin twice and knew what to expect. The other passengers did not. A unique feature of this drive is that once you start descending you can't turn back until the bottom.

We skittered down the incline, the outside tires flirting intimately with the edge of the road. Amy, my beloved wife of seven years, was actually cursing my name. Mark was absolutely silent, his hands the color of snow as they gripped the steering wheel. Beads of sweat were tracking down his cheek.

I have seen Mark climb a sheer 2,000-foot cliff in the Italian Alps. Clinging to the side of the granite wall, with nothing but a quarter mile of empty space beneath him, he was laughing and making jokes and having a good time. Here on the side of the glacial-cut fjord of Lake Chelan, he was not making jokes. There was not a hint of laughter.

Ten long minutes later, we got past the steep part and down to the shore of the lake. The road then jutted back upward to the headland where we parked the car. Meggan was no longer very interested in the cabin. She actually couldn't have cared less about the stupid marmots, or, as she called them, "mountain rats." She was more worried about how we were going to get back home.

"Maybe we could hire a barge to come up and take us and the car back downlake."

This is not an exaggeration. She actually said that. She actually meant it.

We all made the delightful trip down the 600 steps to the lake and admired the waterfront. On the not-so-delightful trip back up, Amy paused at the three hundredth step.

"What were you thinking?" she said.

Otis narrowed his eyes at me.

"Look at this view," I said.

Nobody looked.

"Look at the marmots," I said.

Nobody looked.

Needless to say, we opted not to buy that cabin. Everyone agreed that it was a spectacular place, but probably just not the right fit for us.

"I love it up here," I said. "If we could just find a place like this 15 miles closer to town on a cliff about half this high, it would be perfect."

It was the middle of June when I put that sentiment out into the universe. By late June, the universe responded.

Driving through Lakeside on our way to downtown Chelan, Amy spotted a new road carved into the hillside on the north shore. This was in a section of the lake she had long admired. She had pointed it out to me previously on numerous occasions. What happened after she spotted this new road was reminiscent of a phenomenon I had witnessed years earlier when we were still in college.

Amy and I had gone digging for garnets in the mountains of Idaho. I say that "we" were digging for garnets, but what I really mean is that I was up to my shoulders in a muddy hole toiling with a shovel while Amy sat five feet away on a camp chair drinking iced tea and reading a magazine. After hours of digging, I had harvested half a dozen pretty purple garnets, some of them approaching the size of baby mouse teeth. A fellow garnet digger wandered by.

"Any luck?"

"A little," Amy said. "How about you?"

"Yes, I got a few," he said, and then produced a bag brimming with grape- and golf-ball-sized stones.

He went on his way. When Amy turned to me, there was a look in her eyes that frightened me to my very core. It is a look that still haunts me sometimes in my sleep. This is probably the look a ground squirrel sees in the eyes of a falcon the second before being snatched up and eviscerated. I would describe it as a blazing, covetous, piercing stare underlined by a greedy and sinister grin. She appeared to be possessed.

"Get in there and keep digging," she said through gritted teeth. She had the same voice that the girl in *The Exorcist* used, right before her head spun around and she barfed up green gravy. I think Amy was close to putting her foot on my head and stomping me down into the hole.

Years later, driving through Lakeside and looking across at the new road on the hillside, I was suddenly witnessing this transformation again. The look was back in Amy's eyes. The voice was back.

"Go over there right now," she said, in a low-pitched, terrifying rasp.

We arrived ten minutes later and parked in front of what would soon be our lot. Amy was sold. I was too. Here we were on top of a cliff much smaller than the one in Emerson Acres, and 15 miles closer to town. The sweeping views across Key Bay and up to Stormy Mountain were extraordinary. The cliff was fantastic and half as high, just as I had ordered. It was made of solid dimpled granite, perfect for talking about extensively but not actually climbing. It was complete with rocks to jump off of into the lake. We had found exactly what we were looking for a mile from downtown Chelan on the north shore in a place called Lord's Acres. The road was called Paradise Way. But for the conspicuous absence of marmots, it seemed exactly like paradise.

Two weeks later, we sat in the town of Manson with Mark and Meggan and signed papers. We named the place "Chelan Bluff." By October we were pouring the foundation for our very own lake place.

The Amazing Lakes on the Planet

On my trip to Lake Como, I realized that in order to determine the greatest lake in the world I would need a much stronger assessment of the playing field. There are, as it turns out, a tremendous amount of lakes in the world. Based on my research, if you took all the water in all the lakes in the whole world and put it in one place, what you would have is a really big bunch of water. I wish I could be more precise, but it turns out that would require a lot of math. A rough estimate would be 28,000 cubic miles of water, give or take a few drops.

The definition of a lake is a matter of contention and debate. In general terms, a lake is a standing body of water that has more than one square acre in surface area and is not a part of any ocean. When lakes run together or connect, as they do in the 10,000 Lakes region of Minnesota, for example, it can be difficult to determine just how many lakes are present. Most of us know a lake when we see one. In the final analysis, a lake is a lake largely due to the naming convention. Someone sees a body of water, gives it a name, like Iceberg Lake, or Lake Fred, and just like that, the world has one more lake.

For this reason, it is impossible to determine exactly how many lakes there are in the world. There are well over a million, and maybe more than two million. Further confusing this issue is the question of whether some of the larger bodies of water are lakes or seas. The Caspian Sea frames this debate. It is either the world's largest lake or a small sea. It has no natural connection to the world's oceans and doesn't even have an outlet to the ocean. This would make it seem very lake-like. The water is, however, saline in nature. Being salty does not preclude a body of water from being a lake. The Great Salt Lakes of Utah are examples of highly saline inland lakes. The issue remains not clearly cut and dried.

From my own perspective, I chose to consider the Caspian Sea as a sea, mostly because it is called the Caspian Sea, but also because I felt having fresh water would definitely be a critical component for any lake that would eventually be crowned the Greatest Lake in the World.

Among the one million-plus freshwater lakes around the globe, there are some very clear standouts. Some of these lakes are famous. Others are relatively unknown. Each requires serious consideration when trying to assess which lake is the fairest of them all.

The first lake that demands attention is Lake Baikal in Russia. This lake is also known as the Blue Eye of Siberia. The ancient Chinese called it the North Sea.

Lake Baikal is enormous. It is the deepest lake on the planet. From surface to bottom, there is an astounding 5,290 feet of water. That makes it exactly one mile and ten feet deep. It is the most voluminous freshwater lake on the planet. It contains more water than all the Great Lakes combined. A total of 20 percent of the world's fresh, unfrozen surface water is contained in this lake.

Lake Baikal is 395 miles long and 49 miles wide. It is known to be among the clearest of all lakes in the world. It's also believed to be somewhere between 25 and 30 million years old, making it one of the most ancient lakes on the planet.

The lake was formed by a rift valley. This is a depression that occurs in places where the crust of the earth is pulling apart. The bottom of Lake Baikal is 3,893 feet below sea level, and beneath the bottom is an additional 4.3 miles of sediment, meaning the floor of the rift is over five miles deep. This makes it the deepest continental rift on earth. The rift still widens about two centimeters a year, creating frequent notable earthquakes in the area.

Lake Tanganyika is the second largest freshwater lake by volume, and second deepest behind Baikal. Known as the Great Lake of Africa, it covers part of four countries: Zambia, Tanzania, the Democratic Republic of Congo, and Burundi. This lake was also formed by a rift valley. It is 4,800 feet deep.

If you consider the Caspian Sea a lake, then it would be the third deepest, at 3,336 feet deep. The Caspian, along with the Black Sea, was once part of an ancient ocean, until shifting tectonic plates lifted and isolated it. The Caspian Sea falls into a category called an endorheic basin lake (if it is, in fact, a lake). Endorheic basins are non-porous depressions in the earth that have no natural outflow of water. As such, all water that falls within the basin accumulates as a lake at the lowest point. It is not uncommon for these lakes to be high in saline content or have mineral compositions suspended in them.

Rounding out the top five deepest lakes are Lake Vostok in Antarctica and Lake O'Higgins/San Martin which covers parts of Chile and Argentina. Lake Vostok is 2,950 feet deep and is roughly the size of Lake Ontario. Complicating its appeal to tourists, however, is its location; it is buried in 13,000 feet of frozen water under the central Antarctic ice sheet. This also calls into question whether it should be considered a lake. Subterranean aquifers do not generally qualify as lakes. Ice is not earth, however, so the lake is not technically subterranean. Still, 13,000 feet is a lot of ice. Considering Vostok a lake is a conclusion that falls squarely in the category of "gray area."

Lake O'Higgins/San Martin is the deepest lake in the Americas, at 2,742 feet deep. The name of this lake is confusing in that it really has two names. The Argentine side of the lake is generally referred to as San Martin, and the Chilean side is referred to as O'Higgins. Both names are to honor independence heroes: José de San Martin of Argentina, and Bernardo O'Higgins of Chile. South Americans excessively celebrate their liberators and these two men are venerated as such.

Glaciers calve right into this lake in a truly rugged section of the Andes Mountains. The Southern Patagonia Ice Field extends from the lake for almost 200 miles.

In North America, the deepest lake is the Great Slave Lake. This massive waterway in the Yukon Territory of Canada is 2,015 feet deep. It is the eighth deepest lake in the world. The name comes from the North American Slave Indians and has nothing to do with slavery.

The ninth deepest lake in the world, and the deepest lake in the United States, is Crater Lake in Oregon. Crater Lake sits in a caldera, a cauldron-like volcanic feature. The formation of a caldera usually occurs after an eruption when the land around the volcanic vent collapses. This happens because there is a void left from the ejected molten rock, and the surface caves in to fill the void. The caldera was formed about 400,000 years ago by the eruption of ancient Mount Mazama.

Crater Lake is 1,949 feet deep. Because it has no outlet, the water level can fluctuate from year to year based on how much water is evaporated from the lake relative to the influx of water from rain and snow melt. Conceivably, it could trade depth rankings with other lakes in the world during high precipitation years or drought years.

The second deepest lake in the United States is Lake Tahoe. Tahoe was formed about 2 million years ago by a process called geologic block faulting. This is a fascinating event in which a fracture in the earth's crust causes a block of land to raise or fall. In this case, the block fell, creating a huge depression. The Carson Range to the east and Sierra Nevada Range to the west form the boundary of this fracture. The downward falling block of earth, called a graben, is now the bottom of the lake, which has a maximum depth of 1,644 feet.

The third deepest lake in the United Sates is Lake Chelan. Over a quarter of a mile deep, it is the tenth deepest fjord lake in the world, the sixth deepest lake in North America, and the 25th deepest lake on the planet if you consider both the Caspian Sea and ice-buried Lake Vostok. I reject both, and consider the lake to be the 23rd deepest lake in the world, but I'm willing to split the difference and proclaim it the 24th deepest lake, which was the ranking it was traditionally given until someone recently got clever and decided to include that pesky Lake Vostok in Antarctica.

Talking about the size of lakes based on surface area creates a whole separate list with different names and locations. It is this list where the Great Lakes of the Midwest figure prominently. Lake Superior takes the number one spot for freshwater lakes with a surface area of 31,820 square miles. Lake Huron and Lake Michigan are both in the top five. Lake Chelan doesn't figure so prominently in this category, but it is definitely in the top million.

All of these lakes are unique and fascinating, but there are a variety of other lakes that don't fit into the top one hundred list of any category. Still they remain noteworthy due to their quirkiness, structures, formation, and sheer beauty. The lakes of the Alps, for example, are gorgeous. The same can be said for the lakes of the Canadian Rockies and Montana's Glacier National Park.

Flathead Lake in Montana is the largest freshwater lake west of the Mississippi River and sits in an astounding broad valley that epitomizes the phrase, "Big Sky Country." For sheer beauty and the romance of the American West, this is a lake that is beyond compare.

In New Zealand, Lake Wakatipu was described to me as being very similar to Lake Chelan, residing in a beautiful setting. It is a 50-mile-long lake that is narrow and deep. It is set up against a sharply rising mountain range that is known as the Remarkables. That fact alone seems remarkable.

In Guatemala, Lago de Atitlán was famed for its beauty. After seeing it, Aldous Huxley wrote, "Lake Como, it seems to me, touches on the limit of permissibly picturesque, but Atitlán is Como with additional embellishments of several immense volcanoes. It really is too much of a good thing."

Another interesting lake of the Americas is Lake Titicaca, located on the border of Bolivia and Peru. At 12,500 feet of elevation above sea level, it is the highest commercially navigable waterway in the world. This giant high altitude lake is also significant because, of all the lakes in North or South America, it is by far the lake with the silliest name. If you don't believe me, try sitting alone at a bar, and then, when someone sits down next to you, turn to them and say loudly,

"Titicaca." You can't help but notice the amusement in people's eyes as they back slowly away from you.

Incidentally, all of the water from the surrounding Peruvian mountains flows into Lake Titicaca and then leaves from a single outlet through Bolivia and into Lake Poopó. This is clearly the second silliest name for a lake in the Americas.

Despite the massive quantity and variety of lakes throughout the world, they are, by their very nature, an anomaly. Gravity is constantly pulling on water and trying to move it as expeditiously as possible downward. "Water," as the phrase goes, "seeks its own level."

It takes an event of some kind to create the conditions that can arrest water, pool it, and hold it within a confined space. There are really only a few natural processes that can accomplish this. Almost all are fueled by the dynamic nature of the earth, the molten core, and the motion of the tectonic plates. By lifting and deforming the crust of the earth, this plate movement creates the conditions for rift valleys, block faulting, volcanic calderas, endorheic basins, and glacial scouring.

Climate changes are also a key spoke in the wheel of lake formation. Most of the world's lakes are the result of simple uneven terrain, deformities, and dimpling of the earth's surface. These were created by the advance and retreat of continental ice sheets during the ice ages.

A few more obscure lake forming events exist, including oxbow lakes created by the wandering of slow-moving rivers. Some lakes pool behind natural dams created by landslides or even glaciers. These are called barrier lakes. There is a small lake in China believed to have been formed by a meteor strike.

What all lakes have in common is that they are as dynamic as the processes that created them. A few lakes, such as Lake Baikal, are still being created, but the vast majority are actually in the process of erasing themselves. Water is constantly tearing at the earthen surrounds that hold them in place. Water is also continuously ferrying in sediment to fill the concavities. All lakes are impermanent structures.

Fortunately for us, this happens on a grander geologic time scale. By and large, in the short span of a human life lakes remain relatively permanent. Occasionally there will be a daramatic event. During the 1959 earthquake that rocked Yellowstone National Park, for example, a mountainside gave away, and the resulting landslide dammed the Madison River, creating Quake Lake.

Yellowstone Lake itself is perched on the top of a grand caldera that is actually bulging and tilting, due to the deformations of the magma chamber, faults in the earth, and hydrothermal vents on the lake bottom. This has created noticeable changes in a more human scale of time. There are now large sandy beaches growing on the north shore of the lake, while areas once dry in the southern arm are under water.

Another beautiful lake, and relative neighbor to Lake Chelan, was dramatically changed in an instant. This alpine gem was nestled in the heart of the Cascade Mountains and towering above it was a picture-perfect snowcapped mountain whose pointed summit was said by many to resemble Mount Fuji. The lake was a popular tourist destination. The beautifully timbered shores hosted campgrounds for the Boy Scouts, the Girl Scouts, the YMCA, and a public campground as well. There were rustic old lodges that catered to visitors who came to fish, swim, and take in the gorgeous views of the cinder cone mountain that reflected so perfectly off the water. This was Spirit Lake. The volcano that loomed above it was Mount Saint Helens.

When the mountain erupted on May 18, 1980, the beautiful lake was changed forever. The north side of the mountain collapsed, creating the largest recorded landslide in history. Superheated lahars and pyroclastic flows tore into the lake. The lake water was sloshed, sending a tsunami-like wave over 800 feet up the opposite mountainside. The cataclysmic blast laid waste the surrounding forest, blowing trees down like matchsticks.

When it was over, and the lake emerged from the ash cloud, it was a reservoir of highly toxic water that oozed noxious volcanic gases from its depths. The surrounding hillsides were a barren moonscape covered in seared toppled logs, ash, and debris.

The lake surface was 200 feet higher, owing to the new earthen dam that blocked the Toutle River. It was also ten percent smaller and much shallower. The water was covered in floating logs, stripped clean of branches and drifting around like giant ghost booms. The area was unrecognizable.

The beautiful and oft photographed summit of Mount Saint Helens was no more. In its place was a barren horseshoe-shaped ridge that wrapped around a steaming crater and reached up only 8,365 feet into the air. This was over 1,300 feet lower than its elevation prior to the eruption. The Spirit Lake of old was erased.

These are some of the exceptions. In general terms, lakes are fairly enduring, as they are the result of extremely powerful slow-moving geologic events. To understand lakes better, I wanted to see one of these processes first hand. Watching a rift valley or block faulting event occur would probably be about as exciting as watching my wife shop for ripe fruits and vegetables, although the rifting of continental plates might actually progress at a little faster pace. Being in the right place to witness an earthquake-induced landslide, or perhaps seeing a meteor strike, seemed unlikely and fraught with the potential for an agonizing death.

Watching a caldera forming process was a little more promising. Crater Lake, in Oregon, is a great example of a caldera lake. The collapse of prehistoric Mount Mazama would have been an incredible sight. The highest point on the rim of Crater Lake is now 8,159 feet. Before the mountain collapsed, it is believed to have been around 11,000 feet tall. The eruption that preceded the collapse is thought to have been 42 times as powerful as the eruption of Mount Saint Helens. That eruption was sometime around 5,700 BC. Additional eruptions and subsequent collapses deepened the caldera. The problem with Crater Lake is that the volcano hasn't had much activity in the last 400,000 years.

The caldera in Yellowstone National Park is still an active hot spot on the planet. Yellowstone is, of course, fascinating, but in terms of actively displacing magma and voiding the chamber, no significant event has occurred for 640,000 years. When Yellowstone displaces its magma, it does so explosively, in an event that has been coined a "super-volcano." This has happened three times over the last 2.1 million years. If you were driving through Yellowstone when the fourth one happened, it would undoubtedly lessen the enjoyment of your visit.

A famous caldera that seemed worth a visit was the Greek island of Santorini. This four-mile-wide crater was caused by a cataclysmic eruption 3,500 years ago. What makes the Santorini Caldera exciting is that it has a still-active volcano rising right from its center. This cinder cone island has been growing in a series of eruptions over the last 300 years, the most recent of note being in 1950. What also makes this caldera exciting is that it is in Greece, as opposed to, for example, the frozen wasteland of Siberia.

The problem with Santorini is that it is not a lake. When the caldera collapsed, large sections of the rim fell below sea level, allowing the marine water to flow in and flood the depression. Thirty percent of the circumference of the crater is open to the sea. I thought it would be a fantastic way to get a good look at an active caldera up close, but seeing as my book was actually about lakes, it seemed that a more useful trip would be to go see the largest freshwater lake in the world.

I decided the lake-making process that I should go see would be a rift fault. As a sign of my commitment to this project, I would brave a trip to Siberia and go have a look at Lake Baikal. It would be spectacular. It would be exciting. It would be cold.

I decided not to break the news to Amy right away.

The Crystal Blue Water of Lake Chelan

As all water flows into Lake Chelan somewhere to the west and exits at the eastern terminus, one generally refers to the eastern end, at the city of Chelan, as "downlake," and the western end, at the town of Stehekin, as "uplake." Because of the extreme terrain, roads extend only 20 miles up the north shore and 25 miles up the south shore.

The remainder of the lake is largely undeveloped rugged shoreline, much the same as it was when William Sanders and Henry Domke encountered it so many years ago. The small town of Stehekin is a remote outpost accessible only by boat, floatplane, or via a hiking trail that begins 40 miles away on the other side of the mountains. Although a popular summer tourist destination, it is not uncommon for the town to be buried under four to six feet of snow in the winter. Hearty winter enthusiasts still make the trip to enjoy the snowy solitude, but only about 80 people live there year-round.

From "uplake" Stehekin to "downlake" Chelan, the distance is so long that the lake exists in two distinct climate zones. At the western end, it exhibits all the characteristics of an alpine lake. The shores of this region are covered in Douglas fir, spruce, and ponderosa pines from the water line up the mountains to the tree line. Five major creeks and more than 50 smaller ones flow out of the hills, some ending in cascades and waterfalls as they drop into the lake. At the tip of the lake, the largest tributary, the Stehekin River, drains a broad area of mountainous terrain fed by the winter snowfall and the glaciers in the region.

It is from these glaciers and the topography that Lake Chelan gets one of its signature features, its incredible blue color. Deep clear water will reflect back blue naturally as the water tends to filter out the other colors in the visible spectrum. It is the clarity and depth which gives Chelan much of its blue color, but there is also a process unique to mountain lakes that contributes to the stunning turquoise tint of the water.

As the glaciers high above the lake grind across the mountains, they tear off small granules of rock and then carry it away in the melt water. This debris is often ground up quartz and feldspar. Collectively it forms a powder called rock flour that gets suspended in the water. The result of this is that the brilliant blue water takes on a lighter, more turquoise hue. Diablo Lake in the North Cascades National Park is an excellent example of this process taken to extreme. At times, Diablo Lake is a milky turquoise, as the rock flour is stripped away from the towering peaks near Park Creek Pass and the Boston Basin and washed down Thunder Creek. Park Creek Pass is on the divide between the Stehekin drainage, which flows into Lake Chelan, and the Skagit River drainage to the north.

On the Skagit drainage side, the amount of rock flour that is scoured from the mountains is profound. Tons of particulates are swept down the mountain every year. On the Chelan side of this same ridge, the rock flour is more subtle. The massive drainage systems dilute the floury colored creeks such that only a hint of the suspension is left. That hint of rock flour is enough. It gives Lake Chelan the regal blue tint for which it has become famous.

This is not to say that Lake Chelan is not clear. The lake is very clear. It is often called one of the most clear and pristine lakes in the country. I got to wondering about that as I stared into the blue depths of the lake on a bright spring day. While sitting 80 feet up above the lake on a deck and watching giant fish as plain as day cruising along the sandy bottom in 30 feet of water, I was struck by the incredible clarity. I decided to do a little research into exactly what it means to be one of the clearest lakes in the nation. I wondered if this was just an opinion or a quantifiable fact.

Here's what I learned: There is a system used to identify the clarity of lakes, and it involves a tool called a Secchi disk. (Father Pietro Secchi was an Italian astronomer. He is credited with being one of the first scientists to state authoritatively that the sun is a star. In 1865, he created his eponymous disk to measure transparency in oceans and lakes.)

The disk is painted in four segments, two black and two white. To establish clarity, the disk is lowered on a pole or line down into the water. The Secchi depth is reached when the reflectance from the disk is equal to the intensity of light backscattered from the water. I believe this means when the disk is no longer visible, but I could be wrong.

This depth in meters divided into 1.7 yields an attenuation coefficient (also called an extinction coefficient), for the available light averaged over the Secchi disk depth. The light attenuation coefficient, k, can then be used in a form of the Beer–Lambert Law.

The Beer–Lambert Law is probably important to this discussion as well. Unfortunately, I got so bored reading about the Secchi disk that I couldn't continue reading about the Beer–Lambert Law. Basically it relates to the absorption of light to the properties of the material through which the light is traveling. For our purposes, that material is water, and anything suspended in the water.

The disc is 20 centimeters in diameter. It should be noted that the Secchi disk depth is a bit inexact owing to different light angles and disbursements, wave action, glare, and to better eyesight among the observers. Personally, without wearing my contact lenses, I would probably not be able to see the Secchi disk if someone walked right up in front of me and smacked me in the face with it on a bright sunny day. My wife Amy, on the other hand, could probably spot it five miles away on a bushy hillside in a rainstorm.

The Secchi depth on Lake Chelan measured in 1990 ranged from 42 feet to 55 feet over the course of the summer. This is very clear. In the state of Washington, only Lake Crescent was found to be clearer, with a mean summer average of 79 feet. I think it is fair to say that, if not for the tiny particulates of rock flour, Lake Chelan would probably blow away that measly Lake Crescent. For comparison's sake, Crater Lake in Oregon is thought to be the clearest lake in the world with a Secchi disk depth of 142 feet. Lake Washington, near Seattle, has a Secchi depth of about 20 feet.[4]

Lake Chelan also had the lowest concentration of total phosphorous of all the lakes monitored in the state during 1990. The lake is classified as oligotrophic, which means it is lacking in plant nutrients and has a large amount of dissolved oxygen throughout its volume.

The Washington State Department of Ecology said that "Several water quality studies determined that Lake Chelan is one of the most pristine water bodies in North America due to low concentrations of nutrients and other pollutants."[5]

Just how much crystal clear, slightly blue-tinted oligotrophic water is there in Lake Chelan? As it happens, there is a lot. As previously mentioned, it is the third deepest lake in the United States. It is also the 24th deepest lake in the world. This is a fairly notable characteristic, especially when you consider that North America doesn't have a single mountain summit high enough to be in the top 100 tallest mountains in the world.

Within the cavernous fjord resides over 25 billion cubic yards of water. Ninety-two percent of that water is in the deep Lucerne Basin. The hydraulic retention is 10.6 years, based on an average of 2.4 billion cubic yards flowing from the lake every year—this is the theoretical amount of time it takes for 25 billion cubic yards of water to flow into, and subsequently out of, the lake. All together, there is enough water impounded by Lake Chelan to cover an area the size of the entire state of Washington with 4.4 inches of water.[6]

In my notebook, I jotted down two new sets of criteria for the greatest lake in the world. First, it had to be a lake of some significance. It didn't have to be oceanic like one of the Great Lakes. It just couldn't be small. I thought ten billion gallons might be a nice minimum size. I chose that number for no particular reason other than it seemed big. A lake, in its truest sense, consists entirely of water. It seemed like in order for a lake to be the greatest in the world, there ought to be a lot of water in it.

The second was more of an observation than a criterion. I simply noted that in order for a lake to have the brilliant blue color that I felt was important, it would probably have to be glacier-fed. I didn't know this to be true, but I suspected it. I also felt it would be an added bonus if you could see the glaciers from somewhere on the lake. In this way, I moved a step closer to drawing up my list of contenders.

Lake Project

Day 120: Maligne Lake

When I was ten years old, I stumbled across a painting at a garage sale. It was done in oil on canvas, and it depicted an incredible alpine lake with prominent mountains covered in snow on either side. In the middle of the picture, there was a small wooded island, a peninsula really, with a tiny little strip of land connecting it to the mainland. The minute I saw that painting, I had to have it. It seemed to represent everything I wanted in a lake. I bought the painting for five dollars and took it home and put it on my wall. I would stare at it and imagine myself canoeing across the reflective waters, swimming, and camping there for weeks. I wanted so badly to find a place just like it.

By chance, while visiting a friend's house many years later, I noticed a coffee table book called the *Canadian Rockies*. I was thumbing through it, glancing at familiar pictures like Lake Louise, Peyto Lake, and Mount Robson, when suddenly, there it was. In living color, there was a photograph of the lake from my painting. Unbelievably, it was a picture taken at what was apparently the identical spot from which the painting was made.

The picture was taken at Maligne Lake in Canada's Jasper National Park, and the island even had a name. It was called Spirit Island. At last, I could visit the fabled place and live out the dream that had captivated me for so many years.

"We're going to Jasper National Park in Canada," I told Amy when I got home that night. This time, she almost betrayed her excitement. She had to turn the pages of her magazine, without even looking at me, so that I wouldn't notice the enthusiasm that must have been welling inside of her.

A month later, we were speeding through the Canadian Rockies, blurring past Lake Louise and Peyto Lake. We rocketed down the Banff Ice Field Highway and came at last to the town of Jasper. We checked into our hotel, and I lay awake all night, with thoughts of the next day drifting through my head. Spirit Island, it was called. It was probably named by Canada's First Nation People, because, I speculated, they had done their vision quests there for centuries. No doubt there was a profound nexus of cosmic energy right at that spot. I would likely have some incredible spiritual revelation of my own.

I knew there was a small national park center run by Parks Canada on the lake. I felt certain I would be able to talk to the lonely ranger and convince him to loan or rent us a canoe. Then, I would paddle into the lake until I found this mysterious sacred island. Once I located it, we would spend the night right on the shore of the island. My childhood dream would come true.

"The plan is perfect," I told Amy as I gathered up stuff in our hotel room the next morning.

She looked up from her coffee.

"Undoubtedly," she said.

We headed out of the town of Jasper toward the remote and desolate Maligne Lake. We pulled up near the shore an hour later. The first thing I noticed when I arrived at the lake was that, for a remote and desolate lake, it had an awfully big paved parking lot. Further investigation revealed a bustling lodge, complete with restaurants, gift shops, and an ice cream parlor. My lonely ranger did not appear to be very lonely, as he wandered amongst the throngs of tourists milling down by the giant docks from which the tour boats departed. The destination of these giant tour boats: Spirit Island. I stood in line at the ticket office staring across the mob with my jaw slack, my mouth slightly open. Amy approached from the lodge.

"Ice cream?" she asked as she handed me a cone.

I took it wordlessly.

We boarded the boat and took the 25 minute cruise to Spirit Island. We shuffled along with the crowd off the gangplank and onto the dock, which was built on the shore right by the island. Then we bumped shoulders up a small trail and waited in line to stand on a viewing platform that looked out at Spirit Island, about 100 yards away. The viewing platform was the site from which my picture had been painted. People weren't allowed past the guardrails or anywhere near the island to avoid overuse and erosion.

I stood at the rail and got my picture taken, which seemed achingly similar to having my picture taken in Mexico with an iguana on my shoulder. I felt like I could have saved some time and money by going to a photography studio in Seattle and having my portrait done in front of a pull-down mountain screen. The lighting would have been better.

"I don't understand," I said to Amy as they herded us around the small loop and back toward the dock.

"Of course you don't," she said, and she took my hand and led me back past the T-shirt vendors to the boat. I felt slightly sick that day, as my inner child received a solid kick in the crotch. Back at the head of the lake, Amy ducked into the gift shop and bought me a commuter mug with a picture of Spirit Island printed on it.

It turns out Spirit Island was named Spirit Island because, visually, it captured the "spirit" of the Canadian Rockies. It was part of a tourism campaign that took place in the late '60s and early '70s. The photographed image from the viewing platform was broadcast and distributed to hundreds of millions of people around the world to encourage them to visit Maligne Lake, which, apparently, they all decided to do on that exact August day when I arrived.

Later, I looked up the translation of the French word "maligne." It means shrewd, cunning, sly, mischievous, or wicked. Alas, those evil French Canadians had put one over on me. Sacré bleu!

I don't mean to malign Lake Maligne, so to speak. The lake is singularly extraordinary, and the scenery could compete with any in the world. I simply relate the story to touch upon one of the sad truths about our world's natural wonders. That truth is, as any park ranger will tell you (ad nauseam), we simply love them to death.

This is pretty much the answer a park ranger will give to any question you might ask. For example:

> *"Why is there no camping on Sahalee Arm?"*
> Ranger: "We are loving our natural wonders to death."
>
> *"Excuse me, is this where you get wilderness permits?"*
> Ranger: "We are loving our natural wonders to death."
>
> *"Is there a bathroom here at the lodge?"*
> Ranger: "We are loving our natural wonders to death."

I jotted a sentence down in my notebook. It said, "The Greatest Lake in the World must be more than just a tourist trap."

At that point, I realized the implications of one of the extraordinary aspects of Lake Chelan. As wilderness areas go, particularly in the lower 48 states, the Chelan Valley is extremely pristine. Of the 952 square miles in the Chelan River drainage, just three percent is used for residential homes, vacation homes, and agriculture. Four percent of the area is covered by the lake.

Both sides of the valley are flanked by national forest lands. Moving uplake, the entire wilderness flows into the North Cascades National Park complex, which encompasses 1,069 square miles of rugged mountain wilderness. These adjoin to vast tracks of wilderness areas and undeveloped Crown Lands in British Columbia. Adjacent to all of this, on the Washington side of the border, is the Lake Chelan–Sawtooth Wilderness, the Pasayten Wilderness, the Mount Baker Wilderness, the Noisy–Diobsud Wilderness, the Glacier Peak Wilderness, and the Henry M. Jackson Wilderness. North of the border, these wild lands flow into Manning Provincial Park, Cathedral Rocks Provincial Park, and Skagit Valley Provincial Park. All of these converge with one another, separated only by lines on a map.

Until the completion of the North Cascades Highway in 1972, this area held the title of the largest roadless area in the lower 48 states. Because of huge amounts of snow, and because of avalanche danger, the North Cascades Highway is shut down every year for three to six months. I like to think that during that time it reclaims its roadless status again.

This is wild and lonely country. Unlike other more popular national parks, visitors to the North Cascades are measured in thousands each year, rather than millions. Of those that do come, only a fraction of them ever venture more than a few miles off the highway into the woods and mountains. This leaves Lake Chelan surrounded by a nearly untracked void of ridiculously beautiful desolation. This is certainly a worthy attribute if one were tallying up the score in a competition for the greatest lake in the world.

All of this is the overblown gossamer of a lake that has many spellbinding features further to the east, where the mountains rise only half as high. It's there, at the more populated end of the lake, where the sun shines 300 days of the year, that most people cultivate their love of the lake. What this part of the lake lacks in dramatic mountain peaks, it more than makes up for with pastoral beauty. For those who love the sweeping gentle views of the Napa Valley or the rolling hills of Tuscany, the lower Chelan Valley has set the table with a feast for the eyes. Adding a crystal blue lake to the center of it all seems almost like the valley is just showing off.

A Brief Geologic History

The directions east, west, north, and south are sometimes not very useful in and around Lake Chelan. Confusing to a lot of people, but known to the locals, is that the lake runs at an angle as it cuts back into the mountains, such that, although it meanders northward, the predominant direction of the lake is really from east to west. This seems to cause people a lot of consternation when they come to the lake, and I think it relates to the tendency we have to attribute higher mountains, cold, and snow with the north and warmer, milder weather with the south. When they see the far remote end of the lake, buried in the mountains, it seems to make sense that this would be the north end of the lake, which of course it is, but it is more prevalently the west end of the lake. The more populated part of the lake, then, is the east end.

This is important in that, whenever you are given directions to a place, the first bit of information anyone will give you is whether it is on the north shore or the south shore. All that information is still pretty irrelevant because, due to the topography of the area, especially on the north shore, many of the roads are a tangled and weaving rat's maze. If you don't know where you're going in the hills above Manson, no amount of directions will keep you from getting lost. If you do know where you're going, you might still get lost. Even if you can establish that you are on the north shore or the south shore, this doesn't really help you determine compass directions, since the lake runs on a winding serpentine path.

The lake floods the remnants of two distinct glacier basins. The longest and deepest of these is the Lucerne Basin. The Lucerne Basin ends about 12 miles uplake. Where it begins, one could say, is at Stehekin, but the basin is really more than just the lake, so it might be more fair to say it begins 30 miles past Stehekin, up the Stehekin River, where a wall vaults up from the rounded sides of the valley. Above that wall is the Pelton Basin, which is really sort of a hanging glacier basin. Along the way up the valley, other hanging basins open up, all part of the massive system of the glacial river that scoured this area over the millennia, most recently between 40,000 and 10,000 years ago during the last ice age.

This process occurred in several places throughout the eastern front of the Cascade Mountains and the Coast Range of British Columbia. The Coast Range is really the same chain of mountains as the Cascades, distinguished only by the fact that it is situated north of the Frasier River and has a different nomenclature.

(Lake Chelan is not technically a fjord in the English sense of the word. Although there is some debate about this, a fjord is, by definition, a deep valley that is flooded by seawater, the glaciers that formed it having pushed all the way to the sea. The word finds its origins in Norway, however. There, the Norwegians themselves have referred to a number of glacial-cut valleys full of fresh water as fjords. Still, it is incumbent upon the English speaker to designate Lake Chelan more specifically as a fjord lake. The term freshwater fjord is probably also acceptable.)

The same process that created actual fjords up and down the coast of British Columbia on the western side of the mountain range was also active on the leeward side of the range. Here, however, there was no ocean to flood into the fjords, only the Columbia Plateau. Just north of Lake Chelan, in British Columbia, is Okanogan Lake, the first North American lake to be described as a fjord lake. Along the inland lee of the Canadian Coast Mountains and the Cascade Mountains a number of these lakes were formed, including Seton Lake, Chilko Lake, Atlin Lake, Kootenai Lake, and Slocan Lake as well as Okanogan Lake and Lake Chelan.[7]

Of these many freshwater fjords carved into the Cascade Mountains, Chelan represents the southernmost of them all. This is one of the more unique characteristics of the lake. It is one of the qualities which distinguishes it so significantly from its sibling lakes to the north and east. Because of its latitude, Lake Chelan plays host to a different climate, water temperature, and topography.

Left to its own devices, the alpine glacier which surged down the Chelan Valley would have ground its way straight into the Columbia Valley, as it did in the many partially glacier-cut valleys to the south.

The Entiat River Valley and the Yakima River Valley are examples. They remain merely river valleys, relatively shallow when compared to the gaping scar in the continent that is flooded by Lake Chelan.

The alpine glacier was not given free passage, however. The Pleistocene and late Pliocene epoch witnessed a series of glacial advances that began 2.5 million years ago and lasted until about 10,000 years ago. During this time, huge ice sheets slid down from the north, covering large parts of the North American continent.

About 80,000 years ago, one such sheet, named the Cordilleran ice sheet, covered southwestern Canada and the northern areas of Washington, Idaho, and Montana. It was approximately 3,500 feet thick.

A southern-reaching lobe of this ice sheet, known as the Okanogan–Columbia Valley Lobe, pushed down along the eastern ridge of the Cascade Mountains. (Opinions vary as to how far south the lobe stretched. It is known that it reached further south than the outlet of Lake Chelan, but to what extent is a matter of debate.)

It was the presence of the Columbia Lobe of the continental ice shelf that distinguished Chelan from its neighboring drainages to the south. This massive sheet of ice, which towered above the present-day Columbia River, pushed a giant finger of ice up the Chelan Valley. Somewhere in the vicinity of Wapato Point, that finger likely encountered the alpine glacier which was moving down from the mountains. An unfathomable collision took place. This was the proverbial unstoppable force hitting an immovable object.[8]

Much in the way that tectonic plates collide and crumple upward to form mountains, these two glaciers would have crumpled together in an awesome up-thrust of ice. Likely, the finger of the Columbia Lobe would have subducted under the downward-moving alpine glacier and a massive range of jagged ice would have towered into the sky.

All the while, this would have backed up increasing quantities of ice moving down from the higher mountains, creating more and more pressure in the Lucerne Basin and pushing and gouging ever deeper into the bedrock.

The glaciers represented two massive opposing forces pushing mindlessly up against each other and creating a tremendous amount of noise but not making any perceptible progress one way or the other. It was like an ice age version of the United States Congress.

The Columbia Lobe made the carving of the Lucerne Basin possible.

It was the Columbia Lobe itself that created the smaller and shallower Wapato Basin.

Where the two glaciers met, or perhaps, more specifically, where they parted company, is the sill that separates the two basins. Throughout the process, these glaciers would have butted heads up and down the valley, scattering and then re-scattering glacier till, and scrambling it in every direction. When it was all over, the division between the basins was left right near the narrows of the lake. There, the depth of the water is only 129 feet.

Eventually, the continental ice sheet prevailed. This was a glacier, fed by a quarter of the North American land mass, facing off with an alpine glacier, fed by 900 or so square miles. A unique result of this was that the Columbia Lobe formed a giant ice dam at the end of the lake for many years. The water that pooled behind this dam was forced to find other escape routes, and the evidence remains in Knapps Coulee and Navarre Coulee above the south shore of the lake. These ancient riverbeds are suspended over 500 feet above the current surface of the lake. They are indications of a time when water exited freely from the lake, likely through one first and then the other, as the Wapato Basin finger of ice retreated east. One wonders if Lake Chelan, at that time, might not have been the deepest lake in the territory that would later become the United States.

Lake Project

Day 210

"I have some exciting news," I told Amy while she was in the kitchen making fajitas. Whenever I tell Amy I have exciting news, she fails to react with anything resembling anticipation. For some reason, she tends to lean more toward skepticism. I imagine this has something to do with how she was raised, but I'm only speculating.

She didn't even inquire what the exciting news might be. She just stood there quietly while the fajitas sizzled. I took it upon myself to break the suspense for her.

"As part of my research, I think we should go to Lake Baikal in Siberia. It's the largest freshwater lake in the world."

She made a funny pursed-lipped expression.

"You want to go to Siberia to do research on a book about Lake Chelan?"

"I think it would help," I said.

The fajitas sizzled some more. She seemed to be staring at them very intently. I was starting to wonder if maybe I hadn't sold this trip very well. Maybe I should have looked up resorts or spas at Lake Baikal and done a better pitch job. It occurred to me that I should have looked up whether Lake Baikal even had resorts or spas. I was suddenly realizing I had come to this moment a little ill prepared.

"I suppose we could go to Santorini in Greece to research calderas instead," I said.

Fourteen minutes later, she had a preliminary itinerary mocked up with potential places to stay. The fajitas were half-cooked and cold, sitting on a side burner. Amy was now surfing the internet for swimsuits.

"People swim in Siberia too, you know," I wanted to say, but I actually wasn't sure if that was true, so I kept quiet.

We discussed the trip with Mark and Meggan. Convincing Meggan to go on a trip is about as difficult as convincing a dog to eat bacon. She is the impetus of most vacations, and after she gets a trip in her head, particularly a trip to Europe, she will generally have a 30-minute Powerpoint presentation assembled within a day as a recruiting tool. These are usually set to music and tend to get better and more elaborate with each trip. I suspect within the next few years she will probably incorporate a laser show, live musicians and a fireworks display. She is shameless in her attempts at persuading people to jump on board.

Meggan is a school teacher. She's one of those school teachers who wins awards for teaching and loves her job. She really takes joy in shaping young minds and is often excited to go to work. This is, of course, extremely annoying. She and Mark are great travel partners, though. Rounding out the team of caldera explorers were our friends John and Kerry. Kerry and John travel all over the globe, and Kerry had already been trying to talk us into going to Greece for quite some time. They were committed to the trip before it was even proposed.

I didn't mention to my friends that the trip, for me, was largely motivated by the fact that I was writing a book. This is because only Amy knew that I was writing a book. Over the years, I have found it best not to announce to my friends that I'm engaged in any project because, due to circumstances beyond my control, 90 percent of them never come to fruition. It becomes cumbersome fielding questions about the progress of endeavors that have long since gone extinct. Also, my friends are all quite adept at the structuring and implementation of sarcastic remarks. It had not escaped my attention that my research on lakes was taking me to an arid island that had not a single lake and really very little fresh water. Santorini was at least 150 miles away from the nearest lake, which was located across the Aegean Sea on a different continent.

I imagined such not-very-amusing comments as: "It's too bad you're not doing a book about icebergs, we could have gone to Egypt."

Or, "This Greek music is fantastic. I might dedicate a chapter to it in my book about squirrels."

I am not exaggerating when I say such comments would have numbered into the hundreds, had I exposed the true motivation for my heading to Greece. Only Amy knew. She kept it quiet, probably out of gratitude for the fact that we weren't going to Siberia.

Over the next few weeks, the trip steered in a little bit more lake-oriented direction. Meggan, a history teacher, was showing the movie *The Sound of Music* to her students, and mentioned she would one day like to go on a *Sound of Music* tour.

Much of the movie was filmed in the Lakes District of Austria, known locally as the Salzkammergut. Many people consider this area to be the most beautiful place in the world. Austrian emperor Franz Joseph I once described the region as "an earthly paradise." This is actually an understatement. It encompasses many of the most stunning lakes on the planet. Lake Halstatt, in particular, had crossed my radar several times as a possible contender for the greatest lake.

Heading to Salzburg, Austria on the way to Greece seemed to be a non-sequitor of sorts, but since we were flying all the way over the Arctic Circle anyway, it didn't seem so terribly out of the way. By the time the trip was booked, our schedule permitted four days to wander the Lakes District of Austria before continuing on to Athens. My next foray out into the world in an attempt to secure evidence of the supremacy of Lake Chelan was now officially on the books.

Chelan Butte

Lake mile 0

If you spend some time in and around the town of Chelan, or really anywhere at the eastern end of the lake, you find your eyes frequently drifting up to Chelan Butte. This prominent rise on the south shore frames the lake and the Chelan River. It stands at 3,825 feet above sea level. This is a foothill of sorts when compared to its lofty Cascade neighbors, but there is almost 2,700 feet of vertical relief when viewing the butte from downtown Chelan, and over 3,000 feet when viewed from further below along the Columbia River. In many ways, it dominates the landscape in the lower section of the lake.

The Butte is a promontory of land that is constantly in flux. In the springtime, it is dressed in brilliant green, as if a giant golfing fairway has been manicured along its flanks.

By early summer, the grass is the color of dusty wheat, with the mottled shadows of undulating draws giving it a silky and sublime texture. On bright moonlit nights in August, it can reflect back so much light that it appears to be blanketed in snow. If you're sitting on the north shore after midnight on a windless summer night, the coyotes on the Butte will sing so clearly, it sounds as if they are floating in a canoe in the middle of the lake.

Some winters it can be blanketed in snow, so much that it looks like a destination ski area should adorn it. Other winters, the snow comes and goes, and the Butte can appear like an old yellowed photograph, almost sepia toned. On cold winter days, not cold enough for snow, swirls of mist curl up through the draws and ghost across the summit. Always, sparse pines dot the hillside and crown the summit, as the Butte stands watch over the lower part of the lake.

The house we were building was located directly across from the

Butte on the north shore. I spent dozens of hours there digging in the dirt to build a trail down to the shoreline. The Butte was a constant companion looming above me. I was amazed at how different it would look from hour to hour, as the light and weather constantly changed the shadows.

In the evening, after working on the house, I, along with Amy, Mark, and Meggan, would adjourn to the deck and watch late-flying hang gliders circle above the Butte. We'd sit there for hours drinking wine, as the sunset and the Butte slipped into darkness. We'd watch the brilliant white moon surface from right behind the ridge. One evening, four bottles of local wine empty on the table, Mark turned to me and said, "We should climb that sucker."

He didn't actually use the word "sucker."

I enthusiastically agreed.

We set out on the trail early one Saturday morning in June, intent on beating the heat. The local guidebooks referenced a trail just outside of town that would take us all the way up to the top. We were all smiles as we pulled into the parking spot and donned our sunscreen and packs.

"If we hustle," I said, "we can be back at Campbell's restaurant in three hours sipping on bloody marys."

"Let's hit it," Mark said, and we headed off at a brisk pace.

The golden summer grass was a blur as we dashed up the dirt track, eating up yard after yard of trail for approximately 14 yards. Then the trail turned steep. Then it turned steeper. The grass was suddenly no longer a blur.

I hesitate to even use the word trail. The route up the Butte is a slippery dusty gash in the grass that goes straight up. One section appears to approach vertical. Mark dubbed this portion of the route "The Elevator Shaft." Sweat and groans and curses were flying about the hillside like a swarm of angry gnats, while we progressed upward with the velocity of a herd of snails.

We did not, as was our plan, beat the heat.

Undaunted, and with the conviction of two men who were not so many years away from a cataclysmic midlife crisis, we endeavored ever upward. At about a quarter of the way up, I got the first call from Amy.

"Are you at the top yet?"

"Almost."

This was the first of seven calls. When we made the ridgeline at last, the trip became appreciably more enjoyable.

One of the first things you notice on the Butte is that what appears to be a silky hill of grass from below is actually an honest-to-goodness mountain up close. Rock abutments jut out all across the Butte, covered in a forest of lichens and dry moss. Living trees are stunted and windblown from the constant battle with the elements. Dead trees are gnarled and weathered, silver gray in color.

The second thing you notice, once you regain the strength to lift your head, is the incredible view. Below, in every direction, is an astounding panorama. The lake is brilliant blue and, in places, looks like the Caribbean Sea, as the sand along the shoreline weaves ribbons of turquoise and green.

Standing up there, Mark and I surveyed the town of Chelan, which was hugging the end of the lake and framing the Chelan River in picture-perfect repose. In a bend of the river, just near the dam, three fan-shaped baseball fields formed a semicircle right at the edge of town. Behind them, perfectly laid out streets delineated properties crowded with an assortment of evergreens and deciduous trees. Beyond the town, more foothills rose up to form the perfect backdrop. Over near where the river exited the lake, two beautiful bloody marys were waiting to be poured. They seemed very far away.

When we made our first climb, they were spilling water over the dam so that the river was racing down toward the Columbia. In the hot still air up on the Butte, you could hear the steady hiss and rumble of the rapids below. The river was a jumble of blues and whites and greens as it made its way toward the violent plunge down through the gorge. In every direction we looked, the surrounding countryside put on a wonderful show.

The Butte is the perfect place to observe the vast agriculture that surrounds the Chelan region. Looking to the east, you are high enough to see the wheat fields that blanket the Columbia Plateau right to the rim of the Columbia River Valley. This is the western edge of a giant swath of wheat-producing land that extends to the east and curves to the south, all the way to the rolling Palouse region of southeastern Washington, central Idaho, and northeastern Oregon.

From the Butte, the magnitude of the Cascade Mountains begins to come into focus. Many of the snow-capped peaks that aren't visible from lake level begin to emerge to the west. The drier mountains of the east give way to more and more trees with each successive ridgeline. Rising up out of the amphitheater that cradles lower Lake Chelan, the Butte allows one to see the extent of the wilderness that rolls out to the west. From up on the Butte, the mountains seem endless.

As striking as the views are from the top, they become even more impressive as you move above the Butte. This is the esoteric realm of the hang gliders and paragliders who frequent the area. To many of these pilots, the Butte is a venerable standout among launch points. They will tell you it's one of the best gliding spots in the country. It has, on several occasions, hosted the World Hang Gliding Championship.

On hot afternoons, the warmer air rises and creates spiraling updrafts called thermals. These often manifest visibly as dust devils on the Butte itself and on the wide plains of the Columbia Plateau. The dust usually indicates just the base of currents that can rise up thousands of feet. As far as thermal riding and cross-country gliding, Chelan Butte is a world-class place to fly.

Amy and I are paraglider pilots. We cut our teeth and got our first solo flights launching from the flanks of Tiger Mountain on the western slopes of the Cascades. There, the skies are filled with pilots of extraordinary talent. Most of them rave about Chelan Butte.

Amy was the driving force behind our foray into paragliding. She took one flight and was hooked. She dreamed of soaring in the air currents of locations all over the world. My goal was a little narrower in scope. I wanted to learn how to glide so I could spend afternoons flying off the Butte. I had passed many hours on the deck of our house, watching people ply the winds above the lake. They would slowly arc higher and higher until they looked like tiny bright fruit flies over a giant wine glass. I had to know what they were seeing up there.

At Tiger Mountain, I would constantly ask people about the Butte.

"Fantastic," they would say, "wonderful flying, but..."

"One of my favorite places to fly, but..."

"It's gorgeous up there, but..."

Inevitably, there was a "but."

That "but" would be phrased in many different ways, all of which amounted to the same sentiment. The Butte was not for beginners.

"But you have to be careful."

"But you better know what you're doing."

"Nine times out of ten, you're going to be fine, but..."

My personal favorite was, "The Butte is a kick in the pants, but it's 'Big Boy Air' up there."

A lot of pilots use the huge field down at Chelan Falls Park for their landing strip. One pilot told me about his experience landing there.

"Everyone says to watch the lake," he told me. "If it starts turning dark blue uplake, it means waves are forming and the winds are going to be kicking around down below real soon. You want to get down quick."

On his first flight off the Butte, the lake started turning dark blue.

"What nobody told me," he said, "was how quick it happens."

He was 4,000 feet above the Butte when he first noticed the change. He started coasting quickly down toward the Columbia River. As it turned out, he didn't coast quickly enough.

"When I started down, the river looked as flat as a mirror. By the time I was a thousand feet above the landing zone, the river had whitecaps."

Gliding into a buffeting wind that kept curling his glider and dropping him in violent descents created by wind shear, he made a hasty decision.

"At the last minute, I said, 'to hell with this,' and I turned and splashed, paraglider and all, right in the shallows of the river. I had a hard fight to get myself and my gear to shore."

This was a happy end to an encounter with "Big Boy Air." The Butte has racked up its share of injuries. On at least one occasion, a helicopter has been called in to evacuate a downed and injured pilot from the desolate hillside far below the launch point. Veteran gliders will always emphasize it takes experience and common sense to fly there.

Despite the sometimes challenging conditions, the local gliders have taken flying off the Butte to a near art form. It is incredible to watch the paragliders as they lift off effortlessly and then dip and soar around the top of the Butte. They come down and hover motionless, just inches from the ground, only to twitch the risers and vault up into the sky again. It is amazing to watch the hang gliders take off and start spiraling upward so quickly that it's difficult to believe they are flying without engines.

I practiced flying at Tiger Mountain. I practiced kiting, which is pulling the glider up in the wind on flat ground and balancing it in place without leaving the earth. I would kite in the field behind my parents' place at Lake Chelan. I would kite at the park down at Chelan Falls. Back home, I would kite at Lake Sammamish when the winds came down from the north. I would kite at Gasworks Park in Seattle when the wind came up from the south.

I really wanted to fly off the Butte. I really didn't want to die. By late August, I felt ready to take my first glide out over the Columbia River. I consulted the local experts.

"Make sure you are up there between 12:00 and 2:00 in the afternoon," they said, "That's when the good winds and lift come through. Otherwise, you're in for a quick and boring ride."

"Great," I said. "Thanks for the info."

That settled it. I would be taking off no later then 10 a.m. A quick and boring ride sounded just right.

I made my maiden flight. It was quick. It was not boring. In gliders' vernacular, a "sled ride" is a flight with very little lift where the pilot descends in a relatively unblemished glide rate of six feet forward, one foot down, straight to the landing zone. That is what best describes my first flight. That is what best describes my second flight, and my third. Each time I would push the departure time a little later, finally moving up past the noon hour.

On my fourth flight, I happened across Alex and Nik Peterson. These two brothers are among the many local flyers who have mastered the terrain and temperament of the Butte. Nik was lifting gently off the ground in the wind and then swooping back and forth above the grass before landing and then taking off again. Alex was on the hillside taking some video. When his brother drifted too far down the ridge, Alex took a moment to chat with me.

"Dusties are coming up," he said, "should be some powerful lift pretty soon."

"Great," I said out loud.

"Crud," said the voice in my head (it didn't actually use the word crud). "Big boy air."

"I know," said the other voice in my head.

"Probably going to have to bail into the river," said the first voice.

"Shut up," said the other voice.

I've never been sure if it's my ego or my id, but one of the two is a particularly pessimistic fatalist.

Alex and his brother were going to catch the thermals and go cross-country to the east. They were just waiting for more lift. He watched a dust devil, a thin little tornado of detritus, spiral around on the hill below us. He nodded as if this was his cue, and began to set up his paraglider.

I nodded as if this was my cue too, even though it wasn't. Then I got my glider set up. I watched Alex lift effortlessly off the Butte without so much as taking a step forward. I launched, with considerably more effort, and then tried to follow him and see if I could mimic his skills for catching thermals. I couldn't. He quickly soared up and away.

I wasn't completely skunked though. The thermals were there for the catching, and I had some luck. I almost immediately started moving upward as well.

From the launch zone, Amy yelled up to me, "Good job."

There was a slight tone in her voice that reminded me of the way someone sounds when they are congratulating a toddler for getting most of a spoon full of applesauce into his mouth. Still, the encouragement was appreciated, and hardly necessary. I was already ecstatic about finally catching some updraft.

Above me, Alex spiraled ever higher until his wing was a small butterfly in the sky. Although clearly not a master of the air currents, I was inching up as well, circling in the thermals and then losing them. I would sink a little and then stumble into the next one. These vortexes carried some power. They would ruffle the wing when I entered them like a billowing sail, and then hook the fabric firmly and throw me down into the harness with strong force. The void of empty air between me and the summit of the Butte grew increasingly larger.

I had been focusing so hard on catching the thermals and actively flying that it was quite a while before I felt I was high enough to relax, coast, and look around. What I saw was so spectacular that it caused the hair on the back of my neck to stand up.

Realtors use a term called "outclassing the neighborhood." This happens when a giant fancy house is built in a neighborhood of more modest homes. A mansion nestled in a trailer park, for example, doesn't quite work. One of the things that I find appealing about Lake

Chelan is that, as extraordinary as the lake is, it doesn't outclass the neighborhood. The lake is surrounded on all sides by incredible natural wonders.

As I rose higher above the Butte, one of these extraordinary features came into view. Clearly visible were the northern reaches of the famed channeled scablands of eastern Washington. This is the description given to one of the most unique geologic structures on the planet. It was a fascinating vantage of a place with an even more fascinating history.

The channeled scablands are the product of two incredible geologic events. The first occurred between six and sixteen million years ago. During that time, lava flowed out of giant vents near the Blue Mountains in southeastern Washington and northeastern Oregon. What resulted was one of the world's largest accumulations of lava. Geologically speaking, this is a very young lava flow. It created a formation called a flood basalt which coated the region of the plateau from Oregon and Idaho, across most of eastern Washington. Thick layers of overlapping basalt flows cover a total area of about 63,000 square miles.

The second and no less astounding event that shaped the scablands was the Missoula flood. This flood, or probably series of floods, occurred as the last ice age was drawing to a close. While our friend the Columbia Valley–Okanogan Lobe of the Cordilleran ice sheet was working its magic to help create Lake Chelan, another lobe, the Pend Oreille Lobe, was creating some mischief to the east. This finger of ice moved down the Idaho panhandle and dammed the Clark Fork River, creating an enormous prehistoric glacial lake known as Lake Missoula.

The ice dam was some 2,000 feet high, and the lake flooded the lowlands and valleys of western Montana to as much as 200 miles eastward. The surface area of the lake was 3,000 square miles, with a volume about half the size of Lake Michigan.

At least once, and probably several times, this dam ruptured, and the result was a cataclysmic flood. It's estimated that when the dam of Lake Missoula collapsed, water escaped at a rate of ten times the combined flow of all the rivers in the world. Water was moving at approximately 65 miles an hour, draining the lake in just a couple of days.

These floods across the grand basalt structures of the Columbia Plateau are what created the channeled scablands. This area is characterized by its unique flat-bottomed valleys with sheer vertical walls. Also across this region there are massive potholes and strange ripple marks in the earth.

Some of the more famous structures are the Grand Coulee, the Moses Coulee, Palouse Falls, and Dry Falls. Dry Falls, created by the Missoula flood events, is the largest waterfall in North America. Unfortunately, it draws considerably fewer tourists than other famous waterfalls because, as the name implies, it is dry. However, if one were to witness the runoff that once flowed over this cataract, they would see a waterfall three times as wide as Niagara Falls and about two and a half times as tall. Because of the arid nature of Douglas County, however, the honeymooners, as a general rule, have stayed away.[9]

From the air, these gashes in the land and tabletop mesas created bizarre images as they stretched off into the hazy horizon. The patchwork of farmed fields morphed around the strange formations like oil slicks slithering across rippled water. Some of the landscape appeared to be from a different planet.

Turning the glider back toward Chelan, another highbrow neighbor of the lake came into view. Stretching from north to south, as far as I could see in either direction, was the incredible panorama of the Cascade Range. On that particular cloudless day, the visibility to the west was unlimited. Lake Chelan was a beautiful shimmering strand. Peak after peak lined up, gaining subtle stair steps in elevation and displaying mantles of snow. From where I was sitting, it was an illustration of how much of the lake is truly buried in high mountains.

Five volcanoes rose above the Cascade Crest. To the north, the pure white crown of Mount Baker reached 10,778 feet into the sky. Directly to the west, just a fingernail away from the lake, was the sharp cone of Glacier Peak that juts 10,541 feet upward. Far to the south was Mount Adams, a perfectly symmetrical ice cream scoop of a mountain. To the west of that was the yawning open mouth of the Mount Saint Helens crater.

Much closer, dominating the middle distance to the south, was the crown jewel of the range, Mount Rainier. At 14,410 feet, it was a massive dome of glaciers and rock that dwarfed all the mountains around it.

I am probably joined by almost all of my fellow Washingtonians when I express a feeling of reverence toward that particular mountain. For all of us who live in the surrounding lowlands, the mountain is a sacred natural monument. I have always been enamored with Mount Rainier and had even attempted to climb it on two occasions, but success had eluded me.

Moving in a southwesterly direction now, I was heading right toward the massive strata cone that stood in white and slate blue majesty. Although a long car ride away, from the air the mountain appeared remarkably close. It looked as if you could reach out and touch it. It had been three years since my last attempt to climb to the summit of Mount Rainier. As I coasted down toward the Columbia River, the sight was mesmerizing. It seemed to beckon me.

When I landed down at Chelan Falls, I was overwhelmed by the flight. I had spent so much time learning to paraglide and waiting for the right opportunity, just so I could soar above the Butte and know what all of those glider pilots were feeling and see what they were seeing. For all the anticipation, the flight was more memorable than I could have hoped.

I looked at the Butte, and I thought about Mount Rainier. Somehow, in that moment, the two seemed connected to me in a way that I couldn't really explain. I decided right then that I would make another attempt to climb Mount Rainier, and that Chelan Butte was going to be my training hill. The dreaded trail that Mark had referred to as "The Elevator Shaft" was going to become the proving ground for my journey to the highest point in the Cascade Mountains.

To that end, I started my first training trudge up the Butte the following week. In my ensuing conditioning hikes, I began to develop an intimate relationship with the tall grassy abutment.

The Butte is littered with tiny tokens of the people who have passed over it. Miners have put pick and shovel to the flanks in search of gold and silver. A small gold rush was touched off in 1907 with the discovery of trace amounts of precious minerals. Claims were staked, and small fortunes were made and lost. Two mining claims were sold for $20,000 in 1908.[1]

The base of the butte, on the north side, was bored out in 1927 to create the two-mile penstock that conducts water from the lake down to the PUD powerhouse in Chelan Falls. Radio towers extend up from the summit. A tangle of crisscrossed old wires can be seen emerging from the dirt all over the mountain. Orchards have been planted up the sides, torn down, and replanted again. Jeep trails, dirt bike trails, and access roads sprawl sparsely through the dry grass. A large collection of white rocks is arranged into numbers, broadcasting to the town below that the most recent senior class has graduated from the local high school and left their mark.

Still, the Butte is a quiet and lonely place. Wandering along the empty trails, you feel far removed from the people and the town below. There's often nothing but the sound of wind, the call of birds, the occasional whistle of a marmot or exploding wings of a grouse. There is wild solitude to be found on the Butte. Always, the beautiful swath of Lake Chelan stretches out below. Day to day, even minute to minute, the water presents a different visage that encompasses an infinity of blues, from the palest reflection of the sky to the darkest navy blue that hides in the shadows.

I made several trips up the Butte that spring. The thing that I always pondered, as I wandered on and off the dusty trails, was what a truly tough little mountain it was. Over the ages, glaciers tore at it from every angle. Water carved its way into the Butte constantly and still does today. The continental ice shelf would have completely covered it, or come close, as it scoured down the eastern front of the mountains. I had to admire this rugged little butte for standing up against a quarter continent of ice and holding its ground. It is the base of the Butte, ground together with glacial till under unimaginable pressure, that held strong and formed up the earthen dam that still impounds the lake.

As I would hike along the ridge of the Butte, I wondered what it would have been like to stand up there at the end of the ice age. Might the great Missoula flood have come roaring over the eastern lip of the Columbia Valley, full of ice chunks and debris, howling down through McNeil Canyon and then surging like a tidal wave up the base of the mountain? Did this happen more than once?

The Butte is the keeper of an interesting tale. It presided over the incredible collision that formed the lake. Now it stands as a steadfast sentinel over her lower shores, a worthy guardian of the lake it holds so firmly in place.

Lake Project

Day 340: Austria

One of the most sweeping depictions of Austria's Salzkammergut region occurs in the opening scenes of *The Sound of Music*. An arial montage, shot by helicopter, portrays soaring views of the Austrian Alps and the beautiful glacier-cut lakes in the region. Most notable is a straight down look at Fuschlsee, a radiating topaz blue lake nestled in the mountains just outside of Salzburg. The collection of images culminates with the universally recognized flyover scene of Julie Andrews singing and twirling in a high mountain meadow. It remains, to this day, one of the most dramatic introductions in film history. I couldn't wait to get a firsthand look at Emperor Franz Joseph I's "earthly paradise."

On a late fall afternoon, Amy and I found ourselves driving along the sun-kissed shores of the many lakes dotting the Salzkammergut. Our friends Mark and Meggan and John and Kerry rounded out our intrepid group of lake explorers. We passed by Fuschlsee and stared at the gray wands of the alpine range, clothed in evergreens and reflecting, picture-like, off the glassy waters. We stopped and had lunch at Lake Wolfgangsee, enjoying wiener schnitzel with cranberry jelly while gentle waves lapped against the bulkhead and sailboats darted about in the early afternoon breeze. The mountains on the far shore were a decoupage of green. It was the first days of October, but the sky was cloudless. The air was warm and slightly balmy.

After a leisurely tour over winding mountain roads and through broad lake-filled valleys, we arrived at our destination. We were staying at Lake Halstatt, nestled at the foot of the Dachstein Range, in the heart of the Austrian Alps. The soaring Dachstein massif is one of the most prominent in Austria. It is steeped in ancient myth and legend.

The lake lies against such vertical looming mountainsides that, at times, it seems the imposing rock walls might just smother it outright.

The small medieval town of Halstatt is so pinned against the mountains that the inhabitants over the ages could scarcely find room for a cemetery. The result is that bones were exhumed after ten years of burial and then entombed more economically in the ancient church to make room for the recently deceased. A tour of the crypt treats visitors to a room full of bones and skulls with dates and painted decorations on them, a heartfelt if slightly macabre tribute to relatives lost.

Throughout many of the world's alpine lakes, including most of the lakes in the Salzkammergut, there is a familiarity. The shores of Lake Chelan, though on a different continent, bear strong resemblances to many of the mountain lakes of Europe. There are similar colors, sounds, and even smells.

Halstatt is a distinct exception to this. The lake is extraordinarily unique even to its nearby sisters. It is more hemmed in, encased, at times shadier, and slightly less blue. Beyond that, there is also something not so tangible. There is the palpable feel of ancient history. The oppressive weight of the towering mountains looming overhead seems to have locked Halstatt into isolation and secluded it from the modern world. The tiny hamlet on the shore appears lost in time. Ancient buildings, dating back before the renaissance, stand perfectly preserved.

We enjoyed ourselves immensely on the shores of Lake Halstatt. My friend Kerry is an adorable woman with boundless energy. When she is around, it frequently feels like life is your sport, and she is your cheerleader. She is so charismatic that she could inspire a raucous party to break out within the walls of a cloistered nunnery. By the end of our first night, she had befriended half of the locals. One bartender asked for her hand in marriage.

Her husband John is a man's man who is happiest in life when he is catching or throwing a ball. I have heard him described by others as "a good dude" more than anyone else I've ever met.

Mark and Meggan bring the party with them wherever they go, but perhaps even more so when they are in Europe. Meggan is never happier than when she's in the old country.

We spent the evening in the town bierstube having a singalong and playing acoustic guitars with the local college rock band. We learned many of the Austrian drinking songs and even made up a few. We stumbled home through empty cobblestone streets to take a midnight swim in the frigid waters of early October.

In the daytime, we walked down quiet country lanes with quaint old cottages that seemed like they were torn from the pages of a Brothers Grimm tale. We hiked high up the side of the Dachstein, following a brilliant blue stream into a deep cool forest and then crisscrossing over a terrace of waterfalls that carved grotto-like channels in the ancient smooth rock. We paused high on the mountainside and looked out across the giant cirque that cradled Lake Halstatt. From every angle, the lake was magnificent.

I found myself wishing we had more time. It seemed as though we had only just scratched the surface of this mountain-rimmed natural wonder. On the morning we left, I wandered down to the lake shore and sat in the warm sunshine. I closed my eyes and imagined Lake Chelan. Then I opened my eyes and gazed across Lake Halstatt. The two seemed impossible to compare. This was something I would have to ponder in the coming days. The true difficulty of my lake assessment quest had now become apparent.

We left the town of Halstatt and headed back toward the city of Salzburg. We had already been on the shores of Wolfgangsee, but I was hoping to find a place where we could get more of a birds-eye view. To that end, we stopped and rode a cable pulley up the mountains above the broad waters of the lake. As we moved up the mountainside and looked down across the valley, we watched the late afternoon sun reflect brilliant shards of sunlight off the surface of the lake, like myriad flashbulbs going off in a crowded stadium. In every direction the Alps rolled upward, brilliant green, capped by naked pale gray rock. It was an astounding sight.

To get back to our car, we tried our hand at the luge on a track that snaked its way down the steep mountain. The attendant who sold us our tickets and gave us our luge sleds looked at us with a stern expression and said, "There are two kinds of people who ride down the luge. One kind is careful, and uses the braking mechanism, and never flies off the track and gets seriously injured. The other kind is a group that we simply call Americans."

"He was laying it on pretty thick," I said to Mark right before I set off down the track. "It has to be at least pretty safe."

"Of course it is," Mark said. "They're not going to let us kill ourselves."

I was about to learn an important lesson in cultural differences. It seems in Austria's less litigious society they consider individual people to be, at least to some degree, responsible for their own safety. It sounds absurd, but it's true.

Fifteen seconds later and 200 feet down the track, I was screaming up the side of the luge berm on a hairpin turn and watching the right runners pop up over the edge of the track. I don't mean screaming as in I was going extremely fast. I mean screaming as in I was actually screaming while I looked over my right hip and saw no track, but only a rock strewn hillside and the lake far below. I imagined the old bones of missing American tourists scattered in and around those rocks. I pulled as hard as I could on the brake. I contemplated the two remaining runners that were the only thing keeping me from flying free of the course and hurtling into empty space. I willed them to adhere to the track.

I arrived at the bottom shaking, breathless, and with a slight case of laryngitis. Above me, I heard another terrible scream, and another one shortly after that, as my friends Mark and John both enjoyed a similar brush with death on the wicked curve.

"The hills are alive...with the sound of terrified American idiots," I thought to myself. The cable operator was looking at me with a mirthless expression. He shook his head and then walked away.

Later, Amy, Meggan, and Kerry wandered out into the meadow and did their obligatory tribute to Julie Andrews, running across a field in the high Alps, extending their arms out, spinning, and singing. As the afternoon grew late, we reluctantly departed the Lakes District, the girls now alive with the sound of music, the guys just happy to be alive at all.

For me, it was a valuable look at some truly magnificent lakes. Back at the hotel, I took an hour to write down some notes about the lakes we had seen and the mountains through which we had traveled. Then we spent our last night in Austria, out on the streets of

Salzburg, celebrating the incredible Salzkammergut, and anticipating the second half of the trip.

As we wandered up ancient castles and into centuries-old breweries, I found my mind drifting to Lake Chelan and the central question motivating my trip. Did Austria have the greatest lake in the world? Had anything I encountered overwhelmingly outshined my own champion of lakes?

Halstatt was an extraordinary lake to be sure, with an incredible, almost haunting history and a mythical ancient charm, but there was, in my mind, a slight touch of claustrophobia to the lake basin. Lower Chelan was a sweeping broad valley with gentle rolling sunny hills. Halstatt was a deep rock-lined bowl. It was stunning in its appearance and dramatic in the severity of its placement within the Alps, but perhaps just ever so slightly too severe.

As John Muir once observed, "Sometimes the mountains are more enjoyable when viewed from afar." As a result of the incredible slope of the mountains that surround the lake, it was difficult to truly take in the scope of the mountains themselves. The incredible massif of the Dachstein, shrouded in glaciers, loomed almost directly above Lake Halstatt, but because of the giant walls that rose straight up from the lake, there was no point on the lake from which the upper, slightly more distant peaks of the Dachstein could be viewed. No glaciers were visible from the lake.

Still, the lower sides of the mountains were incredible. There was a point, at the extreme end of the town of Halstatt, from which one could look up the lakeshore at the tiny village, with its ancient stone church belltower protruding above the buildings. The image was framed by the immense front face of the Dachstein massif. This particular view might rank as one of the most stunning vignettes in the entire world. The town of Halstatt is a world heritage site, and for obvious reasons. The lake itself is also nothing shy of breathtaking. Taken as a whole, however, it simply could not lay claim to the greatest lake in the world.

I considered a section of Chelan deep in the mountians near a place called Safety Harbor where the lake runs relatively straight for about 17 miles. It occurred to me that if you could somehow pick up that section of Chelan and drop it next to Halstatt, you would be looking at two pretty comparable pieces of real estate. If there was a way to isolate that section of Chelan and remove it from north central Washington, however, you would be leaving 38 miles of additional lake behind. In that sense, Lake Chelan was miles ahead of Halstatt, so to speak.

More importantly, many of the sections you left behind would look nothing like Lake Halstatt. Some of it would be framed by snowcapped peaks. Some of it would be surrounded by beautiful arid landscapes. Parts of it would have a grand gorge carving away from them. Other parts would have tumbling creeks and waterfalls that dropped right into the lake. There was no way to ignore the fact that Lake Chelan was simply blessed with a plethora of diverse natural wonders that Lake Halstatt could not supplant.

The Salzkammergut is more than just one lake though. It is the extraordinary sum of all its parts. It is the collection of ten major lakes and countless smaller ones, set amongst extremely beautiful and impressive mountains. I could speculate that a book about the greatest lakes district in the world might very well crown this region. I couldn't say that for sure. I would first need to visit South America and Switzerland and northwest England, among other places. I could say for sure that I had just visited one of the most amazing places on the planet, and I knew that I would return. But I had other matters to attend to first. We were now leaving Austria and heading on to see one of the great lake-making processes in action. The following day, we would be heading to Santorini.

The Town of Chelan

The town of Chelan is a friendly place. When William Sanders and Henry Domke made their trip in a makeshift canoe down the lake, they were greeted by the native people with warmth and given food, clothing, and shelter. They were actually encouraged to settle near the site of the current town. This is the first record of what seems to be a longstanding tradition.

Early settler Don C. Mathers arrived in Chelan in 1893. He recorded the altruistic nature of the already established homesteaders.

"The People in Chelan gave us a welcome we never forgot," he said. "In the many years I have lived here, there was always a friend when we needed one."[10]

Shortly after his arrival, his family moved to 160 acres up near Cooper Gulch. They made a deal with their neighbor Charlie Schofield to haul logs onto the site to build a cabin. Mr. Schofield instructed the Mathers family to let him know when they were ready. When they had prepared the foundation and informed Mr. Schofield that everything was prepared, he replied that he would be there two days later at six in the morning.

The Mathers were amazed when the appointed hour arrived and the whole neighborhood showed up with axes and tools. They built the entire 18' x 30' cabin before nightfall. It was a good old-fashioned barn raising of sorts. No thanks were required or accepted. They told the family "it was a custom of the country to help a newcomer build his homestead cabin and to let him know he was one of the neighbors."[10]

This spirit of friendship and cooperation still seems prevalent in the town of Chelan. The whole area was built on a pioneering sense of enterprise that is hard to fathom in the modern age. The obstacles that needed to be overcome to get a foothold on the shores of the wilderness lake seem almost insurmountable by today's standards.

In 1889, Lewis Woodin and his partner A.F. Nichols devised a plan to bring their mechanical equipment (including an 8,500 pound boiler) halfway across the continent to create a sawmill. Everything was brought by train to Ellensburg, then by horse- and mule-drawn wagons up over the mountains to Wenatchee. It then continued on by river boats. Finally, horse power was used again to haul it all up the steep hill and into the Chelan Basin. The huge boiler was winched up using block and tackle in a process that took three days. An account of this entire journey seems so fraught with difficulty and setbacks that it reads like an epic Greek poem.

The whole town was founded on a sense of optimism and industriousness. In 1890, the newspaper called *The Chelan Leader* captured this sentiment.

> At the foot of beautiful Lake Chelan, where the Chelan River begins a terrific plunge to the Columbia, a little more than three miles in an air line from the last named stream, surrounded by majestic mountains and with an unhindered view for a dozen miles of the blue waters of the lake, on the north bank of the river is the prosperous and promising town of Chelan.

Promising it may have been. Prosperous is a statement that might lend itself to debate in the clearer eyes of retrospect. Some early business did thrive. One such business is Campbell's hotel. Completed in 1901, it was the dream of Judge Clinton C. Campbell to "erect a hostelry that was a credit to the community."

The resort still endures, surviving bust and boom cycles including the Great Depression. The original building stands nobly on the shore where the river exits the lake. It remains in the Campbell family to this day.

Likewise, there are orchards in the area that date back generations and continue to produce lucrative harvests. Most historical accounts, however, detail the difficulties of commercial success in the remote and initially untamed wilderness. The lake itself was the biggest draw of this region, rather than any single compelling economic opportunity. This is illustrated by the early Woodin–Nichols sawmill. Years after the mill had closed, their longtime employee Chris Robinson made this observation:

"Mr. Woodin, I think, was more impressed by the magnificent setting of the lake than by the business possibilities, such as the difficulties of logging and the finding of a market."[11]

Hard work and perseverance were the order of the day. Often, as is detailed in stirring accounts by early entrepreneurs, when one effort proved untenable, the new residents would ambitiously throw themselves into another, continuously searching for a way to create a life for themselves in a part of the country they had come to love. The abundance of fish in the lake, wild game in the area, and land that, when irrigated, produced ready crops, was an ever-present aid to help make ends meet.

Enterprise is still, at times, a challenge in the region. A major part of the economy is based on agriculture, with its susceptibility to market forces and the intermittent attacks of nature's uncooperative elements. Another large part of the economy is based on tourism, which is so seasonal that it often creates difficult barriers to longevity.

Then as now, there were occasional quarrels, but the spirit of cooperation still reigns supreme. While starting my own small business in the valley, I was often astounded by the welcoming spirit of people who already lived by the lake, and by their willingness to lend a hand. In all of my dealings in Chelan, I recall being involved in only one quarrel, and that was related to a homeowners association. Since homeowners associations exist specifically to ensure that neighbors won't get along, I don't consider this in any way to be a reflection on the Chelan community. As I recall, every single homeowner in that association was not actually even from Chelan.

Perhaps the welcoming and friendly spirit of the area comes from the gratitude of people who are so lucky as to be living in general proximity to one of North America's greatest treasures. Maybe it has to do with the 300 average days of sunshine every year.

Talking about her arrival at Lake Chelan, early pioneer Mrs. Ben F Smith remarked:

> The weather was simply delightful all the following year. The sun shone from a cloudless sky day after day and week after week until we almost wished for a rousing thunderstorm to break the monotony. And when the gently falling rains did come, how different from the roaring, splashing downpours of Iowa.[1]

Perhaps it's the unique location, a town set in a desert-like environment, but still reposing next to billions of gallons of water. Maybe it's the town itself. In July of 1889, with great foresight, it was surveyed by Henry Carr and laid out by Probate Judge Charles H. Ballard, who included unusually wide roads to allow for stagecoaches to turn around. These broad streets give the downtown what might now be referred to as good feng shui. It allows the pedestrian, right in the heart of downtown, to remain connected visually to the lake and the surrounding mountains.

The town moves at a slow pace. Coming across the river into town on the Woodin Avenue Bridge, drivers are directed to go only 20 miles per hour. In our culture of on-the-go, fast, frenetic movement, this speed seems almost painfully slow. It takes an act of will and serious concentration to restrain the accelerator and keep under the legal speed limit.

This deceleration is in keeping with a longstanding tradition. Visitors a century ago, crossing the original bridge in a horse-drawn carriage, were greeted with a sign that stated, "Anyone crossing this bridge at faster than a walk is subject to a $10 fine."

The 20 mile per hour speed limit sign that exists today sets the tone for anyone entering the town. To me it seems to say, "Welcome to Chelan. Slow down and relax. You're here now. There's no need to hurry."

Things simply run a little differently and at a different pace. A T-shirt that appears from time to time, proudly worn by the locals, is a testament to this. It bears the slogan, "I don't care how they do it on the west side." This refers to the greater Seattle area on the other side of the mountains.

There is a way of getting things done here that harkens back many generations. It is small town America at its best. For an outsider, it can take some getting used to.

Chelan is, at times, such an amalgam of a storybook country town that it can seem made up. On a warm Sunday in late spring, Mark and I were working at the Bluff when we had to run into town for supplies. We drove down the narrow country lane called Dietrich Road, where Dilbert Dietrich, a septuagenarian orchardist, waved at us from his tractor as he moved among the tress. We turned right on the highway and drove past Vin du Lac vineyard. Stopping to let a dog cross the road, we could hear the sound of live bluegrass music from the shady side lawn of the winery.

A half mile down the road, we entered downtown Chelan only to find dozens of girls in cheerleading outfits and young boys in high school lettermen jackets sitting on the lawn of the park eating burgers from the lakeside burger drive-thru. They were laughing and giggling while a group of high school band members sat in the shade playing the song "Tequila." Everyone was happy and smiling and picnicking. We had apparently come across the end of the Memorial Day parade.

Back then, Mark and I spent most of our time in Seattle. It felt like we had stumbled into a movie set, or some kind of Potemkin village. It was so picture-perfect it almost seemed like we were in an episode of the *Twilight Zone*, and something bad was about to happen. This was far beyond our comfort zone. I wanted to race back over the mountains to the city, speed right to Pike Place Market, run into Victor Steinbrueck park and smell the garbage in the overflowing cans while listening to the bums yell at their imaginary friends. With luck our car would get stolen.

As it was, we drove, eyes straight forward, past old couples holding hands and kids riding bicycles with clickers in the spokes. (Clickers in their spokes. I'm not kidding.)

This is the near perfect small town charm of Chelan. The people who live there are just plain friendly. The people from out of town seem to become more friendly while they are there. Well-maintained facades in the business district speak of a bygone era. Kids play in the parks. People stroll beside the river. Dogs chase sticks in back yards with low fences. The town is postcard perfect. If there had been a cloud in the sky that Memorial Day, I'm sure a rainbow would have arced its way right down onto Woodin Avenue. This is the town that one would hope to find at the base of a lake, if one were trying to prove that lake was the greatest lake in the world.

> In every community there were both Joys and sorrows and Chelan was no different. I remember that the concern of one was the concern of all. There were no organized charities, but if anyone was in need at Chelan, the need was supplied.

—Christopher Robinson Switzer, born in Lake Chelan in 1895.[11]

The Lower Wapato Basin

Lake mile 1 to lake mile 8

As our house at the Bluff was nearing completion, I spent many hours building a trail down to the lake. My partner in this effort was my faithful dog Otis. He would sit and watch me for hours at a time. He seemed unable to comprehend why anyone would commit so much time to hard labor when there was a beautiful shimmering lake just 30 feet away.

On occasion, he would come and nudge my legs toward the water with his muzzle. At other times, he would come next to me and begin digging in the dirt with his paws to hurry the process along. When I would stop to take breaks, he would sit next to me and rest his head in my lap. He would let out quiet little whimpers. Loosely translated, I think he was saying, "Hey idiot, did you happen to notice the beautiful lake right there?"

I did notice the beautiful lake all the time. From my vantage point on the ever-lengthening trail, I could look straight uplake across Key Bay, all the way past Wapato Point. This is the widest section of the lake, and it is encompassed by incredible rolling hillsides of farm country. The backdrop to this was the forested mountainsides of Slide Ridge and Stormy Mountain.

The surface of the lake would reflect the hills and mountains back, brightening them with golden halos of light. At the point that the landscape transitioned from brilliantly colored farmlands to unblemished forested mountains, it looked very much like the Piedmont region of Italy, where the hill country ascends into the Alps. I would think this from time to time, and then I would stop myself, because it seemed in a way to cheapen what, to me, was an extraordinary display of nature. It was a scene reminiscent of the dramatic landscapes of Europe, but this seemed to be almost a thin veil that was draped over the true essence of the landscape. That essence was the unique characteristics of the American West.

The hill on which I was working was largely a cliff of barren white and pink granite. It was an arid environment found throughout the western Unites States and Canada known as a sagebrush steppe. Brown, bone-dry bunchgrass, native buckwheat, sagebrush, and tumbleweeds covered a landscape that could only be described as a desert. One could easily confuse a snapshot of this area with a picture from New Mexico or Palm Springs.

The farmlands and hills across from me, and the vast Columbia Plateau to the east, were the epitome of North American cowboy country. This dry landscape is distinct from anywhere else in the world. The mountains uplake were simply the perfect depiction of the mountains of the western United States. The land that Lewis and Clark passed through on their journey from the eastern front of the Rocky Mountains to the eastern front of the Cascades was all markedly similar to the diverse mix of land that surrounds lower Lake Chelan.

After the Nez Pierce lost their storied battle with US cavalry forces, their leader, Chief Joseph, was expelled from his homeland in central Idaho and eastern Oregon to the Colville Reservation north of Chelan. When he visited Lake Chelan, in the final years of the nineteenth century, he would most certainly have felt a fondness for the landscape that so closely mirrored the place of his birth.

The incredible bowl of lower Lake Chelan was a definitive depiction of the western continent. Unfortunately, one cannot describe a place by referencing it to itself, and so the similarities of many European locations kept creeping into my head whenever I gazed across the water. It looked like Tuscany. It looked like Piedmont. It looked like lower Bavaria in the Lake Constance region. It was all these things wrapped in the romance of the wild, and still largely untamed, American West.

When the days came to an end, I would strip off my work clothes and then take a running leap off the rocks into the aqua blue waters of the lake. I would float there, with my face to the sky, and let this tiny little portion of the billons of gallons of crystal clear lake water wash away the dirt and dust. Otis would swim lazy circles around me.

"You can't do this in Tuscany," I frequently thought.

I'm not the only person who has noticed the similarities of European locations to the Lake Chelan area. In the eastern end of the lake, on the south shore, sits a winery called Tsillan Cellars. The tasting room is a Tuscan style building, and the winery is billed as "An Italian country retreat recreated on the gently sloping shores of deep water Lake Chelan."

Bob Jankelson is the owner and creator of the winery. Having spent a lot of time in the hill country of Italy, he immediately recognized the similarity of scenery in the lower Chelan Valley. He set out to create the Italian winery experience at Lake Chelan. This was a monumental effort. The tasting room is a striking villa-inspired structure with over two tons of marble imported from Italy. The view from the grounds is breathtaking.

Originally, the wine industry in the Chelan Valley was a small consortium of grape growers with nascent vines and quaint tasting rooms. That charm is still present, but the wine industry along the sides of the lake has matured. Bob Jankelson stated that his goal was to create a world-class winery. Considering the incredible vineyards, grounds, and structure at Tsillan Cellars, it is clear to see that he has succeeded. His award-winning wines seem to punctuate this accomplishment.

Many other vintners have matured as well, with a host of highly recognized wines and a collection of ever-growing and impressive vineyard properties. When referring to the region, Jankelson describes it as being "like Napa Valley, but with an incredible lake."

The ratio of vineyards to apple orchards began an impressive shift over the years and appears to be headed toward parity. Perhaps the crowning achievement of the collective vineyards in the valley was the success of a hard fought campaign to have the Chelan Valley recognized and designated as a unique American Viticulture Area. This was a strong testament to the quality and uniqueness of grapes grown in the area and the impressive vintages being produced. The Chelan wine industry had slowly come of age, and the world had taken notice.

As I thought more and more about how I would designate the greatest lake in the world, I felt it would be important not to put too much weight on the attributes the lake had which were the result of human development or intervention. The things that people build along the shores of a lake are relatively impermanent. The attributes which make a lake the greatest lake in the world needed to be attributes that would endure through the millennia. Still, I had to admit that being able to enjoy award winning wines from the numerous world class vineyards in the valley was nice. It didn't really set Chelan ahead of any other lakes in the world, but it certainly didn't suck.

Manson and the Upper Wapato Basin

Lake mile 8 to 15

Building a house is like having a baby. I don't mean having a baby as in giving birth. It's like having a newborn baby in the house. It sounds like a fun and exciting thing to do, but the reality is not quite so romantic. The reality is months and months of drawn-out misery. You lose night after night of sleep. The house is full of crying, only when building a house it's not the baby who is crying. It's you, every time a new and unanticipated invoice arrives.

Then after the baby has accomplished a few months of growing, he or she starts to be fun. By the end of the first year, the baby is a twenty-pound bundle of cheap entertainment. You start to think nostalgically about the first few months, somehow convincing yourself that it wasn't really all that bad. If you are not careful, you can make the critical mistake of opting to have another baby. Then the cycle of misery reignites.

This was how building a house was for me. Shortly after we broke ground on our house at Chelan Bluff, Amy and I had purchased a second piece of property in Lake Chelan, right next to my parents' farmhouse. We thought it would be fun to one day build our dream house there, near what was becoming our family compound.

One fall day, after our first year of renting out the Bluff as a vacation rental, I announced to Amy that we should build another house on that lot.

"Really?"

"Yes," I said. "Since we have a successful rental business, why not replicate the same thing at our other property?"

"Doesn't a successful business usually make a profit?"

Amy is always harping about these kinds of boring details. She is, however, well aware that, once I have committed to an idea, nothing can stop me, except possibly another idea for another project. This second idea almost inevitably appears once the first project is about twenty percent underway. That's the exact moment when you still have the immense and daunting bulk of the first project ahead of you, but you've gone too far to cancel it.

With the paint still drying on our first Chelan house, we started construction on our second home, and, as spring follows winter, a third project poked its head up out of a muddy hole and, not seeing a shadow, decided to present itself. My parents announced they were selling their house and buying another place six doors downlake and that their farmhouse was going to be sold as well.

The farm, with its rustic old house, aging barn, small orchard and garden, had found a special place in my heart over the years. I couldn't bear to see it go. Also, unbeknownst to my parents, I had secretly stored all of my old junk in the barn. I didn't want to be forced to move it. I really hate moving. Purchasing the Farmhouse from my parents seemed like a much easier option.

Amy loved the farm, but she was concerned we were over-committing.

"Come on," I told her. "It'll be fun. We'll restore the house to its former glory. It'll be like our own version of the book *Under a Tuscan Sun*."

As it turned out, I was to be reminded of that comment on several occasions in the ensuing months. To facilitate the purchase of the farm, my younger brother Jim and his wife Kris became our partners in the new house we were building next door. This house sat about 60 feet back from the lake with a year-round stream that ran through the property. We named that house the Lazy Creek Lake House. Usually we shortened it to Lazy Creek. In retrospect, Jim and I don't recall having much time to be lazy during or after the construction, but the name remains.

With our partnership in place on the new house and construction underway, Amy and I sat down and signed papers on my parents' old house a month later. We had now officially "bought the farm," so to speak. To assuage Amy's concerns I told her, "Relax. It's real estate. What could go wrong?"

This was another pearl of wisdom that would be repeated back to me on several occasions in the coming years.

The Farmhouse was built in 1919. I could talk about the frustrations of old wiring and aging plumbing. I could lament the restoration of ancient lath and plaster and the myriad other challenges related to an old house, but the truth is, we really enjoyed our time working on the Farmhouse. It was the first time we lived full time in the Chelan Valley. It took many months to spruce up the place.

This was during the warm sunny days of spring. In the afternoons, we would sit in the lounge chairs on the covered patio beneath an old wisteria tree and work our way through a bottle of wine. The late afternoon sun would glitter off the lake, and the flanks of Stormy Mountain and Slide Ridge to the southwest would glow in brilliant green springtime regalia.

Every morning, we would take a break, go grab coffee, and then drive through the maze of country roads in the low hills behind the town of Manson. I imagine this area was a seething disarray of violence and pressure when the two glaciers collided here during the last ice age. That event left the area with distinct hummocks, ridges, and hills that cradle three smaller lakes and numerous wetlands.

Orchards, vineyards, and even a berry farm blanket the hills, and a warren of narrow roads winds through them all. Horses and livestock graze sporadically in small pastures, and tractors move slowly down the lanes. There are no through-roads in this area. No one is passing by on their way to somewhere else. People are here because they live here, or they work here, or they are enjoying the fantastic scenery, quaint wineries, or the small fish-filled lakes. This is the country, quiet and off the beaten path.

Amy and I found a spot where a small army of marmots had built a village. We would sip our coffee and watch them scamper around the hillside in their happy marmot way. I had always felt that our house on the cliff in Lord's Acres was just ever so slightly lacking because of the conspicuous absence of marmots. It was clearly prime marmot habitat, and yet no marmots had ever taken up residence. As I watched the dozens of chubby little rodents, I secretly plotted to trap one and transplant him to the rocks above our house. Maybe I would find another marmot community and trap a female and create my own thriving marmot haven.

Amy was extremely supportive of this plan.

"Absolutely," she would say, or, "Let me know what I can do to help."

When Amy demonstrates enthusiasm and gets behind a project that she cares very little about, this generally means that she really thinks my plan is stupid and she firmly believes that I lack the resolve to follow through. This is only a theory of mine, however, because on the several occasions I have tried to call her bluff she has never flinched from her supposed support. By sheer coincidence, on those particular occasions in which I have tried to call her bluff, I ended up lacking the resolve to follow through. Therefore, my theory that she is actually not being genuine remains unproven.

On other days, when we would take our morning breaks, we would head through downtown Manson and up to the ridge above Lake Chelan on Summit Boulevard. From there, we could look down at the deep narrow chasm of brilliant green water that stretches between the north shore and Slide Ridge. This is one of my favorite views, and one of my favorite parts of the lake.

In most cases, when I think of Lake Chelan, I think of a bright blue sapphire color. From this vantage point, the lake often looks more like a deep brilliant emerald. The narrowness of the channel, the steepness of the shore, and the denser evergreens across the way all lend a hand in this vibrant dark green hue.

Looking across to the south shore from Summit Boulevard, the mountains begin to assert themselves. Slide ridge is a 5,800 foot high spine that soars above the lake. It takes its name from the reddish orange scar that is gashed down its face, evidence of old landslides that occurred there over the ages and continue when heavy rains or large amounts of snowmelt scour the hillside. There is a large alluvial fan of ancient debris that spreads into the lake, and it is easy to see exactly where the debris peeled away from the mountain centuries ago. In the middle of this fan, a rock and dirt wash cuts through the trees at the lake shore. This is the outlet for the tons of debris that still slough off the mountain during extreme weather events.

This large fan of earth and rock creates the setting for a section of the lake that many people adore above all others. It forms a gentle slope and flatter shoreline than the steep valley walls that dominate the shore both uplake and downlake. This flatter, shadier delta allows the forest to get solid purchase so that the entire section is a carpet of green that rolls up to the more sheer walls of the ridge.

The waterfront homes and vacation getaways in this area have an authentic mountain lake feeling. They are scattered amongst the forests and shaded by the stands of pine. Log homes, rustic wood cabins and A-frames are common throughout. Deer are so abundant in the area that seeing them starts to seem as mundane as spotting a squirrel. If you're used to the more arid environs near Manson and Chelan, this area can make you feel like you're at a completely different lake. In this portion of the south shore, you are really in the woods.

Near the western end of this lakeside forest is Kelly's Resort. For generations of people, Kelly's Resort *is* Lake Chelan. This quaint wood and stone house looks like it fell off the pages of *Sunset Magazine*. It is frequently featured in lifestyle and travel publications. The resort was opened in 1948 by the Kelly family and is still run by them today. The lodge is the quintessential old lakeside dwelling. The rocks and shingles are covered in climbing ivy. The lobby hosts a coffee shop, store, and attached view balcony that defines the genre.

If ancient towns and villas are the human contribution to the charm of European lakes like Como, then old lodges like Kelly's Resort are the equivalent representation of our own more abbreviated new world history. These lodges are distinctly North American. From the historic lake lodges in the Catskill Mountains and Adirondacks to the grand old lodges of the National Parks, rustic lake resorts are architectural mainstays embedded in our culture.

There are few things better than sitting on the deck of Kelly's Resort with a cup of coffee in your hand. You look out across the lake, and listen to the gentle "galoop" noise the water makes as small waves push up under the dock. The warm air carries the scent of the pine trees down from the woods behind you where small rustic rental cabins dot the hillside. This is when you feel all the nostalgia of an old time lake resort, the kind which once dominated the vacation proclivities of many Americans.

All of this, viewed from across the lake, can only be described as idyllic. Sitting on the north shore looking over at it, Amy and I would often ignite an age-old debate, one in which I have heard many people engage. The opinions vary as to whether it is better to be on the south shore, in the woods, enjoying the shady tress, pine scent, and frolicking deer, or to be on the north shore, looking across at this beautiful display of mountain and forest scenery.

I am incapable of forming my own conclusion. I have had the opportunity to spend time on both sides, and they are truly different experiences. One can genuinely believe that they are at two distinct lakes in two distinct regions.

Another gem that catches the eye when looking across the lake from Summit Boulevard is the headland that rises up off the shore between the state park and Cove Marina. The South Shore Road comes up off the lake and cuts a deep swath, exposing the pink and white granite along the downlake shoulder of Slide Ridge. This rise in the road is necessitated by the near vertical exposed rock cliff that drops straight down to the water. The area is sometimes referred to as the Jumping Rock.

As a youngster, I spent a great deal of time around these rocks. My cousin Kelly was my partner in crime. He and I spent many hours scrambling up and down these cliffs and hurtling ourselves from dizzying heights. I say partner in crime because, as it turns out, we did commit a crime. In the state of Washington, it is illegal to jump from a height above 50 feet, even into water. The crime committed under this statute is called attempted suicide. I imagine we blew by the 50 foot mark before either of us turned 15.

For reasons I will discuss later, I have to go on record as saying that I would in no way endorse jumping off these cliffs. I've seen at least a dozen people hurt doing it. Most of them got bloodied up trying to climb the cliff, slipping and skidding down the rocks, banging off jutting abutments as they fell. Others have been hurt just from the impact of the water.

With the infinitesimal wisdom I've gained with age, I have come to believe the Revised Code of Washington might not be so out of line. People have died hitting water from as low as 35 feet. For a skydiver in an arched position, terminal velocity is about 120 miles per hour. For a cliff jumper, it can be much faster. The vertical position of the body creates less drag. In theory, in low air pressure, a person in this position wearing only a bathing suit could move past 150 miles per hour. The peregrine falcon can approach 200 miles per hour using gravity alone when it curls its wings and dives for prey. Generally a person falling reaches 50 percent of terminal velocity in about three seconds, and 90 percent in about eight seconds.

It's hard to survive a fall that generates speeds of 100 miles per hour, even if you're hitting water. The body can defend itself and maintain healthy functions throughout the fall. It's the conclusion of the fall that doesn't always work out so well. It gets harder to escape injury with each increment of increased velocity above that. Simply stated, cliff jumping is dangerous. To any kids who may be reading this I say, never ever, ever, ever do it, ever.

Despite the obvious danger (and clearly defined risks and warnings stated herein and expressly written such that no prudent person would or should ever consider cliff jumping) kids have been jumping off these rocks for decades. The cliff is decorated with painted signs and graffiti that indicate the various launching points from the rock. People familiar with the area have developed their own vernacular related to these rural art installments.

"Have you jumped from the Jobe?"

"No, we jumped from the Rainier."

"We both launched off the Westgate."

"Dude, we took off from the JK."

These are discussions I've heard amongst people in Seattle, Pullman, and as far away as San Francisco. The cliff has earned for itself a small measure of fame. It's not uncommon to see a cluster of boats gathering at the base of the cliff on warm summer days to send jumpers swimming in toward the rocks, or merely to watch.

Over the years, Kelly and I worked our way higher and higher up the cliff, achieving ever-lengthening periods of freefall. I felt we had reached our apex when we vaulted from a 75-foot-high ledge above a prominent sign that displays the well known Rainier beer symbol, a large cursive *R* on a white background. It turns out we had not.

In an act that I'm not too proud of today, we decided that we too would leave our mark on the rock. I have to mention that I despise graffiti in all its forms, and so I cringe to even relate this story. I think because we were young, and also because the rock was already so marred with the signs, scribbles and scrawls of those who came before us, it seemed like it was an acceptable thing to do.

Fresh off our leap from above the Rainier sign, we returned the next day and scaled back up the cliff with paint in hand. Above the Rainier sign, we looked for suitable flat faces of unpainted rock. There were very few. We moved along the ledge and upward, over 20 feet higher, until at last we found a nice granite canvas to record our passing. In bright yellow and brilliant blue, we assigned our initials to the rock.

Our task complete, we turned to look out across the lake. What we saw was mortifying. An armada of boats had accumulated nearly a hundred feet below us. Our location for the sign was predicated on availability of space, not from an interest or willingness to jump from that particular location. Not that we were totally averse to it, but the difference an extra 25 feet can make when you're talking about vertical empty space that you intend to hurtle yourself into can be quite dramatic.

A roar of encouragement went up from the boats below.

"Oh crud," said Kelly.

He didn't really use the word "crud."

Of the many reasons to undertake anything, especially anything dangerous, doing it just to look cool is probably about the worst of them all. Still, here we were above an increasing flotilla of boats, many of them filled with cheering girls in bikinis. I will acknowledge that we were pretty crazy kids at that time. We were rock climbers, and we were skydivers, and we were risk takers, and we had rubbery bones and a misplaced sense of immortality. Backing down from the challenge did not seem to be an option.

To complicate matters, the ledge we were on was extremely narrow and uneven. Fifty feet below us, the cliff jutted outward well over 12 horizontal feet, so we both needed to get a good jump and make some lateral distance just to make sure that water was the first thing we hit. We labored to find good solid footholds that would allow us to lean forward and then get a strong outward push. At last we were situated in what felt like a workable stance for both of us. With a high five and a deep breath, we flung ourselves from the cliff.

And we fell.

We circled our arms in rapid gyroscopic motions to keep our bodies straight.

We fell some more.

We accelerated, but the water did not appear to be getting any closer.

We were still falling.

Galileo first observed that all objects (in a vacuum) accelerate at the same speed when falling. I got a firsthand observation of this myself. Looking down and toward the cliff, I could see Kelly hovering eight feet below me, in lock-step motion, while the cliff blurred by.

We fell some more.

It began to occur to me that we were in the air a long time and moving very fast, and that when we entered the water there was probably going to be a fair amount of pain involved. I was expecting a body-jolting impact, probably having the wind knocked out of me, and likely an extreme amount of discomfort in the crotch. My expectations were exceeded on every account.

Upon reaching the water, we had a real intimate encounter with a phenomenon known as rapid deceleration. I could best describe the splashdown as the feeling you might get if you were simultaneously electrocuted, punched in the teeth and kicked hard between the legs. It was similar to running at full speed to catch a Frisbee and hitting a tetherball pole concurrently with your nose, sternum, and pelvis. I know. I've accomplished that feat as well.

With all the air knocked out of me, it was a long swim back up to the surface. When I got my head above water, I thought maybe I had hurt my eyes, but in actuality, the water had just folded both of my eyelids inside out. This is not an exaggeration. I rubbed them, and they flipped back into the correct position. My ears and cheeks were stinging.

For my efforts, I was rewarded with dark purple bruises under my arms, thighs, chin, and on the bottoms of my feet. I had made a very clean entry in the water. My cousin Kelly fared a bit worse. Because of the thin and erratically textured ledge we had launched from, his right foot slipped coming off the rocks at the top. He barely cleared the rocks below, and he was never able to get fully straightened out as he accelerated downward. He entered the water at ever so slight an angle. He received such a jolt that he actually had a difficult time swimming back to the boat. Where my bruises were purple, his bruises were black, and he was in pain walking and laying down for almost a week.

Neither of us cared very much. We had made the jump. We went back by car the next day to retrieve the paint cans, and we took a fishing pole and dangled the line down over the cliff to see just how far we had fallen. When we got home, we laid the line out and measured it. The distance was 97 feet.

"Do you want to go back and try and make it an even 100 feet?" I said.

"Crud no," said Kelly.

He didn't actually use the word "crud."

He knew I was bluffing anyway. Neither of us had any intention of jumping from that height again. Neither of us have ever done it since. The cliff, however, has always held a special spot in my heart.

On other days during our morning drive behind Manson, Amy and I would head back into the three lakes area. Roses Lake, Wapato Lake, and Dry Lake nestle comfortably into the surrounding fruit trees. We watched, each day, as the apple orchards began to bud, and then eventually blossom. The entire area came alive with brilliant white and delicate pink petals. The apples were returning to the valley.

It seems there is no more enduring symbol of the Chelan Valley than the apple. It is a part of the region's history. As early as 1890, Peter Wapato and Ben Martin were growing and harvesting apples in the Manson area. When the area was opened up to homesteaders, land developers were quick to seize on the potential for successful orchards in this area. They were prophetic in this assessment.

They built incredible flume systems out of lumber to bring irrigation down to this area in the early 1900s. In July of 1916, the Lake Chelan Land Company auctioned off plots of the now irrigated land and an already burgeoning production in the region reached critical mass. The fruit growing industry was firmly rooted in the valley.

The Chelan Historical Society has some literature that was distributed as part of a marketing campaign during the World's Fair in Saint Louis. Excerpts from the literature paint a picture of lake living that sounded almost too good to be true. Knowing the lake as I do now, they actually weren't too far off.

Along with a stack of polished apples and pictures of the surrounding landscape, marketers at the World's Fair tried to lure potential landowners to head west and take up the utopian life of an apple farmer on the shores of Lake Chelan. The farmers came. With the irrigation in place and the fertile glacial till, the areas around Chelan and Manson soon became a Mecca for growing apples.

Apples are a part of the local culture now. A common sight in almost every home is the framed designer labels that adorned the apple boxes from the various growers, packers, distributors and co-operatives of the region. Local businesses are named after apples. Trucks full of apples rumble down the streets. The apple is even celebrated each year in the Manson Apple Blossom Festival, complete with a parade.

Along with apples came migrant workers. Many of these people, from Mexican or Central American descent, came to the valley to pick apples, and eventually stayed year-round. They gained proficiency in tending to the orchards, and branched into other businesses as well. There are formerly migrant families who have now lived in the area for three and four generations, and who have become some of the longstanding old-timers of the Manson community.

Their presence has also helped to facilitate more people moving into the area from Mexico and places further south. It is not uncommon to hear Spanish being spoken as frequently as English around town. This has created a rich and unique culture in the Manson area. There is a hint of the exotic, almost authentic Mexican feel in the Red Apple Market in town.

Over the years, this small town mercantile, set in a compact cinder block structure, had become a blend of what felt like a small country grocery and a Mexican tienda. Locals and longtime vacation visitors alike had come to adore this eclectic blend of cultures in Manson, of which the store had become an unofficial epicenter. When owner Jack Courtney announced plans to build a new and more modern store, there was great concern that it would lose this quirky, familiar feeling.

He had to assure people (my dad for one) that the new store would not lose track of this unique feel. To that end, he succeeded. The store and its attached coffee shop remains a bustling town gathering place. It is a large, beautiful new building, and yet it continues to be an intimate and inviting place that captures the cultural blend of the area, complete with piñatas above the display racks and a taco truck in the parking lot. The familiar greetings of friends and neighbors in English, Spanish, or a combination of the two are more common than they ever were.

The walls of the Red Apple Market are covered in fascinating historical pictures of Manson. If one were to look at the large prints that captured Manson in the middle of the last century and then wander a short way along the road to downtown Manson, they would be taken aback by how little has changed over the years. Billed as "The Village on the Bay," Manson has maintained its small town charm decade after decade. Sitting right on the shore of such an extraordinary lake, it has to be one of America's best hidden treasures.

Most days, we would have to stop working on the Farmhouse and wander next door where construction was finishing up on our new house. After meeting with sub-contractors, we would sit on the front patio and watch the water come a little higher each day, as the PUD was bringing the lake level up to full pond for summer.

The lake shore and the creek next to the house seemed like an unofficial bird sanctuary. Two or three times an hour, great flocks of Canadian geese would soar overhead in classic *v* formations. You could hear the whistle of wind across their feathers, the thump of wing flaps, and a garble of goose chatter that sounded like a hundred rusty gates swinging shut at the same time. If they landed on the lake in front, it was in a mighty succession of splashes, almost like a small wave breaking on an ocean beach.

We counted five different types of waterfowl floating next to each other peacefully at the same time in Mill Bay. Three distinct families of ducks would make the short pilgrimage up to our patio in search of an easy meal. I declined to offer charity on philosophical grounds, but I suspect the workers at the house had been doling out bread crusts on their lunch breaks.

Bald eagles would perch in the cottonwoods, and then lift off every hour or so to go hunting on the lake. I was hoping to see them pull a mighty fish from the surface of the water right in front of our house, but instead they tended to favor the smaller waterfowl that congregated here. Watching them catch, depilate, and then eat a bird was not quite as romantic as watching them catch a fish might have been, but it was no less fascinating.

The creek was a resting place, hunting ground, and nesting site for too many birds to count. One that frequented the stream was so colorful that I thought it was a tropical pet bird that had escaped its cage. It was brilliant yellow with a red head and black wings that I later identified as a western tanager.

We saw swallows, and blue jays, and magpies, and hummingbirds, and yellow finches and sandpipers and hawks, and sparrows, and swifts, and golden eyes, and quail in the thousands. One night we saw a barn owl sitting right on a street sign. Those were just the ones I could identify. As spring moved on, more and varied species would arrive, while others would disappear. Dozens upon dozens of different kinds of birds moved through the area.

I had never been much of a bird enthusiast, but being surrounded by so many, and watching their strange behaviors and incredible feats of flight, it was impossible not to be captivated. The area was an ornithologist's dream.

"I should start a bird journal," I said to Amy.

"You should."

Her voice was full of enthusiasm.

"I'll help you," she said.

I very much doubted her sincerity, but again, was unable to prove it since the journal never actually came to fruition for reasons totally unrelated to my commitment or resolve.

As spring drew to a close, the renovations on the Farmhouse property were complete. The house was fixed up, a new swimming pool was in the ground, the garden was planted, and the property was ready to host summer vacation renters. The new house next door was finished as well. The first renters of the season had already taken up residence there. For Amy and me, it was a sad time. We had enjoyed our months living in Manson so much, it was difficult to pack up and get ready to leave.

Amy took comfort in the knowledge that at least our projects were complete and we could relax for a while. She was particularly excited for a break. She's such an adorable optimist.

She could not have known at the time that a large tempest cloud was brewing just beyond the horizon. On the other side of the lake, a very serious and complicated project was forming in the lower atmosphere and moving our way. This was maybe a class four or even a class five event on the ECLIPS scale (Extremely Complicated Life-altering Impending Project Scale). Poor Amy was completely naïve to the perfect storm that was gathering on the opposite shore.

Lake Project

Day 345: Santorini

Twenty hours after leaving Salzburg, Austria, our team of six lake explorers was moving across the crystal blue waters of the Aegean Sea toward the Cyclades, a circular chain of Greek islands that includes Santorini. Like Crater Lake in Oregon, and the grand depression that is home to Yellowstone Lake in Wyoming, Santorini encircles a massive caldera, the result of a still active volcano. We first saw the caldera from the back side. Approaching by ferry, we rounded the northern tip of the crescent moon-shaped island and passed between the headland and the smaller island of Thirasia. We were suddenly inside a giant amphitheater.

From the west side, Santorini presented huge walls that leapt up from the water nearly a thousand feet to the crater rim. These walls were layered with different colored strata ranging from beige to red to black, evidence of the volcanic origin of the island.

Villages stretched out along the upper edge of the island and, with the classic brilliant white painted buildings and cave houses that are ever-present throughout the islands, it looked exactly as if parts of the caldera were capped with snow.

We made our base camp in the northernmost of these towns. I immediately began doing research. Here's what I learned on day one:

> Santorini does appear to be a caldera.
>
> One should go a little easier than normal when drinking Santorini wine.
>
> Santorini has a lot of cats.
>
> Hot dusty donkeys don't smell very good.

None of this seemed particularly relevant to a book about Lake

Chelan. However, day two was the crux of the trip, and the real reason why I had come. We headed out on a boat into the middle of the caldera to an island known as Nea Kameni. This is the hot steaming cinder cone of the Santorini volcano. This was where we could see the caldera building process in action.

Crater Lake in Oregon has a similar cone in the west end of the lake known as Wizard Island. This cone was built up over successive eruptive periods and now towers like a perfect little tree-covered pyramid from the water. There is even a small volcanic crater at the summit of the island. The problem is the Wizard Island crater, known as the Witches Cauldron, is cold and quiet.

Nea Kameni is very much alive. Built up over the last 300 years, the volcano has extruded dacite lava and ash, pushing up multiple small islands that eventually grew together to form a larger island. As recently as 1950, a small eruption extended the lava dome, further enlarging the island. The area is now constantly monitored by scientists and produces numerous small earthquakes every year.

The two craters on the island announced their presence before they even came into view. The smell of sulfur was thick in the air. After we arrived, we hiked to the top of the island and stood at the edge of the crater to watch the show. Steam issued from numerous vents around the edge. These holes, known as fumaroles, seemed to take turns hissing and sometimes growling in a deep throaty tone. Occasionally, the entire crater grew quiet, and then re-energized, as if the earth was breathing in an erratic sleep apnea kind of way. Other times, steam ushered out with such force that the entire crater edge vibrated and small rocks jarred lose to skip down into the hole.

I was hoping to get a sense of one of the great processes that deforms the earth and gives rise to lakes (or in this case, a sub-marine crater). The volcano of Santorini did not disappoint. With the ground vibrating beneath me, I looked across the steaming small crater and took in the immense caldera rim that cradled the entire inlet. The ocean-filled concavity was over four miles across, and the sea dropped down below us to a depth of 1,300 feet.

All of this was the void left by the expulsion of magma, and here we were, standing on the lava dome created as more of this molten earth was pushed up in fits and starts. Trying to imagine the eruption and collapse of this island was difficult. It was, perhaps, one of the largest eruptions the planet has ever known.

There are many scholars who believe that Santorini, prior to the eruption 3,500 years ago, was the location of what was later called the lost city of Atlantis. This was in the centuries leading up to the height of ancient Greek civilization, and it is not a stretch to imagine an idyllic utopian society, rich in culture, inhabiting this large mountain in the middle of the sea. Like other Greek societies of its time, Santorini would have been developing advanced cities with ornately decorated three-story buildings, temples, and monuments.

While Greece was moving toward its golden age, the mountain grew restless. The inhabitants fled to the sea. Then the volcano blew up, and the island collapsed. The tsunami it caused is known to have been devastating to the surrounding seaside villages on islands beyond Santorini and may have completely destroyed the Minoan society that was flourishing on the island of Crete. Santorini was uninhabitable for over 200 years.

In the evening, back on the main island, Amy and I sat in the balmy air at the Santorini Winery. We were perched on the very edge of the crater, with a cliff dropping away from us over 2,000 feet to the crater floor. A searing red sun was sinking behind the steaming crater of Nea Kameni and painting the entire horizon scarlet, purple, and pink. A flight of various glasses of wine sat on the table, glowing in the warm evening light. Amy was looking to the west, content and smiling. If she was at all unhappy about missing the opportunity to go to Siberia, it was not evident at that moment.

I gazed across the caldera and thought about the incredible events that had formed it, and the other amazing ways in which the world's lakes have come into being. In my notebook, I wrote a few lines about the manner in which these events dramatically shape human history, human culture, and our daily lives. The process that created the Santorini caldera may have wiped out an entire society. It may have spawned the myth of the lost city of Atlantis. This myth would later be the motivating factor of numerous explorations across oceans to terra incognita.

The process that created modern day Santorini is the same process that created the super-volcano that would eventually become Crater

Lake. It also created Yellowstone Lake and the Yellowstone caldera, with geothermal activity so unique that it became the world's first national park. This would lead to conservation efforts on a global scale.

Almost anywhere a lake-making process occurs, it dramatically affects humanity. Giant cities grow up on the shores of lakes, and commerce moves across them. People rely on them for food, fresh water, and livelihood. They affect the weather in places far distant from where they are located. They are a constant, if unseen, force in almost all of our daily lives.

I thought about how Lake Chelan affected the history of the Pacific Northwest. It formed a transportation route that allowed the early Native Americans to access and trade with the tribes that inhabited the lowlands of Puget Sound. The lake was the carrot that lured European settlers further east to settle in north central Washington. It spawned the vast agricultural infrastructure that lines its shores. It continues to irrigate the orchards and vineyards today. It has also drawn millions of tourists to come relax, swim, and explore. At Chelan, as in all the world, the often slow, occasionally dramatic processes that create these lakes leave an indelible impression on human history.

As we left Santorini, I already knew I would have to see more of these lake-making processes. I would need to see a glacial fjord lake still being carved by a glacier, probably Lake O'Higgins/San Martin. I wanted to see a barrier lake and an endorheic basin lake. I was also going to have to visit a rift valley, either in Africa or Siberia, maybe both.

I decided to keep this information to myself. I didn't even tell Amy. I certainly didn't want to give her time to research reasons why we should go to a tropical beach instead. I was sure she would appreciate another trip much more if I sort of sprung it on her with short notice. Spontaneity, I had been told, was the soul of romance.

On the flight home, we went back up over the Arctic Circle and came down directly over Canada's Great Slave Lake. I knew it was the deepest lake in North America. I watched the lake approaching for an hour on the airplane's live video computer map with anticipation. Finally, I saw a large body of water looming in the distance. The lake was huge. It was a brilliant blue in the late evening sunshine of the northern latitudes. Most striking was that it seemed not to have a shoreline, but rather to dissipate into swamps, and then marshy tundra. There were very few trees. The surrounding country was as flat as the lake itself. There was barely a rise of land to be seen anywhere. The north end of the lake extended over the horizon and out of sight. It was a mind-boggling display of trackless nothingness.

I pulled out my notebook and flipped to the page with the header "Greatest Lakes in the World." The list of possible candidates had been growing longer as I did more and more research. It was now a daunting collection of many lakes around the globe. It had stretched to three pages. I traced my finger down until I found the Great Slave Lake. Then I took a pen and crossed that giant crap hole right out. At last I was making some true progress. The trip to Austria and Greece was looking like a success on many levels.

The Wilderness

Our friends Tim and Melissa have a house on the shore of Lake Joy in the western Cascade foothills near Duvall. This is a quiet, peaceful lake, surrounded by miles of timber. That peace and quiet was upset one night when their three-year-old son started screaming from his bedroom. He was the apparent victim of night terrors. When they entered his room, he was very upset because he had observed a monster.

They did everything they could to calm him down, assuring him that monsters did not exist. Finally pacified, Grant lay back down, and they took their leave, only to be called back 20 minutes later. The monster had made another appearance, and Grant was not pleased. This time it took even longer to calm him down. At last, they succeeded and left again.

Shortly thereafter, Grant screamed out in alarm again, and they returned to his aid. "Where is the monster?" Tim asked.

Grant pointed his trembling finger toward the closet.

"Okay," said Melissa, "we'll check the closet and show you there's no monster in there."

They opened the closet door with calmness and composure. That calmness and composure was very short lived.

There emerged from the inky black depths of the closet, at full speed, with fangs exposed, hair bristling, and claws extended, a giant chiropteran. This frightful beast of the night is more frequently referred to as the common brown bat.

Anyone who has ever had a close encounter with a bat already knows what happened next. Both Tim and Melissa ran from the room, screaming with arms flailing wildly, leaving three-year-old Grant to fend for himself. If the lesson for Grant was that monsters don't exist, this was a situation in which that lesson was quite improperly taught.

There could have been no other outcome to the drama that played out. As someone who has come into very close contact with these leathery winged night demons, I can assure you they are sufficiently terrifying. I have seen firefighters who would not think twice about running into a flaming building cower and bolt from a swooping bat. A certain business partner of mine, who will remain unnamed, was opening an umbrella at Chelan Bluff when a bat dropped out and landed on his head. He responded with a series of motions that resembled a stiff-jointed zombie trying to break-dance across the deck while simultaneously fighting off a swarm of angry invisible bees.

When it comes to bats, Chelan has plenty. At the time my dad first purchased the old farmhouse, the barn could best be described as a bat preserve. If you happened to walk by right at dusk and look up at the roof, you would see a dark cloud of bats emerging from under the eaves in nightmarish quantities reminiscent of the introduction sequence for the old Scooby Doo cartoons. Pyramids of bat poop stacked up in the unfinished loft below the rafters.

My dad installed some electronic sonar emitters to discourage the bats from roosting there. These actually worked rather well. After I bought the farm, I became concerned because it seemed that North America was having a bit of a bat crisis. There were mysterious colony collapses happening around the continent. Bats being an important part of the ecosystem, this had biologists concerned.

Knowing that the barn had, at one time, provided refuge for bats, I decided to unplug the sonar deterrents. It took a while for the bats to return. By my estimate, it was roughly nine minutes. Even in daylight, when you went into the barn you could hear their high-pitched squeaking and leathery demon wings fluttering. The effect of this was similar to the feeling of the hair on the back of your neck standing up, only more intense, as if someone was collectively grabbing each hair with needle nose pliers and pulling on them while pouring ice cold water down your back. One or both shoulders would inevitably twitch up uncontrollably toward your ears as you tucked your head down and strained your eyes upward in preparation for an attack.

A fear of bats is somehow hardwired into human DNA. This is not learned behavior. This is pure instinct. What that instinct says is that if there is a bat coming at you, every impulse for self-preservation needs to kick in instantly, or else you are undoubtedly going to die.

Humans respond to life-threatening stresses in two ways. They either fight or they flee. The problem with a bat attack is that, for some reason, it triggers both the fight instinct and the flee instinct simultaneously. The result is something that can only be described as the most amazing and silly display of human activity, bar none. It is not uncommon to see flailing bodies actually levitate and fly laterally. This motion is always accompanied by punching and kicking at thin air in spastic motions. Plastic outdoor furniture and picnic tables can be flung out of the way of a fleeing-fighting bat attack victim as if they were children's toys.

I have seen this behavior many times. It is possible that I have witnessed this behavior more than anyone on the planet. This is because once, while at a Halloween store, I happened across a very realistic toy bat made out of wire, cloth, and fake fur.

I consider myself a bit of a scientist. This is despite having no formal training or real knowledge of anything scientific that goes beyond what I have read in *National Geographic*. As a self-proclaimed pseudo scientist, I felt if I could simulate this bat attack response on a repeated basis and study it up close, it would somehow be useful. I didn't know how it would be useful, but I was pretty sure it would be a lot of fun, and that I could worry about the usefulness part later.

It was in this way that I introduced my sisters, my brothers, my nieces, my nephews, my friends, and my neighbors to the "Simulated Human Automatic Bat Avoidance Maneuver," also known as SHABAM.

In general terms, the experiment to induce a SHABAM goes like this: The realistic bat is tied to the end of some fishing line on a fishing pole. The apparatus is stored just around the corner behind where everyone is sitting looking out at the lake. Around dusk, the scientist—in this case me—comments that there are a lot of bats out. Ten minutes later, as the evening grows darker, the scientist says, "Wow, they sure are swooping low." He does this while simultaneously ducking his head, as if he has been startled by a low-flying bat.

He then excuses himself to get a fresh beer. Really, of course, he is going back to get the fake bat apparatus. This is where some skill comes into play. First of all, the scientist must sneak up, unobserved, to a position right behind the subject intended for study. In order to get an effective response, the fake bat must be maneuvered properly. Generally, the best technique is to swing the bat once right in front of the subject's face very close, and then swoop it around in a tight arc and smack it directly into their head.

At this point, the scientist needs to be alert. In most cases, the chair the subject is sitting on will come rocketing backwards, so the scientist must be careful not to be injured. The subject will likely scream like a girl, even if the subject is, in fact, not a girl. It is not uncommon for a chain reaction of panic to erupt amongst the group. This can result in an array of beer and pop cans hurtling into the air and raining back down. With so many arms and legs punching and kicking blindly at nothing, some of these cans can ricochet wildly and caution avoiding these projectiles must be exercised.

If done correctly, the scientist can run after the subject and continue to bounce the bat repeatedly off of his or her head until the subject collapses from exhaustion or runs into the lake. Obviously, it is important to make sure that all participants are not carrying cell phones or expensive electronics. It is also important that the escape corridor be cleared earlier of dangerous obstructions such as cars, bonfires, or tetherball poles.

Be prepared for nieces and sisters to be unwilling to talk to you for a few days. Also be prepared for wives and mothers to call you childish and immature. Scientists throughout history have often been made to endure such ridicule and ostracism.

I personally witnessed, and others will corroborate, an incredible display of the human survival instinct while at my parents' house in Mill Bay. After the fake bat collided with the face of my niece Ashley, she preformed a dramatic SHABAM right across the sandy beach. Not content to stop at the water's edge, she proceeded to take three complete steps across the surface of the lake. She didn't run into the lake. She ran on top of the lake. These were long, purposeful strides. Finally the laws of physics reasserted themselves and she collapsed in a spray of water exactly like one that is made when a water-skier takes a nasty fall. She ended up 12 feet from shore.

"What kind of a sick person gets a thrill from terrifying people with a fake bat?" my mother asked, or something like that. I wasn't really paying attention, because I was laughing too hard.

If this sounds slightly mean spirited, you must keep in mind that I come from a large Irish family. Irish people take great pleasure in scaring the bajeebers out of each other. It's simply part of our culture.

There are very few of my relatives who wouldn't do the exact same thing given the opportunity.

Growing up, I was constantly assaulted by uncles jumping out of the woods on dark trails. Older brothers would lunge from hidden corners wearing authentic movie horror masks. Cousins would bang on windows from the ebony night right at the climax of ghost stories. This is what Irish families do. For this reason, it is important that I take the opportunity to terrorize my relatives, particularly the younger ones, so that I can continue the frightening cycle for generations to come. People are lost without their heritage.

I have, on one occasion, been the victim of my own bat apparatus, which I was careless enough to leave accessible to my younger brother Jim. My observation is that, in this particular experiment, one should opt to be the scientist rather than the subject.

As scary as a fake bat attack can be, a real honest to goodness live bat attack can redefine the meaning of the word terror. I was the victim of one such attack, right in my very own barn. This one was of notable duration. We were having a pool party with some friends one late summer night at the Farmhouse. I left the pool and went down to get some float toys that were stored in the barn. I was wearing only a swimsuit. I flipped on the light and headed toward the back storage room, when down from the rafters descended a mighty winged behemoth of the night. What's amazing is if you see a bat in North America, in daylight, curled up, it's unlikely it will look bigger than a piece of charcoal. At night, wings fully spread, ears flared, claws extended, it appears more like a fully matured pterodactyl.

In retrospect, I imagine I frightened the bat as much as he frightened me. Probably both of us misinterpreted who was chasing who. The result was a highly spirited struggle for survival that involved numerous laps around the inside of the barn, wings flapping, bat squealing, me squealing, arms punching, paint cans flying, garden tools scattering asunder. It ended with me clutching a tennis racket in front of my face and backing slowly out of the barn.

I returned to the swimming pool gasping for breath, hair sticking in every direction and covered in cobwebs.

"Are you okay?" Amy asked.

"Fine."
"Where's the air mattress?"
"It wasn't there."
"It's right on top of the—"
"No," I said, "it wasn't there."
I re-installed the sonar bat deterrents the next day.

I really do love bats. As long as they don't sneak up on me, I think they are one of the most interesting animals around. In order to reconcile my distaste for bat attacks with my love for bats, I finally installed some bat boxes on the upper outside of the barn. These are like birdhouses, but designed specifically for bats. There is now a very healthy population of bats peacefully coexisting with us at the Farmhouse.

When viewed from a distance, the bats at Lake Chelan are fascinating. There are twelve species of bats believed to live in the various habitats of the North Cascades. All are insectivorous. They work the sky endlessly at night, displaying incredible aerobatics. I like them because they are one of the reminders that Lake Chelan is still very much a wild place. [12]

I'm not referring only to the stretches of mountains and forests. The wilderness, in many ways, integrates right into the places where people work, live, and play. At the Bluff, we would frequently watch bald eagles come right next to the house, riding the updraft from our cliff just 15 feet from the deck. Behind the Bluff is an orchard filled with wild rabbits. Where there are rabbits, there are coyotes, and we've often seen them working the fields in the early morning, just a half mile from downtown Chelan.

A black bear wandered right down the fence line of the Farmhouse in broad daylight on a recent Memorial Day weekend, where it either sniffed around peacefully or tried to eat my friend Meggan, depending on who you talk to. It loitered for five minutes before we finally shooed it down to the beach. From there, it ambled casually down the lake shore, through yard after yard of homes.

In the late fall and during the winter, the south shore is crowded with mule deer that wander down amongst the vacation homes to nibble from the flower boxes. Just east of Chelan, between the downtown and the airport, is a sign that says "bighorn sheep crossing." I've never seen them there, but I assume they must have wandered through from time to time to necessitate a sign. I have seen bighorn sheep many times along the Columbia River between Chelan and Wenatchee, and we've frequently followed a herd of them by boat on Lake Chelan, as they wandered along the shore up beyond Mitchell Creek.

These are just the critters in and around town. The surrounding wilderness and the ecosystem of the North Cascades National Park are home to nearly all of the great land mammals of the temperate North American continent.

In what my wife has described as "a strange quirk," I am a person who believes that artwork and decorations in a home need to capture the essence of the region in which they are located to some extent. I find it weird, for example, when people who own a ski chalet pick tropical fish paintings and seashells to spruce up a room. Leave the pictures of the palm trees down in your Mexican cabana. Mount the killer whale photo in the kitchen of your beach house on Orcas Island. Hang your oriental artwork in the study at your townhouse in one of the large Pacific Rim cities. Make sure all the southwestern Indian artwork stays in your winter hacienda next to the golf course outside of Phoenix.

I should mention that, in terms of decorating skills, I have a natural talent that would be on par with a monkey flinging poop at a wall. Saying that might actually be unfair to the monkey. That's not to say I don't know what I like when I see it. I just lack the ability to conjure it up. However, as we were starting to accumulate houses in Chelan, it became necessary for me to do more decorating than I would have anticipated doing in my whole life. My "quirk," as Amy called it, began to manifest.

I want my mountain cabin to be decorated with broken old skis, rusty old logging equipment, old snow shoes, broken mountain climbing gear, and paintings of tall peaks and rivers. Give me a lake place with weathered signs that say, "This way to the lake," and have old fishing gear on the wall and pictures of the surrounding hillsides.

Important to me, and this is where Amy thinks I jump off the rails a bit, is if you're going to put up paintings of wildlife in a house, it has to be wildlife that actually inhabits the region in which the house resides. In the spirit of tolerance, I will accept wildlife that "traditionally" was native to the region.

Amy and I butted heads over this issue with regards to a really neat painting of a moose we had acquired. The painting had the perfect color scheme to fit prominently on a wall in the living room of the Farmhouse. It captured the mood of the rustic country setting that we were trying to instill in the room.

"But wait," I said indignantly. "The problem is, it captures the rustic mood of a different part of the country. There are no moose in the North Cascades."

"Who cares?" Amy said.

"I can't imagine many people who wouldn't care."

Amy set the painting down on the carpet and walked into the next room humming. She does that sometimes right in the middle of a conversation. It's strange, especially since she's the one who accuses me of having quirks.

I knew, from firsthand observation, that there were moose in Wyoming, Montana, and Idaho. In what I felt was a bizarre story, my aunt Barb and uncle John had a moose living in their yard for three days in the flat rural plains of North Dakota, miles from any forest. I had heard there were moose in the northeast corner of Washington and in British Columbia. In the North Cascades, however, I was not so sure. This was an issue in need of researching. I consulted my Time Life animal flash cards. They were ambiguous.

I consulted the internet. The North Cascades National Park website listed moose as occasional residents, but I have great skepticism of the North Cascades National Park website (more on this later). The Smithsonian listed moose as residents only of the Selkirk Mountains of northeastern Washington. The results were unclear. I needed hard proof. I asked a North Cascades National Park ranger if he was aware of any moose in the region.

"We are loving our natural wonders to death," he responded.

I spoke to longtime residents and local hunters. For many weeks, no one could answer with authority.

Finally I found a firsthand account. A family friend, a former ATF agent, wildlife enthusiast, and avid outdoorsman, had seen a moose. While on a hunting trip up near Conconully he and a buddy had witnessed two moose come, at a full run, right through their camp. At first they thought they were seeing horses.

This was a valid confirmation that moose were in the North

Cascades in the Pasayten Wilderness. This was promising, but we were in Lake Chelan. Conconully was still quite a ways north. I was ready to concede the point anyway, but an interesting news story happened to pop up that same week. It seems many people had watched a moose standing in one of the backwater ponds of the Columbia River formed by the elevated roadbed. This was on the west side of the river, between Chelan and Pateros.

I had seen moose in the Moscow Mountains of Idaho. This terrain was very similar to the hills up around Union Valley and Echo Valley. With suitable terrain and verified reports of moose in the area, I concluded that the Lake Chelan Valley was acceptable moose habitat and that a painting of a moose would be perfectly appropriate in a Lake Chelan home.

Despite the magnitude of this breakthrough, Amy was still able to mask her enthusiasm when I ran to share the news with her.

"This means we can hang the painting the next time we're at the Farmhouse," I said.

Strangely, when we arrived at the Farmhouse the following week, the picture was already hanging on the wall in its assigned place. It was as if she had somehow already known the valley was acceptable for moose habitat.

With the discovery of the moose in Chelan's back yard, the cadre of the great North American land mammals in the Chelan vicinity was nearly complete. There was one grand icon of the American West, however, that was still in question. I found myself wondering if there had ever been any buffalo in the region. I had purchased some buffalo pictures years earlier in Wyoming, and I was curious if it would be appropriate to hang those on the wall.

I very much doubted there had been any buffalo in the Chelan area, with the exception of some domestic ones that were currently residing on a farm behind Manson. I would have said with 99 percent certainty that there had never been wild bison in eastern Washington. Still, I had to concede that there remained a one percent chance. Buffalo in the Chelan Valley, or even on the Columbia Plateau, would be an extraordinary complement to my beloved region.

I have a warm place in my heart for buffalo. Before Amy and I were married, and shortly after college, we borrowed her mom's car and headed on a road trip out across the American West. In Yellowstone National Park, we were driving down a lonely side road near Old Faithful when a stately buffalo stepped right in front of our car, blocking the way. Almost immediately, a second buffalo blocked the road behind us. Within seconds, we were surrounded by a small herd that was migrating past us. The situation was a bit tense. The herd seemed restless and slightly aggressive, obviously disturbed by our presence.

There was an extremely agitated female making a lot of strange and very loud noises. The noises sounded something like this:

"Get us out of here! Get us out of here! If they wreck my mom's car, I'll kill you!"

From experience, I knew better than to mess with an agitated female, and so, at the first gap in the wandering ungulates, I punched the accelerator and made a swerving escape to safety.

The buffalo had left their impression on me. They really are magnificent creatures. That's why I bought the buffalo pictures.

The Flathead Valley in Montana is the historical home of many buffalo. The National Bison Range is located there today. I knew that, in my efforts to prove Lake Chelan was the greatest lake in the world, I would have to face a mighty contender in Flathead Lake. I knew in the final analysis that Flathead Lake was going to make an extremely strong showing to garner the coveted title. Concerned that the presence in the Flathead Valley of the romantic buffalo, the symbol of the American West, might give Flathead Lake an edge, I looked into whether buffalo had historically roamed the Columbia Plateau. After all, the rich grasslands of the Columbia Plateau, the Palouse, and the Okanagan highlands certainly seemed capable of sustaining large herds.

I read a lot. I scoured many sources. I finally discovered a study done by Lee Lyman and submitted to the Department of Anthropology at the University of Missouri. In it he referred to, "a ratio diagram of measurement data derived from eight zooarchaeological collections of bison remains recovered from eastern Washington, in combination with the presence of both sexes and all age classes of individuals."

I'm no zooarcheologist, but it sounded to me like someone had found buffalo bones. I got a bit excited about this information. I read on, only to learn that "There are, however, a relative paucity of bison remains during the middle Holocene and an apparent 2000-year absence of bison from Eastern Washington at this time."

I remained optimistic. Just because the buffalo had died out in this region 2,000 years ago didn't mean that at least a few hadn't returned. Might some of the herds from western Montana have found their way back during that time?

In the end, my conclusion, unfortunately, was no. It seems they were close, but the string of mountains that ran up the western front of the Rocky Mountain chain proved to be a barrier they never again overcame. Although they were prevalent throughout nearly the whole of the United States, they never made it back into the three west coast states. The Native Americans, particularly the Nez Perce, would actually travel over the Lolo Mountains to Montana to hunt buffalo and then bring the meat and fur back to their villages in western Idaho, eastern Washington and eastern Oregon.

Even the Tsillane Indians and the Entiat Indians are said to have made occasional forays over the Rocky Mountains to hunt for buffalo, after the horse had been introduced into their culture. These hunting trips often lasted longer than a year. No doubt they would have brought back buffalo hides, horns, and skulls. In this way, the buffalo was at least a small part of the local culture, but living herds of bison were not.

Because of a 2,000 year absence of buffalo in the region, it seemed like putting buffalo art up at Lake Chelan would be akin to putting up woolly mammoth art. The pictures would have to remain in the storage room. Clearly I would have to do some digging and find some serious shortcomings of Flathead Lake in Montana in the near future.

What Chelan lacks in buffalo related history, it more than makes up for in the present by being the habitat of other fantastic furry critters. One famous romantic character of the American wilderness is perfectly acceptable adorning the walls of any home in Chelan. This is the gray wolf, sometimes called the timber wolf.

By the 1930s the gray wolves were effectively eradicated from the north and central Cascade region. Fortunately, they were listed as endangered under the Federal Endangered Species Act and also by the State of Washington. This made it illegal for wolves to be trapped, shot, captured, or harassed.

Now, the timber wolf is back in the North Cascades. Unlike Yellowstone, where wolves were reintroduced into the Lamar Valley, our local wolf populations returned on their own four paws from the wilderness to the north in British Columbia.

In the early 1980s, wolf prints were found on the shores of Ross Lake on the Washington side of the international boundary, marking the first accepted proof that they had returned. Wolves were later confirmed to be back and living in the Pasayten Wilderness as well. There are now resident wolf packs living in and around the North Cascades. Near the town of Twisp, they are frequently seen and heard throughout the valley. More importantly, they seem to be rebounding.

There is nothing but 30 miles of mountains, forest, and hills between Twisp and Lake Chelan. It is prime wolf habitat. Doubtless there are lone wolves that wander occasionally into the Chelan Mountains, and it seems very likely that we could see resident wolf packs in the area between the Chelan Valley and the Methow Valley very soon as the population grows and they expand their range.

In addition to the aforementioned land mammals, it is possible to see mountain lions, mountain goats, lynx, elk, bigfoot, skunks, raccoons, river otters, porcupines, beavers, ermine, and a host of other small mammals. The wildlife in the region is abundant and diverse.

Best, and probably most significant, is the presence of grizzly bears. Their residence in the area adds a very special cachet and an incredible romance to the wilderness that surrounds the lake. When Lewis and Clark made their historic journey to the Pacific, they had numerous encounters with grizzly bears. It is estimated that the western United States may have been home to between 50,000 and 100,000 of these stately predators at that time. They ranged as far south as Mexico.

During the century that followed, the grizzly bear population was devastated. Hudson Bay Company trapping records show that between the years 1827 and 1859, 3,788 grizzly bear hides were shipped from the North Cascades area trading post alone. Trapping, unregulated hunting, and loss of habitat all combined to nearly eradicate grizzlies from the southern half of North America. Today, in the lower 48 states, the grizzly bear occupies less than two percent of its original range.

The year 1967 marked the last recorded killing of a grizzly bear in Washington state, near Fisher Creek in what is now the North Cascades National Park. The wild grizzlies of Washington state were moribund, and the region was about to lose one of its great treasures.

In 1975, help arrived. Due to incredible efforts in conservation and education, the grizzly bear was listed as threatened under the Endangered Species Act. By 1983, the Interagency Grizzly Bear Committee was established. Their mission was the recovery of the grizzly bear population in the lower 48 states. Included in this collaboration of agencies were the US Fish and Wildlife Service, the US Forest Service, the National Parks Service, the US Geological Survey, and various state Fish and Wildlife Departments. Recognizing the interconnections of ecosystems, the British Columbia Ministry of Water, Land, and Air Protection was also a part if the IGBC.

Restoring the grizzly population was to be no small challenge. Grizzly bears are solitary creatures that require vast tracts of relatively undisturbed wilderness. After initial studies, the IGBC determined that six locations in four states and British Columbia could provide suitable habitat for sustainable grizzly bear populations. Among these were the large stretches of wilderness in the North Cascades.

This recovery area would eventually encompass over 10,000 square miles, one of the largest in the United States. More than 40 percent of this recovery area is the designated wildernesses that adjoin and abut Lake Chelan.

Grizzly bears were never re-introduced to the region, as they never truly disappeared. Today some estimates put the grizzly bear population in the North Cascades at between five and twenty bears. Estimates by the National Park Service are a little higher, listing between 15 to 30 bears including those that may cross back and forth between Washington and Canada. Sightings with definitive corroborating evidence have been made in recent years on the flanks of Glacier Peak south of Lake Chelan and in northeastern Washington. Numerous reports, not completely confirmed though highly probable, have been made throughout the range as far south as Snoqualmie Pass.

Actual confirmed sightings are rare, given the area and the reclusive nature of the bears. Exciting news materialized, however, in 2011, when a photograph of a bear in the North Cascades was confirmed by biologists to be a grizzly. This was taken in the Cascade

River watershed just a scant distance over the ridge from the Stehekin Valley. It was the first verified photograph of a grizzly bear taken in the North Cascades in almost 50 years.

The presence of grizzly bears in the area is significant. The grizzly bear is aptly described as a blanket species. Because they require so much territory in such pristine condition, they are the best indicator of a truly successful conservation effort. If grizzly bears are thriving in an area, it's a safe bet that the ecosystem is functioning extremely well.

It's most important just to know they are there. It lends a true credibility to the wilderness experience of Lake Chelan knowing that you are in honest to goodness grizzly bear country. It is a wonderful mix of emotions both hoping to catch a rare glimpse of these animals and, simultaneously, praying that glimpse is not too close.

There is also another reason it is critical to keep grizzlies in the North Cascades and to work to expand their population. Grizzlies play an extremely important role in the efforts to terrify young nieces and nephews. Without the grizzly bear inhabiting the area around Lake Chelan, there can be no horrific tales of man-eating bear encounters relayed to young children who feel they are old enough and brave enough to sleep out in a tent by the lake.

There is a far greater degree of doubt about the veracity of a low growl emanating from the shrubbery late at night if the children are allowed to believe that grizzly bears are not actually in the vicinity. This has become even more important in our age of astounding technology where kids now carry wireless smart devices.

With such a wealth of knowledge at their fingertips, it would be very simple for a child to determine that grizzly bears were no longer in the area if we were to make the shortsighted mistake of not fostering their presence here. For this reason alone, it is important that we maintain a healthy grizzly population. Otherwise, we risk debunking the long cultivated myth of the rogue grizzly bear that "just last week was spotted in the apple orchard across the road. I'm sure he's gone by now though. Okay kids, sleep tight."

Lake Mile 12 to 25

About 12 miles uplake, just below Navarre Coulee, is the mouth of First Creek. Although not technically the first year-round creek to enter the lake, it is the first substantial one. It meets the lake right at the state park on the south shore. The state park is a haven for mountain lake recreation, Americana style. Cool shady trees overhang grassy fields. A shoreline with sandy beaches beckons campers to swim and fish. On hot summer days, the whole park is a cacophony of children laughing and screaming with delight.

My own family history at Lake Chelan began at First Creek. My grandfather first brought his tribe of five young sons across the state in the 1950s. On several occasions, they camped on Lake Chelan near the mouth of the stream.

The best part of First Creek, in my opinion, is 300 yards inland, just across the road from the state park at the Alpenhorn restaurant. The restaurant is a decades-old building that resides beneath a canopy of evergreens. It is complete with slightly aged Bavarian gingerbreading. They serve burgers and fries, as they have for years, to be enjoyed right on the side of the creek.

The outdoor creekside dining enclave is not perfect. A cyclone fence sticking slightly over the bushes across the creek hints to a storage business above the opposite bank. The rumble of trucks occasionally reminds you that you're right below the Navarre Coulee Road. Still, First Creek rushes through a cool green gully with fast moving crystalline water cascading down from the mountains over 6,000 feet above. The lush vegetation surrounding the creek is reminiscent of the rivers and streams to the west of the rain shadow, on the other side of the Cascades.

If Chelan represents two lakes, with the drier rolling sienna-colored shorelines downlake, and the steep mountain-rimmed wilderness fjord uplake, then First Creek forms the demarcation line. Sitting in a dome with lush green walls, listening to the noisy tumult of ice cold water racing by, you get the sense that you are not in the foothills any longer. You have left the Tuscan-like rises of the eastern front. You are now in the Cascade Mountains proper, and the mist you feel is snow, only recently melted from shaded pockets on the back side of Slide Ridge or the grand sweeps of Stormy Mountain.

If one allows that First Creek is the first creek (the first substantial mountain creek in all events), then the second and third mountain creeks are not far behind. Only a mile further uplake on the south shore is Granite Falls, the first real waterfall that spills into the valley. Moving further uplake, more creeks begin to flow down the hillsides on both shores of the lake, evidence of the taller mountains that are rising on either side.

Across the water, a little under 20 miles uplake, the roads on the north shore end. Just beyond, Mitchell Creek sweeps down out of a deep canyon that's carved below stark mountainsides. The Mitchell Creek fire of 1970 burned so intensely that the ground was seared clean. The flora has still never fully recovered. As a result, the bones of the mountain can be seen poking through the sparse grass with barren rocks, bleached almost white, protruding from the treeless higher reaches.

The depth and sheerness of Mitchell Creek Canyon is something my family got to experience firsthand. On a snowmobile outing years ago, my younger sister Kim's boyfriend (now husband) accidentally got one of the snowmobiles stuck on a very steep incline just below the trail which cut across the side of the canyon high above the creek. Snowmobiles don't always find great traction in deep snow on steep hills, and they can often just dig themselves right down into a deep ditch of their own making. The location of this particular sled was exacerbating the problem.

"I can get it back on the trail," said my younger brother Jim, after thoughtfully examining the terrain. He got on the sled, grabbed the handlebars and leaned hard into the mountainside while slowly applying gas. The leverage and finesse worked and the snowmobile began moving across the hillside, ostensibly in a gentle upward angle that would eventually intersect the trail.

The snowmobile, unfortunately, had another destination in mind. After a few yards, the heavy engine forced it to lean away from the steep hillside and it nearly rolled over. Not inclined to go somersaulting down a hill embracing 600 pounds of metal and plastic, my brother thought it was the better part of valor to abort his rescue mission and abandon the machine with a hard lunge to the snow.

The snowmobile turned and then rode smoothly down the steep hill away from the trail in a straight line, gaining a fair amount of speed before launching off a ledge. It cut a beautiful and graceful arc out into an abyss of empty space before nosing over into a headfirst dive and disappearing below the cliff edge.

Everyone stared at the clean tracks through otherwise unblemished snow that led down to the precipice. In the still, bright-blue winter day, the engine of the snowmobile could be clearly heard as it grew ever softer, falling away into the deep maw of the canyon. After a painfully long time, the faint but sharp metallic twang of heavy machinery colliding with barren rock made its distant report. The frail sound of the engine was no more.

For a long while, there was stunned silence among the group of snowmobile riders. Finally my brother Jim spoke.

"I'm not sure I can get it back on the trail now," he said.

There was another long pregnant pause, as everyone gazed down at the distant cliff edge.

"Maybe we should have bought that insurance after all," my older brother Mike said.

What was left of the sled was lying so deep in the canyon that it was 500 feet below the snow level. It took a spring thaw, weeks later, and an act of creative engineering to block and tackle the snowmobile, in several pitches, up and out of the canyon.

The upside of this disaster was an opportunity for me to spend several hours down in the Mitchell Creek Canyon exploring the drainage. It was a lesson in how truly rugged the terrain around Lake Chelan is. It's also stunningly scenic. The undulating sweeps of brush and wild grass create a tapestry of earth tones that seem to be pulled right from a Charles M. Russell painting. The deep canyons and draws are lined up and down with striking vertical cliffs and abutments of rock. They have an amazing range of color hues, some grayish black in tone, residing right next to bright pink granite extrusions and white quartz cliff faces. Ribbons and bands of color weave through the exposed mountainside and create intricate mosaics. All of it gives testimony to the fascinating process which raised and folded these former ocean floors into high water-carved mountains.

I was also struck again by the remoteness of the canyon. Because of its steep sides, I would not be surprised to learn that we were some of the few people who had ever been down there. Perhaps some hunters, and likely some prospectors, had made their way through the canyon, but it seemed unlikely that many people would make the difficult trek down the steep hillside except maybe to find wild game, precious minerals, or the occasional crushed tin can-like remains of a demolished snowmobile.

Mitchell Creek is just one of hundreds of drainages and draws that weave up into the hills and away from the lake. Many of the deer and marmots out in these areas probably go their whole life and never see a human being.

Back on the south shore, almost directly across the lake from the outlet to Mitchell Creek, is Fields Point Landing. This complex, which was created by the efforts of the National Forest Service and the National Park Service, represents a fitting debarking point for journeys up into the untamed higher reaches of the lake. The beautiful and storied boat, the *Lady of the Lake II*, makes a stop here to pick up wilderness-bound travelers and ferry them to points deeper in the mountains.

Fields Point is well appointed with the appropriate rock walls, national park facilities, information reader boards, and a topographic relief map, such that it engenders the feeling of being in a national park. Even if visitors to Fields Point aren't technically in the North Cascades National Park complex yet, for many, the national park experience begins here.

A trail that wanders out along the lake shore and connects manicured picnicking lawns showcases the sweeping lake views and the dry barren mountains rising above Mitchell Creek to the north. To the south, above Fields Point, Slide Ridge stair steps down in platform after platform of rocky benches draped with evergreens. The whole grounds of Fields Point and the surrounding mountains are a theater of beauty.

The best part of Fields Point, however, is being there when patrons line up in preparation to board the boat. The air is alive with the crackling excitement of people who are about to go on an adventure. As they wander up the gangplank, there is nothing but smiles from first timers and loyal return visitors. Everyone knows they are bound for one of the prettiest places on earth, heading into uplake Chelan and the beautiful North Cascades.

As the boat sounds the horn and heads off, the buzz of anticipation swirls along with it. There are usually people left on the shore, either because they were dropping someone off or because they just came to Fields Point to enjoy Fields Point. I have been one of those people, on occasion, and among others watching the *Lady of the Lake II* glide away, I have felt the communal sense that we have all "missed the boat," both literally and figuratively.

Those on the boat are treated to a spectacle. Almost immediately, the boat passes by the first waterfall visible from the lake on the north shore. The misty white ribbon of water emerges from a deep rock channel and then plunges straight down, landing just a slight distance back from the lake shore.

The area between Mitchell creek and the waterfall is a favorite haunt of a large herd of bighorn sheep. It's very common to see them working their way up and down the cliffs and hills of the valley, grazing on the dry summer grass or drinking from the lake.

Within a few short miles, the boat moves past the outlet of Twenty-Five Mile Creek. A state park there stands as a sometimes lonely outpost at the edge of Lake Chelan's "civilized" section. At Twenty-Five Mile Creek, the road turns inland and heads up and away from Lake Chelan, toward the Entiat Mountains and the Glacier Peak Wilderness.

Early resident Thomas Dodge arrived at Twenty-Five Mile Creek in 1908. He had left New York and traveled all the way across the country before coming face to face with the high mountains that loom above the lake past the creek. He recalled his reaction in these words:

> The trip uplake and particularly the view uplake beyond 25 mile creek was a crowning joy to me, a young man who loved the beauty of nature and who had reveled in the unspoiled scenery and great open country that had been revealed on this trip.

From this vantage point, the first of the 8,000-foot-high peaks come into view. They form a daunting rampart as they loom high above the narrow lake, pronouncing the fjord-like nature of Chelan.

A short few thousand feet uplake, the last home with road access sits gazing toward the route to Stehekin. As the *Lady of the Lake II* steams past it, the passengers are heading in a straight line directly at the jagged snowcapped peaks of the high Cascades. This is the wild, unmarred, upper reaches of Lake Chelan. Everyone on board is moving beyond the Pale.

Lacu Rosu

A barrier lake

On an inky black night, high in the Carpathian Mountains, I found myself being chauffeured down a narrow, windy switchback road at a precarious speed. I was heading through the lonely heart of Transylvania, the ancestral home of Vlad the Impaler, also known as Vlad Tepes III, but perhaps best known as Count Dracula.

The Carpathians are a land that the modern age seems to have bypassed, a land synonymous with creepiness, shrouded in legends and myths about werewolves, ghosts, and, of course, vampires. My driver, Zolton, was negotiating the road with grand prix velocity, the tires squealing through hairpin turns, the car drifting perilously toward the void that loomed beyond the road's edge. Safety rails were apparently not in the budget during the long dictatorial rein of Nicolae Ceausescu, who ruled the area in a cruel unyielding fashion before the fall of the Iron Curtain.

When the Soviet Union collapsed, it did so in a series of peaceful revolutions that began in neighboring Hungary and spread to other satellite states. These events were given names like the Orange Revolution in the Ukraine, or the Velvet Revolution in the Czech Republic, names which depicted the peaceful transfer of power to a new political system.

The exception to this was Romania, where violent and deadly riots culminated in the storming of the government palace and subsequent execution of the dictator and his wife. Local rumor has it that Ceausescu's head was kicked around a courtyard like a soccer ball, but historical descriptions of the event discount that.

It was within the borders of this newly liberated country that I found myself hurtling into the night at breakneck speed. I think half of me expected to see a menacing figure, cloaked in a black hooded robe, materialize from the woods in the gloom ahead of us at any moment.

Apparently, the other half of me really did not expect to see a menacing figure, cloaked in a black hooded robe, materialize from the woods. I know this because when a menacing figure in a dark robe actually did materialize, the half of me that was not expecting it let out a sharp, staccato screech, like a wounded barn owl.

Zolton swerved around this horrific apparition without tapping the brakes and continued hurtling the car into the night.

"The Romani," he said in his low monotone voice. "How you might to say, the Gypsies. The widows are to wear only the black and they wander the roads at night. It is to be all the time dangerous."

I wanted to respond, but I hadn't resumed breathing yet. At that moment, I wasn't one hundred percent sure I would ever start breathing again.

"I am sorry if that startled you," he said.

"It didn't at all," my brain said, but my mouth actually made up its own sentence that sounded something like, "Urrgal goober fartmint," with the emphasis on the word "Urrgal."

Zolton didn't speak English that well, so he nodded his head and pretended to understand.

My trip had started out a little rough. I had missed a connecting flight, and been delayed in Vienna. I finally arrived in the capital city of Bucharest, but, unfortunately, my luggage had not. As nearly as I could understand, my bag was somewhere in Istanbul, and would be there for the foreseeable future.

"Do you think they will be able to deliver my bags to your village?" I asked Zolton.

He looked at me as if I had just asked him whether we might see any dinosaurs on our trip.

I was in Romania for a variety of reasons. The first was to assemble a team of data entry personnel that would work in conjunction with an American company to compile, filter, categorize, and disseminate fixed income financial information to a proprietary database. If that doesn't sound like the most boring task in the history of the world, then I have not properly described it.

The second reason I was there was to asses the possibility of investing in a ski resort. As Romania was getting cozier with the European Union, the gold rush was on. Anything that could compete with Western Europe, but at Eastern European prices, was a "can't for you to miss," endeavor, as Zolton was more than happy to inform me.

Secretly, however, I had a third agenda, and one that was most important to me. There were two lakes I wanted to see. One was fairly well known, and although it probably wasn't going to be the greatest lake in the world, it was historically important, and rumored to be "enchanting."

The second lake was not very well known, particularly in the west. From what little I had heard, it had a sort of mythic quality to it. Most importantly, it was a great example of a barrier lake. It was a young barrier lake at that. The landslide that formed it occurred in 1847. According to Zolton, it was "an important lake" in Romania, whatever that meant. It was rumored to be full of mineral waters that had curative powers. There was not much more information available, but firsthand reports from trusted sources had led me to believe that it was also one of the most beautiful lakes in the world. If the lake could cure ailments, that certainly would give it a leg up in a competition for greatest lake in the world.

We had already driven by the first lake earlier in the day. It was known as Lake Snagov. This lake is beloved by the Romanian people. It is a beautiful pastoral body of water, just north of Bucharest. It is a relatively small lake, only about six miles long.

The lake encircles a small island that is home to the Snagov Monastery. Built in the fourteenth century, the monastery may or may not have a particular claim to history. It is rumored to be the original burial place of Dracula. Emphasis must be placed on the word "original," because, according to legend, he might not have remained buried there for long. He may not currently be buried anywhere.

On the morning we were there, it was a beautiful sunny day, but the lake itself had thin tendrils of fog that were slithering erratically across the water. They seemed to materialize and evaporate spontaneously. They stretched up and ghosted around the island with its ancient monastery. It was the perfect eerie touch to this storied locale.

Although Lake Snagov was beautiful and certainly a striking piece of the Romanian countryside, I found it to be located much further from the Carpathian Mountains than I had expected. It could not really be classified as a mountain lake. I decided almost immediately that it would not make it onto the short list of the greatest lakes in the world.

Nevertheless, it was a beautiful place. My expectations hadn't been set all that high, so I wasn't in any way disappointed. Besides, Zolton assured me that when we got to the second lake, I would be "very joyousfull."

The spooky fog on the lake set the tone for our drive through ancient hamlets filled with gothic architecture. Old houses had extensive gabling that dripped with ornate iron latticework. There were crucifixes on the roof peaks of every home. There were crucifixes in the iron railings. There were crucifixes in the corbels under balconies. There were crucifixes in the end trusses. As we began our ascent into the Carpathians, there were mountains that leapt up to needle-sharp rock summits, copiously adorned with large crucifixes.

"You are, of course, must to be thinking the crosses are for the vampires," said Zolton, "and you are to be right. They are for the keeping away of all evil spirits. People in Romania are very superstitious."

It was on the heels of this prelude that I arrived at our near collision with the gypsy widow on the dark mountain road. With Lake Snagov and the haunted Romanian countryside on my mind, my near cardiac arrest from this encounter had been hours in the making.

We continued on without incident and arrived late at night in Zolton's village. There, I spent two days in the small town in the Miercurea-Ciuc region. I was incarcerated for hours in a large soviet era cinder block apartment building, engaged in an insidious endeavor known as work. I was overwhelmed with anticipation for our trip up to the second lake.

At last, the day came. Still without my luggage, I was now wearing a pair of canvas pants and an industrial, thick, plaid shirt I had borrowed from Zolton.

"I have swimsuits, shirts, pants, whatever you need. Is no problem," he assured me.

We departed for my visit to the second lake. It was known as Lacu Rosu, the Red Lake. Zolton was at the wheel again, and now we were accompanied by his wife Anna Marie, and her cousin Annicue. The two girls looked like they could be sisters. Both had pretty Slavic features, slightly olive skin, and long raven-black hair. Zolton was more blond, and had the look of a professional German cross country ski racer. All three were very pleasant, and extremely nice, but I had found there is a reserved, serious nature to the Romanian people. They were not what I would call, "quick to laugh."

We headed out of the farmlands and back up toward the Carpathian Mountains. We first drove through the stunning Bicaz Pass. This gorge, with its monolithic peaks and broad canyon walls, is sometimes called the Yosemite of Romania. I found this description to be a bit inappropriate in that Yosemite is a broad valley. Bicaz is a narrow slot carved through rock. The height of the wall, combined with narrowness, makes it extremely dramatic. There was no question that the Carpathian Mountains were home to amazing scenery.

We wound around and up to Lacu Rosu. One of the first things I noticed is that, after driving through a wild collaboration of rock walls and bony peaks, when we dropped into the valley that contained the lake the scenery sort of just stopped. There was one rather fetching broad rock face that rose up above the lake, but the bulk of the shore was hemmed in by lower tree-covered hills. After the grandeur of Bicaz Pass, this was a bit of a letdown.

We stopped on a grassy shoreline where a lot of swimmers and bathers were congregating and lounging in the sun. The lake itself was sort of a black brown color, not really what one would call visually stunning. Because the lake had been formed so recently, it was still full of dead trees that protruded, like skeleton fingers, from all over the surface. The evergreen trees that surrounded the lake had thin branchless trunks that rose to a dense but sickly looking canopy, making the woods seem like a hollow, dark, and foreboding place.

"Is this Lacu Rosu?" I asked Zolton.

"Yes," he said, sweeping his arms with a look of pride, "this is it."

There was something else a little disturbing about this beach. There were lots of Romanian women on the beach, many of them very pretty. They were all wearing very conservative one-piece bathing suits. There were a lot of men on the beach as well. Tragically, all of them were wearing swimsuits that were not very conservative. Every single one was scantily clad in a hideous, small, European-style swimsuit.

Americans, statistically speaking, are said to be more portly than other countries in the world, but to our great credit, when an American gentleman finds himself a few doughnuts past his ideal weight, he doesn't go parading himself around in a string bikini bottom. The same cannot be said in Romania. The tight brief-style swimsuit is the bathing accessory of choice, without exception. There were men crammed into this flimsy lingerie who had such large bellies that the swimsuit was not even visible when you viewed them from the front.

To say this was disturbing to my Victorian-rooted cultural sensibilities would be an extreme understatement. In the end it was not vampires and werewolves that would haunt me, but the image of 300-pound hairy Eastern European men splashing around a giant mud hole crammed into women's underwear. There were so many of them that there was really nowhere that one could look away. Three words came to mind: God bless America.

"We will now, then, to go change in these trees," said Zolton, gesturing to the dark Transylvanian forest. I followed him back away from the lake into the woods. The spindly tree trunks seemed to stretch forever into the dark recesses of the mountainside. It took me a moment to realize what it was that made these woods seem so foreign to me. Finally I put my finger on it. There was no underbrush, just earth and pine needles. The woods were picked clean of anything that could be used for firewood. It made the forest seem less like a good place to hide, and more like a good place to be ambushed. I had the surreal sense that I was actually living in a waking nightmare. I had no idea how real this feeling was about to become.

The woods were scary enough in their own right, but it was at that moment that I actually came face to face with a true life horror that I could not have foreseen. What I saw made my skin turn cold. My mouth went dry. Air rushed uncontrollably from my lungs. There in the forest, emerging from Zolton's bag, was a small pair of thin European-style swimming briefs. I want to place emphasis on the word small.

I suddenly was struck with a gut-wrenching realization. When Zolton had offered to loan me a swimsuit, my mind naturally conjured up the image of trunks similar to my own swimsuit. It was in that instant that I came to grips with the fact that we were in Romania, and that's not what Romanian people wear when they swim.

"I think these will for to fit on you," he said.

If I had been in a horror movie, this is the point where an

un-rosined bow would have been pulled repeatedly across the single string of an old violin. In slow motion, he handed me the flimsy shred of fabric. The voices in my head were louder than I've ever heard them before. In unison they screamed one long, drawn-out word, "Noooooooooooooo."

Zolton walked away through the woods, while I stood there speechless, eyeing the garment he had just handed me as if it were a dead rat.

"Wait," I yelled suddenly. "Do you have a towel?"

There was no response. He was gone.

I was trapped, and I knew it. I had been excitedly discussing my trip to this lake for two days. My wonderful hosts were ecstatic about sharing it with me. They had brought me here to soak in and enjoy these curative waters. I had no choice. To do anything else would be rude. I was about to walk out of the woods into a large crowd of people wearing the equivalent of undersized women's underwear.

I took off the canvas pants and put on the bathing suit. I looked down. In truth, it appeared that my new attire really wasn't as bad as I had suspected it would be. It was worse. It was much worse. The swimsuit was probably two sizes too small. Maybe it was three sizes. I really don't know.

It looked ridiculous. I honestly would have been much more comfortable just walking out of the woods naked. Romania is, at its heart, a conservative country, however, with strict Catholic traditions. An American streaker strolling among the beachgoers would not likely have gone over well. There was no alternative. I mustered up all the dignity I could find, which was very little indeed. I emerged from the woods looking like an underweight sumo wrestler.

"At least everyone else is wearing these silly things," I thought. "So I won't stick out."

Anna Marie and Annicue quickly dispelled that illusion. I think the offending circumstance was that I was an American, in the middle of summer, and as an American, I had spent a great deal of time back home in the sun wearing American swimsuits, and American shorts. For this reason, I had a nice dark tan on my legs that ended right at my mid-thigh. With my upper legs roughly the color of snow on a sunny day, not only did I appear to be wearing ladies underwear, but

I looked like I was wearing them on the outside of a pair of bright white, skin-tight, cut-off leotards.

I think it's fair to say that, as far as Anna Marie and Annicue were concerned, the spectacle of me walking out of the woods in a loincloth, with a farmer tan, was the most hysterical image in the history of the universe. If there was a brief second in which they tried to contain their amusement, I certainly didn't notice it. Their mirth and uncontrollable attack of laughter was such that Anna Marie actually sat down in the grass. Annicue remained standing, but she swayed back and forth and clutched her upper stomach with one hand while she wiped steaming tears off her face with the other. This was coming from two people who had barely cracked a smile in three days. I think they actually felt bad about laughing, but were powerless to stop it.

Apparently, when Romanian people do get around to laughing, it is explosive. The two women sounded like a pair of coyotes whooping repeatedly at the moon. They were gasping for breath. This attracted the attention of all the other people lounging about the lake, beautiful women and enormously overweight men alike. The jocularity of the moment seemed to be extremely contagious. They looked at me like I was some kind of clumsy marine mammal that had just flippered my way into a coffee shop wearing a diaper. All eyes were on me. I could tell they were all mortified about laughing, but couldn't do anything to stop it. I was now officially living the dream where you walk out on a large stage, and then realize you are in your underwear.

Any of the remaining dignity I had mustered up quickly evaporated in the thin mountain air. I shuffled into the lake, my pasty white butt cheeks hanging out the back of the undersized suit. Remarkably, the laughing grew even louder, a feat which I had not felt possible. I submerged myself completely in the lake, but I could still hear the girls howling even while I was underwater.

The water felt nice, which was good, because I didn't foresee a scenario in which I could ever come out of it again. It was a long time before the girls stopped laughing. For the remainder of my stay in Romania, they would occasionally have relapses and say things in broken English like, "Your legs, so much white, so much white," or, "Your butt." Then they would break into hysterics again and yammer unintelligibly in Romanian.

As for Lacu Rosu, the water was not the prerequisite blue color that the greatest lake in the world required. Nor was it in any way clear. It was supposed to be colored red, tinted by minerals from one of its tributaries, but I didn't really detect even a hint of red. It was more brownish black. There was thick gooey sediment on the bottom that stirred up in ochre plumes when you waded through it. If the waters were curative, I certainly didn't notice any effect.

Zolton and the girls went swimming as well, and later, when they left the water, I found out that Lacu Rosu had one last little treat in store for me. The three of them stood in a circle and began picking at each other the way monkeys might when trying to rid themselves of fleas. As I waded closer to the shore I saw, to my delight, that they were all covered with tiny little pea-sized black dots. This compelled me to exit the water rather quickly. I, too, was covered in many dozens of little black dots. Lacu Rosu, it turns out, had cute, adorable, little leeches. Apparently, they were particularly drawn to the pale region of my body, and darn it if they hadn't figured out some clever little way to work themselves right inside the scant fabric of my swimsuit. Deep inside! I reacted to this in a way that a person might react if they suddenly found out their private parts were covered in leeches. I would struggle for a better metaphor here, but the reality of what happened pretty much speaks for itself. I stood with my back to the beach and carefully removed every leech while muttering to myself, "I am so joyousfull. What a joyousfull place."

When I was done, Zolton motioned me over, and the girls began de-leeching my back, as if this was just standard practice for swimmers all over the world, like showering or toweling off.

"Now you see," said Zolton, "you can tell to your friends that you did to get your blood sucked in Transylvania."

He said it with a deadpan smoothness that made me suspect he had delivered the line on a few other occasions. I tried to smile, but I suspect my grin looked more like the expression someone might give if they accidentally urinated on an electric horse pasture fence.

Lacu Rosu was not going to be the greatest lake in the world. Lacu Rosu was a parasite-filled swamp. But for an unfortunate landslide, the lake should not even have been there at all. As for the trusted sources that had told me Red Lake was one of the most beautiful lakes in the world, my visit taught me something important—those sources were no longer to be trusted.

The trip, on the whole, was a wonderful experience. Romania was a beautiful country. The people there were the most gracious hosts I had yet encountered. The Carpathian Mountains were captivating at every turn, and Bicaz Canyon was a spectacle never to be forgotten. Some of the lakes there were wonderful, but on a world stage, they were not the attributes in which the country held its distinction.

Flying back home from Romania, I contemplated what the Romanian people considered to be an important and beautiful lake. I thought about some of the other lakes I had already seen that were famously beautiful and well known on a world stage. None of these had unseated Chelan in my mind. A small feeling of wonder and excitement started to creep over me. What if Lake Chelan really was the greatest lake in the world? Perhaps I really was on to something.

"Holy crud," I thought to myself.

I didn't actually use the word "crud."

The North Cascades

It is impossible to extol the greatness of Lake Chelan without considering the North Cascades that embrace the lake. These mountains are responsible for forming the lake, and if the lake, by definition, is billions of gallons of water, it is the mountains themselves that hold this water in place and define its boundaries. Their sturdy flanks plunge all the way down to the bottom of the Lucerne Basin.

The term North Cascades generally refers to the area from Snoqualmie Pass to the Canadian border. From the Canadian border north to Lytton Mountain, the northern terminus of the range, they are simply called the Cascades, since the Canadians don't consider them to be particularly northerly. Strewn throughout these jagged peaks are 519 glaciers, representing a higher number than any other area in the continental United States.[13]

I grew up hiking and camping in the Cascades. As soon as I turned 16, I would constantly jump in my car and sneak off to go explore them further. When I moved to the relative flat of eastern Washington for college, I yearned for the mountains and frequently made the trek west. I often used Lake Chelan as my base of operations. When Amy and I left college, we bought a book called *The Best Short Hikes in Washington's North Cascades and the San Juan Islands*. The book, by E.M. Sterling, is a bible for those who want to explore the mountains.

Along with our faithful dog Otis, we set out to hike every trail in the book. There were 104. Within seven years, we had knocked out nearly half of the hikes. Two of these hikes were high above the south shore of Lake Chelan up the Twenty-Five Mile Creek drainage. One went to the summit of Stormy Mountain. The other was a place called Big Hill near Shady Pass. A third hike began in the Skagit drainage and rose up to Cascade Pass at the extreme end of the Chelan Valley drainage system. From here, the vast glaciers above the Pelton Basin and the Stehekin River Valley were laid out in full panorama. Undoubtedly, the numerous hikes between Cascade Pass and Stehekin would have been grouped into this book as well were it not for their remoteness.

We had hoped to get a little higher up in the hills, and also to knock off a lot more of the hikes in the book, but practical matters interfered. By the time we started renovating the Farmhouse, Otis, our crazy wild mountain dog, was starting to slow down a touch. After years of running full tilt up and down mountains, through woods, and across rivers, his hips were starting to give him some problems. Keeping Otis out of his beloved woods would have been unthinkable. We started to select hikes that were flatter so that he wouldn't put such a strain on his aging joints. This kept us out of the higher hills.

Our hiking book had become a journal of sorts. We would record the date of each hike, trail details, as well as funny anecdotes and comments on what was going on in our lives. One late summer, we took a beautiful hike on a trail beside Baker Lake on the west side of the mountains. On the pages of the book relating to this hike, I recorded the following:

> This was a very nice hike. We found a point of land above the lake and ate handfuls of wild blueberries. Mount Baker was in full view. I'm sad to say this is probably the last hike in this book we will take with Otis. We picked this hike because it is relatively flat, but even a slight amount of elevation was a bit too much for him. I'm afraid his hiking days may be over.

It was a sad milestone for us. It felt a little bit like the end of an era. There was not a checked-off hike in the book that hadn't included Otis as a hiking partner. There were dozens of other hikes in Idaho, Montana, Oregon, the South Cascades, and the Olympic Mountains that he had bounded up and down as well. I'm sure he traveled over a thousand miles through the mountains and woods of the Pacific Northwest.

If it was the end of the hiking era, it was the beginning of the lake era. To keep him active, we were constantly down at the lake shore throwing sticks for him. This was the time when we found ourselves more frequently visiting the park near Chelan Falls. With the flat grass and the river for swimming, it was perfect for Otis. If he missed heading up into the high hills, he didn't seem to show it. His tail wagged every time we were near the shoreline.

I felt myself missing the mountains, though. During our earlier scrambles through the Cascades, the three of us had seen some incredible sights. We were continually encountering new and fantastic places as we worked our way through the hiking book. The more we saw of the mountains, the more I came to believe that in a region of incredible high alpine country, Lake Chelan and the Stehekin Valley were surrounded by some of the best of it.

What is astounding about this area, and really the whole mountain range, is its relative obscurity. Certainly those that live in the Pacific Northwest know and admire the Cascades, but even among the locals there seems to be a marked lack of understanding about just how spectacular this area really is. These are world-class mountains. They have mesmerizing sheer rock edifices, glacier fields, rivers, forests, and valleys that combine to create scenery rivaling anywhere in the world. Amongst this astonishing range, one of the true highlights is the spectacular 8,000- and 9,000-foot peaks that form the upper drainage of Lake Chelan.

Just how spectacular are they? The mountains in the region are so stunning that they were set aside as a national park in 1968. The national park, as it exists now, consists of 684,000 acres. The park complex is comprised of four distinct units, one of which is the Lake Chelan National Recreation Area that embraces the western end of the lake and the Stehekin Valley.

Even this designation as a national park fails to give the North Cascades anything in the way of true recognition. When one talks of national parks, it is the great celebrities of the system—Yellowstone, the Grand Canyon, Yosemite, Glacier National Park, and the Great Smoky Mountains—that garner most of the attention.

Television documentaries about our national parks will gush about the Everglades or Acadia, or Isle Royale. Even the local siblings, Mount Rainier and Olympic National Park, are far better known on a national and even local level than the North Cascades. There are a few other obscure national parks in our system. To avoid offending anyone, I won't name them, because the truth is these parks remain obscure largely because they are sort of duds in terms of visual splendor.

This is not the case with regard to the North Cascades. These are wild, soaring, flower-blanketed, glacier-covered masterpieces. Within the park itself, excluding the wilderness outside its borders, there are 318 glaciers. Compare this to Glacier National Park, the famous cousin to the east. Glacier National Park has only 26 glaciers, the largest of which covers less than a square mile.

Excluding Alaska, if you consider all the area in the United States covered by glaciers, over 90 percent of that area is in the State of Washington, and 60 percent of it is in the North Cascades. Including the glaciers in the national park and other wilderness areas surrounding Lake Chelan, there are 42 square miles of ice in this region.

The North Cascades are buried in glaciers because of a coincidence of geology and geography. Comprised of an ancient seabed, the crest of the range was thrust up by the collision of tectonic plates that began seven million years ago. By far the highest of these continental upthrusts are in the northern part of the range. Of the non-volcanic mountains, ten named peaks rise to a height above 9,000 feet. Five of these are in the Chelan drainage, including the highest, Bonanza Peak, which towers 9,511 feet.

The geographic location is the second component that feeds these glaciers. The proximity to the Pacific Ocean and the prevailing direction of the jet streams force a massive amount of precipitation across the mountains. Mount Baker, located just outside the National Park, logged the highest recorded snowfall in history for the entire world during the winter of 1998–1999. That year 1,140 inches of snow fell. This was 95 feet of snow over the course of a one-year period, almost a ten-story building. That measurement just barely nudged out the prior record of 1,122 inches, which was also recorded in the Cascades at Mount Rainier in the winter of 1971–1972.

These are snowy mountains. The milder air coming in from the Pacific during the summer also helps maintain the glaciers by keeping the mountains cooler than the Rocky Mountains of the interior. The result is massive glaciations.

The glaciers are spectacular. They are twisting, undulating rivers of ice that are hundreds of feet thick. They warp, crack and deform to create fascinating structures like bergschrunds and seracs. These protrude from the mountainside, appearing to be formations of another world. Great cracks in the ice open to reveal glowing blue and green walls that disappear into unseen chasms hundreds of feet down.

They can seem like cold lifeless moonscapes, but they are far from it. They support numerous microcosms of life, from small algae and bacteria to whole colonies of insects, spiders, worms, and other invertebrates.

More importantly, they drastically alter their environment. Their sheer mass and their never-ceasing movement are constantly grinding and reshaping the mountains. Their melt waters create raging rivers that form the basis of entire ecosystems in the broad valleys below.

The glaciers impact the immediate environment by moderating and changing the temperature of the air and water. They create their own weather systems. Cool shading fog and winds increase the variety of microclimates in the mountains around them. In the North Cascades National Park, this diversity of climates has allowed more species of plants to grow than in any other national park in the country. Around 1,700 have been identified, with perhaps hundreds more yet to be catalogued.[14]

Certainly everyone knows about glaciers. Everyone has seen them in pictures, on TV, or in movies. Only a fraction of a percentage of people living on the planet, however, have ever actually been to a glacier and walked across its surface. I remember vividly my first trek across a glacier on the flanks of Mount Rainier. It's something I could never forget. I have also been with many friends who have stepped onto a glacier for the first time and the reaction is always the same. I firmly believe that if there is one experience that cannot be communicated through words or picture, it is a firsthand encounter with a glacier.

The North Cascades are extraordinary because they still remain a haven for glaciers in a world where glaciers are diminishing, and they maintain these glaciers at such low elevations and in such southern latitudes.

The North Cascades have another attribute which makes them exceptional. In a world where one mountain rises above 29,000 feet and many rise above 20,000 feet, it is easy to dismiss the Cascades as falling short of the splendor of the higher ranges. The truth is that they stand out, even among many of these towering counterparts. They stand out because they are a range of incredible relief. From base to summit, the steeply carved deep valleys present massive walls that rival the rock faces of some of the world's highest peaks.

Mount Everest, the tallest of all mountains, rises above the Tibetan Plateau to 29,029 feet of elevation. The plateau itself, however, has an average elevation of nearly 15,000 feet. The actual edifice presented from any nearby vantage point of Mount Everest is a little more than 14,000 feet.

In the Cascades, Mount Rainier displays this same amount of relief when viewed from sea level, or 9,000–12,000 feet when viewed from a closer vantage point that encompasses the foothills at its base. Throughout the North Cascades, the non-volcanic 9,000 foot peaks drop precipitously down to river valleys, many with less than a thousand feet of elevation, creating 7,000 and 8,000 foot ramparts. Combining this with the relatively low elevation of the many glaciers in the range, the Cascades present themselves as visual equals to many of their higher counterparts.

The fact that this same giant relief occurs at a lower altitude serves to distinguish the Cascades from other ranges. This allows for the incredible riot of wildflowers to cover the meadows and the rich blanket of timber to grace the valleys, creating a contrast between lush vegetation and sheer alpine granite that is the delight of artist, photographer, and sightseer alike.

Those that come to know the North Cascades are aware of just how stunning they are. In his book *Encounters with the Archdruid*, Pulitzer Prize-winning author John McPhee wrote, "A great many people believed that [the Cascades] were the most beautiful mountains in the United States. A smaller and more parochial group felt that [they] were the most beautiful mountains in the world."[15]

Talking about the North Cascades National Park in another book, Peter Potterfield described them as "one of the most significant conservation achievements of the modern environmental movement—snatched from the jaws of development and timber interests."

The name of his book is *Classic Hikes of the World*. This book, a revered tome by adventure travelers, is about "23 breathtaking treks on six continents."

The author vetted hundreds of hikes in locations around the globe. Of his favorite 23 treks on the planet, two of those classic hikes are right in the Cascades of Washington. One is the Wonderland Trail that circumnavigates Mount Rainier. The other is Park Creek Pass, which makes the voyage from the Skagit River Valley on the North Cascades Highway up over the mountains and down into the Stehekin River Valley at the head of Lake Chelan.

There are 57 million square miles of dry land on the planet. That two out of 23 of the world's most breathtaking treks should fall in the 10,000 square miles of Washington's Cascade Mountain range is a telling commentary on the beauty of the area.

Lord Shelley wrote his superlatives about Lake Como in 1818. He never made it to Chelan, of course. In 1818, only a handful of Europeans had even seen Lake Chelan. If he had, he undoubtedly would have had a similar impression. His prose about "the appearance of a mighty river winding among the mountains and the forests," seems to be equally appropriate for describing Lake Chelan.

As it happens, the North Cascades would eventually play host to their own famous poets and wordsmiths. Many of the avant-garde poets of the Beat Poet generation spent substantial amounts of time in and around these peaks.

One such author was Kenneth Rexroth. He was one of America's leading poets in the 1950s. His career at that time was at its height, and he is often credited with being the chief architect of the San Francisco Renaissance that spawned the rise of the beatnik culture. The flash point of the movement is considered to be a single poetry reading at the Six Gallery in San Francisco. This event was made famous in Jack Kerouac's book *Dharma Bums*. It was Kenneth Rexroth who organized the event. He was the mentor to many of these artistic visionaries, and, with the help of a weekly radio broadcast in the Bay Area, was the central catalyst of this literary revolution.

He had lived in the North Cascades in 1924. He spent the early part of that summer clearing the pack trail from Marblemount all the way to Stehekin. Later that season, he was part of the team that hauled up the wood and glass to the top of McGregor Mountain to build the fire tower that looked out across Lake Chelan and the Stehekin Valley. In his 1966 autobiographical novel, he tells the story of his North Cascades summer and describes the structure built on McGregor Mountain as "The Siberia of lookouts."

From the summit, he could look north right to the apex of Crater Mountain, where Pulitzer Prize-winning poet Gary Snyder spent a summer secluded in a fire lookout tower in 1952. Snyder was the person who inspired the character of Japhy Ryder in *Dharma Bums*. He spent two and a half months stationed on top of the mountain looking directly at the spine of the Boston Buckner Ridge which separates the Skagit drainage from the Chelan drainage. Snyder would spend an additional summer five miles west at the Sourdough Mountain fire lookout, as would fellow beat poet Phillip Whalen. Both of these writers would later generate a tremendous amount of writing based on their experiences amid the soaring peaks.

Perhaps most famously, on the advice of his friend Gary Snyder, Jack Kerouac took up residence at the next lookout to the north. In 1956, Kerouac spent 63 days at the summit of Desolation Peak. From this vantage point, he looked out at what he called "The Chelan highlands."

The founding father of the Beat Poet culture and a legendary bohemian, Kerouac escaped to the wilderness of the North Cascades in search of quiet introspection. He lived in a 12' x 12' shack cabled to the top of the mountain overlooking miles and miles of the Ross Lake, Lake Chelan, and Pasayten Wildernesses. He wrote about his time there in his bestselling books *Dharma Bums* and *Desolation Angels*.

His experiment with isolation was not necessarily the wonderful adventure for which he had hoped. The many verses he generated relating to his time there seem to be a tug of war between his battles with loneliness and his sheer admiration for the scenery that surrounded him. To read his work, one could surmise that he was profoundly affected by the experience.

"Desolation Peak," he wrote, "sometimes on the alpine grass, hundreds of miles of snow covered rock all around, looming Mount Hozomeen on my north, vast snowy Jack to the south, the encharmed picture of the lake below to the west and the snowy hump of Mt. Baker beyond, and to the east the rilled and ridged monstrosities humping to the Cascade Ridge, and after that first time suddenly realizing It's me that's changed and done all this and come and gone and complained and hurt and joyed and yelled, not the Void."[16]

Even Allen Ginsberg, the most cosmopolitan of the Beat Poets, made the journey up to Glacier Peak in the wilderness that borders the south shore of Lake Chelan. Gary Snyder, who was the most accomplished mountaineer among them, had scrambled up to dozens of summits throughout the Cascades and probably knew the area as well as anyone. When Ginsberg received a Guggenheim grant in 1965, the two used the money to explore the mountains of the west, culminating in a climb up the volcanic cone of Glacier Peak.

The time that all of these poets spent in and around the mountains near Lake Chelan inspired some of the great poetry and literature of the age. Many of these writers, at the leading edge of what would become the Zen movement in America, drew their inspiration from these lonely peaks and shimmering waters. The true power of this gorgeous land inspired them in much the same way as the mountains of Asia inspired the ancient Zen lunatics and enlightened wanderers of history.

That same spirituality is woven into the myths and legends of the Native Americans who inhabited this region for centuries. That same power is still as omnipresent today as it was then. It knows no particular denomination or religion. It continues to draw people every year.

Forty miles up the lake is the small landing at Lucerne. From there, another 12-mile journey up the Railroad Creek Valley away from the lake leads to Holden Village. This small town, left over from the days of the Holden Mine Company, draws hundreds of people of various Christian denominations every year to enjoy the mountains, rest, and rejuvenate their faith. The solitude found among the cathedral-like peaks seems to be the perfect environment for personal introspection.

Whichever lake on the planet was the greatest lake in the world, it had to be surrounded by stunning, world-class, glacier-covered mountains. The North Cascades more than fit the bill. The blazing sunsets reflecting off the calm water, storms rolling down the lake, the raging streams, the tangled forests, and the jagged mountains seem to inspire everyone who has seen them. They are, as Gary Snyder described, "A perfection of Chaos."

Lake Project

Year 2

Springtime came again, and with it, some significant events took place. One of them began on a gorgeous Memorial Day weekend. We were in Chelan staying at the Bluff with Mark and Meggan and our friends Jon, Kerry, Scott, and Trish. We weren't planning on staying all three days of the long weekend. Our plan was to head back to Seattle on Sunday. We packed up our things to head home, but it was so warm and sunny, we thought we would stop at the park at Chelan Falls for a few hours, relax in the sun, throw a ball around, and let the dogs run.

The day was perfect. It was also eventful. Boats were beached on the gravel bar at the mouth of the Chelan River and music was playing. There was a touch of "spring break" atmosphere just across the water from the park. On our side of the river, we had the shoreline and the play field all to ourselves. Mark, John, Scott and I were up in the grass throwing a football while our wives sat down by the water in beach chairs reading celebrity tabloid magazines. That's when a woman came running toward us yelling for help.

Her boyfriend had swam across the Chelan River, and, while swimming back, he had become tired, or too cold, or both, and was now barely treading water moving right toward the outlet of the river. The four of us ran down to the shore, just as he went racing by in the current and got swept out into the Columbia River.

We jumped in and swam toward him while the girls stood on the shore near their beach chairs watching the rescue. The water was cold, and the current was strong, and the flow of the Chelan River water pushed the man well out toward the center of the Columbia River. It was turning into an epic struggle for survival. We finally reached him, put him in a back float position, and began swimming him back to shore.

The first thing I noticed as I swam toward the beach was that the rescue was so exciting that our wives had actually returned to sitting in their beach chairs and were now engrossed in their tabloid magazines again. It was apparent that the old *Baywatch* television-show versions of a water rescue were a lot more dramatic than an actual live open water rescue.

The four of us traded off the task of assisting the exhausted swimmer. We finally had him back on shore, fifteen minutes later and one hundred yards down river. The man thanked us and went on his way with his girlfriend, who had at least had the courtesy to wander down the river as the current pulled us south. I can only assume there simply weren't enough tabloid magazines to go around, or else she likely would have just stayed with our wives on the beach and read, pausing only to discuss fashion faux pas, or which star looked better than the other in a particular dress.

At the conclusion to our apparently less than dramatic rescue, we wandered up, sucking wind, back to our wives, stern looks on all of our faces.

"I don't know what to tell you," Amy said. "It got boring to watch after a while."

We sat in the sun catching our breath.

"Man I really wish we had brought some beer with us," I said.

I was letting the sun warm my chilled bones when, suddenly, something caught my eye, floating down the Chelan River. The cold water had swept up another victim, now bobbing just barely above the surface. I couldn't believe what I was seeing. Another urgent rescue was necessary. This one looked more precarious. I jumped to my feet and ran to the shore. I was still tired from the last recovery as I high-stepped into the water and then dove forward into a crawl stroke. I knew if I didn't get there in time and the current outran me, I wouldn't have the strength to go out into the Columbia River again and make it back.

This time the girls were on their feet. Mark, John, and Scott, who hadn't seen the situation unfold, were too far behind me to be of any help, so they stood on the shore yelling.

"You're almost there. Keep going."

I closed my eyes, gritted my teeth, and with every last bit of strength, I kicked and lunged forward. Then my hand touched something. A moment later, I got a firm grip, and just like that, I was cradling a waterlogged case of Budweiser beer.

A cheer went up from the shore. The cardboard was so saturated that it seemed ready to fall apart at any moment. I had saved yet another victim of the river just in the nick of time. Obviously someone upstream had been storing the beer in the water along the beach to keep it cold when a fluctuation of the river had lifted it loose and brought it to us. One moment I was actually saying out loud how much I wished we had brought beer, and the next minute I was pulling 24 nice cold cans up onto the beach.

My friend Trish was staring at me with an inquisitive look.

"Did you just wish for a beer, and then a half rack of beer floated down the river?" she said.

"I believe that's exactly what happened."

She shook her head slightly.

"That might be the weirdest thing I've ever seen."

"And now I wish I had a million dollars," I said, and then looked expectantly at the river. Nothing floated down.

"I wish this beach had topless women like they do in France," I said, and looked expectantly at the girls.

"Not likely," said Amy.

Apparently the Chelan River was only granting one wish per customer that day. I decided not to take my good fortune for granted. Everyone cracked a can open, and we were suddenly lying in the sun drinking beer by the water, our favorite pastime.

We were all officially having a great outing. Our faithful dog Otis was splitting his time wandering through the tall grass searching for birds, then walking back to the river to wade out belly deep and feel the current flow past his fur. Occasionally he would swim a tiny little circle out in the river and then back. Then he would wade out of the water, come beg for some chips from Amy, and then wander off to sniff the tall grass again.

It was decided that on a day like this, we couldn't possibly get in the car and drive back to Seattle. The Chelan River had lured us into staying one more night back up at the Bluff.

I remember that day very clearly. The river was running so fast, sunlight sparkling off every ripple. The surrounding mountainside was covered in bright green grass, so that it looked more like we were in the Irish highlands than in the arid hills of eastern Washington. The sun was as warm as if it was midsummer.

What I remember most, though, is the deep blue water by the steep shoreline and watching Otis cast off from the river rocks and then paddle in little circles out into the river and back. The water was crystalline, and you could see his legs so clearly, that it looked almost like he was swimming through air. I remember him stepping back on shore, shaking his fur, and showering us all with tiny cold droplets. I remember his tail wagging and casting off long looping lines of water that made a strange figure-8 pattern in the air before breaking into beads and falling to the beach. I remember this all so well because, as it turns out, this was the last time Otis would ever go swimming.

We had learned that winter that Otis had bladder cancer, and we knew that he only had a few months left to live. The doctors told us that the tumor would eventually rupture and that would be that. The doctors had been right. Otis fell very ill late that night. We got up before dawn and carried him to our car and made the drive back over the mountains. On occasion, he would sit up and stare out the window at the trees and peaks of Snoqualmie Pass, but for most of the trip he laid curled up. He could no longer eat or drink.

We tried to offer him a plain cheeseburger, but even this, his favorite treat, had no appeal. He looked at the cheeseburger and he looked at us, and the expression he gave us was as if by not eating the food, he was somehow letting us down. We took him to the vet and while there, a large loss of blood on the cold tiles of the waiting room left no doubt. We went into an exam room, sat down on the floor, and held him while he grew weaker and fell asleep. Then the vet gave him a shot.

With a faint sigh, his sleep became permanent. We were left in the room with a beautiful, funny, furry little animal that was no longer with us. I'll never forget the sadness we felt when we had to get up and walk out of that room, leaving our wild, crazy mountain dog behind.

I went back to my hiking book a few days later and turned to the page that had notes on our final hike with Otis at Baker Lake. I added to the trip details this entry:

> This was the last hike we took with our beloved dog Otis. He was with us on every one of these trips, and he loved going on them more than anything in the world. On May 31st, he passed away. We will miss him so much. He was a part of our family and a constant companion on all of our adventures. This hiking book, the woods, the mountains, the lakes, and streams will always remind me of the wonderful times we had together.

Amy and I didn't have kids. We were devastated. Otis had been with us for as long as we had known each other. Our house felt empty. We couldn't sleep. Everything reminded us of him. I suggested we get outside. Knowing the trails in our area would seem sad without his familiar tail wagging out in front of us, I proposed that we head down to Mount Saint Helens and hike around the blast zone. I thought the dramatically different scenery would serve as less of a reminder than the more familiar deep woods near Seattle. I was wrong.

After a half hour on the trail, we both admitted to being miserable. We turned around. We returned to the car and drove two and a half hours back home.

Even Lake Chelan could not cheer us up. We headed over to the Bluff, but that house felt as empty as our home in Seattle. When Mark and Meggan arrived, their dog Levi wandered around the house, sad, looking for her swimming buddy. She didn't know her swimming buddy was gone. She kept letting out quiet little whines that seemed to put voice to what we were feeling.

It was a long time before we were able to recapture a little joy. Like all sad events, each day helped a tiny bit, and over the weeks, things got a little better. After a while, things even started to seem normal again. It helped that we were a little distracted. As it happened, there were more big changes looming ahead in our lives.

There's no delicate way to say this, so I have to just state it. People get pregnant at the Bluff. This was a phenomenon we had become aware of just a few months after we completed the house and started renting it. Many of our renters, and also a few of our friends, had fallen victim to the strange nexus of fertility that seemed to swirl around the large granite abutment upon which the house was built. I suppose Amy and I should have been more attuned to the risks, but we were not. We learned during the summer that we too had been swept up in this cosmic anomaly. We were going to be parents.

A few months later, back at the Bluff, Mark and Meggan became victims as well. All of our lives were about to change. To cope with this, I did what I always do in moments of uncertainty. I ran out and bought some more property at Lake Chelan.

This time I was buying a real project. The property in question was going to present some challenges when it came time to build. I was convinced that if I ever did decide to put something there, it was going to be the coolest spot on the face of the entire globe. I was purchasing four lots on the very same cliffs from which my cousin Kelly and I had spent so much time jumping as kids.

"What in the world are you going to do with those lots?" Amy asked.

"Rustic cabins," I said.

"Do you really need more houses?"

I paused and considered that. Then I went to respond. Then I paused and considered it some more.

"These are going to be small cabins, but that's not all I'm doing with the property," I said.

"What else?"

I gave her my wise, secretive, knowing look. "I've got some ideas," I assured her. I don't think she believed me. This was bothersome because, although I didn't have any ideas, I certainly could have had some ideas, and I found it presumptuous of her to be convinced that I didn't.

As projects go, this one would have room for all kinds of creativity. It was also going to require far more effort and commitment than my projects in the past. If I'm being honest, it's possible that I might not have properly assessed the cumulative effects of having a brand new baby, a full time job, a vacation rental business, and two brand new construction projects underway. In retrospect, the bulk of that underestimation was related to the commitments of having a new baby. Time having passed by now, we also threw in the addition of a new, untrained puppy that had, by chance, wandered into our lives. We had a lot going on.

It was a fantastic and exciting time. The new dog was named Opal. The new baby boy was named Cooper. The new construction project was named Mountainside. The new lifestyle could best be described as an ongoing clown-like juggling act.

As the days went by, I kept coming up with potential ideas for my new properties. I kept sounding these ideas off of Amy. She kept pretending not to show excitement.

While in Jamaica a year earlier, I had been to a bar that was perched on the edge of a cliff. You could jump off the cliff into the Caribbean Sea and then swim through a cave, where a ladder led up through a hole in the earth and back into the bar. At the top of the ladder, a man would charge you five dollars, and then hand you a rum punch cocktail. People would complete this cycle over and over again. The man sitting next to the hole was doing a brisk business.

I now owned cliffs of my own.

"I've got it," I said to Amy. "We do the same thing at our cliffs. We'll make a fortune." I explained to her exactly how the bar was set up. To add excitement to my sales pitch, I told her about a boat full of topless girls that had shown up while I was there. They were allowed to jump for free.

"It becomes a real fun party atmosphere," I told her.

She gave me a blank hard stare. As I've mentioned, she can be hard to read when she employs her expressionless poker face, but my best guess is that she was probably wondering how she ever got so lucky as to marry such an innovative entrepreneur.

Sadly, my attorney felt this idea was slightly high on the liability scale.

"How high," I asked, "on a scale of one to ten?"

"Infinity."

Thus, another money-making venture befell a premature death.

My real estate agent suggested that I should put a steakhouse on the property. I didn't hate the idea, but I had owned and operated a bar and restaurant a few years earlier in Seattle. Although it was a business I had truly enjoyed, I felt that opening up another one would be like repeating a step. I told him a restaurant was not in the cards. Later, while I was at a hardware store in town, I heard a customer that I didn't know talking to a checkout girl I didn't know and telling her that someone was putting a steakhouse up on the property above the cliffs. I didn't bother to comment.

Two weeks after that, I heard that a large restaurant chain had bought the property and was definitely putting a brand new restaurant there. In the ensuing months, I would learn that this restaurant was going to have the largest inventory of wine west of the Mississippi, that there was also going to be a spa, and that country singer Garth Brooks was somehow involved. I assumed I would be getting a call from this large chain, or possibly Garth Brooks at any moment, but the call never came. Perhaps the deal fell through before they could ever contact me.

We broke ground on two cabins in the fall. I was extremely excited as they rose up out of the ground. I would spend hours wandering on the property below, laying out the trail down to the water. When no one was around, I would employ my horrific opera voice to sing Verdi's "Nessun Dorma" at the top of my lungs because the acoustics of the giant rock were so good. People across the lake probably thought there was a wounded animal dying on the south shore. I was now back scratching around in the dirt next to Chelan, and it was fun to be spending so much time by the lake again.

"Bungee cord jumping," I said.

Amy looked up from her book.

"We buy an old crane, and we put it out over the cliff, and then people bungee jump off the crane. I bet we could charge a hundred bucks each."

After a brief pause she said, "Let me guess, if ladies go topless they get to bungee jump for free."

"I hadn't thought about that," I said (even though I had), "but that's a great idea."

She turned her head back down to her book and continued reading. In hindsight, I was beginning to wonder if my story about the boatload of topless girls in Jamaica was information that I might better have kept to myself.

It turns out cranes are pretty expensive. As a result, another dream of early retirement died a quiet and lonely death. I had more ideas to put forth.

I thought about the winery we had visited in Santorini. The scraggily little grape vines of the Santorini vineyard were grown in flat circles across the parched volcanic rock of the islands. This dry, low-soil, inhospitable region produced some hearty grapes that created exceptional wines.

"We could open a winery," I said to Amy.

"Now that's a good idea," she said. "The only pitfalls I can see are that you don't know how to make wine. You don't know how to grow grapes. You have a hard time brewing coffee."

She was referring to an incident on a kayak trip in the Broken Island Group off the west coast of Vancouver Island where I accidentally dumped a pan of coffee into a campfire, losing the coffee and extinguishing our only source of warmth in the same instant. This was not the first time she had recalled that event.

Still, her points were valid. My garden at the Farmhouse had fared pretty poorly. Owning a winery would probably require an ability to actually grow something, an ability to produce something, an ability to distribute something for wholesale, and the ability to sell something in a retail environment as well. All of those things seemed suspiciously like a lot of work. The part of me that likes to go skiing and paragliding and mountain climbing and fishing was sounding the alarm bells. Trying to open a winery could really intrude on those much more important endeavors.

"But if you're up for it," Amy said, "I'm behind you one hundred percent. I think it would be exciting."

I scanned her face for any sign of sarcasm. I imagine she was laughing hysterically on the inside, with visions of me wandering through a dying vineyard while my customers gagged on glasses of chunky maroon vinegar in the tasting room. Still she stayed in character.

"I think it would be exciting too," I said, "but I do worry about the liability."

By liability, I was referring to the fact that I was liable to waste all of my free time working. A winery didn't seem like the right choice for a person with my unique set of nonexistent skills. So far, the cliff properties were just going to have some quaint cabins.

I was happy with that. It seemed better to leave the wild grassland and exposed granite untouched. I didn't consider myself a developer, but I realized that, with this project, I was actually starting to impact the lake. I remembered the old adage that you have to be careful not to destroy the things you love. I had also heard on numerous occasions that we are loving our natural resources to death. I decided a few little cabins would probably be enough. If Garth Brooks called, I was going to tell him to take his restaurant chain and his giant wine collection and look elsewhere.

Flathead Lake

I first noticed the dead deer around noon. It was laying on the shore half in and half out of the clear green waters of Flathead Lake in Montana. I wasn't sure how the deer got there. Perhaps it drowned. Perhaps it was hit by a car and then made it to the lake before expiring. I only knew that it hadn't been there the day before, and now, there it was, 20 feet away from the dock where we were swimming and playing. I realized that within a day this poor deer was going to become a problem for us.

It was early August in the second year of my lake project, and Amy, Cooper, and I, along with Amy's mother and sister, were staying at our friend's summer house, a sprawling waterfront estate that faced right across Polson Bay toward the majestic Mission Mountains. We've had the good fortune to come visit the lake almost every summer for 15 years. Although Lake Chelan is my personal favorite lake, Flathead Lake has always run a close second. Since I first conceived of a competition for the title of Greatest Lake in the World, I knew Flathead Lake was going to be a formidable challenger.

The deer was going to have to be disposed of, and it appeared the task would fall to me. I hatched a plan to tow the carcass downlake to a long stretch of uninhabited wetlands near the eastern edge of the bay. Of course, everyone knows you don't dispose of a body in broad daylight, and so I waited until the sun dropped below the horizon and a brilliant pink and purple sky presided over my macabre activities.

Using a thin rope, barely thicker than twine, I made a noose and then slipped it over the three visible legs of the deer. I attached the other end of the rope to a wave runner. With an audience of friends and family observing from the deck of the house, I pulled the dead deer off the beach and, at a trolling speed, began rafting him down the lake to his final resting spot. I was afraid the thin rope would break, so I moved very slowly. The deer coasted, mostly submerged, through the jade colored water.

After ten long minutes, the western sky now turning scarlet red, I decided I could probably risk breaking the rope. I figured the deer would just drift into the wetland anyway, so I gave the wave runner a little gas. The deer disappeared beneath a wall of water and the wave runner labored against the increased drag, but the rope held. I gave it a little more gas, and the wave runner labored harder, the bow now pointing up 30 degrees. We were grinding our way through the water, and we were moving significantly faster, so I kept the throttle pinned down. It occurred to me that I should probably worry about the deer's legs tearing off, then rocketing through the air and smacking me in the head. That would be a tough injury to explain on an insurance form. I looked back nervously at the bulging wave of water. That was when I witnessed one of the strangest things I've ever seen.

In a fraction of a second, before I could grasp what was happening, the deer came exploding up out of the water exactly like a water skier who had just yelled, "Hit it!"

The wave runner surged forward, and the deer began skimming on top of the water, sitting on his haunches the way a dog might sit, and skipping across the surface of the lake on his butt. It was (in this order) a horrific, morbid, and fascinating sight to witness. Reluctant to lose momentum, I kept the throttle pegged and looked forward to see how far I had to go before I reached the edge of the wetlands.

That's when I saw the canoe. A couple of campers had apparently decided to go for a sunset paddle. In the fading light, I could just make them out directly ahead of me. Rather than slow down, I opted to curve to the right of them to preserve our momentum. The wave runner made a broad arc, but the deer headed straight for the canoe. To make matters worse, the deer's head was tilted and resting on his right shoulder. When the deer hit the bottom trough of the wake, his head lurched up rapidly and flopped over onto his left shoulder in a motion that I could only describe as being extremely animated. His nose was now pointed right at the canoeists, and his wide glassy eyes appeared to be staring them down as he accelerated past them, a mere ten feet from their canoe. As I turned back toward the wetlands, he made a forceful curve backward, and then jumped the wake again before skidding to the opposite side of the wave runner.

If the whole event seemed strange to me, I can only imagine how it must have appeared to the couple in the canoe. As we moved on by, I caught a glimpse of them, both with eyes bulging out like golf balls, paddles suspended in the air. They looked like floating statues. When I finally got to the wetlands I looked back, and by all appearances their paddles were still frozen in place. I wonder, to this day, if either of them actually spoke about it. I can easily imagine a scenario in which they both just pretended they hadn't seen anything.

I assume, from their reaction, that they were tourists from out of town. If they had been from Montana, they probably wouldn't have been fazed at all. I was in Big Sky Country, after all, and almost nothing seems unusual in Montana. For a local, such a spectacle might have warranted only a brief mention at the coffee shop the next day in Missoula.

"I saw a deer water-skiing up at Flathead last night."

"Is that so? Was he any good?"

"Not bad."

"Hmm, so how's your aunt doing?"

The Mission Valley and the Flathead Valley seem to define the term Big Sky. If one were to go looking for the biggest sky in North America, it seems the natural place to start would be on the flat plains of Iowa, for example, where the horizon looms 40 miles away in all directions unimpeded. The problem with flatlands is that they don't give the observer any perspective. It is the broad valleys curving up to lofty peaks that allow a person to grasp the scope of distance that is spanned by the sky. Montana is blessed with just these types of valleys.

Flathead Lake is spectacular. It is just slightly less than 28 miles long from north to south and over 15 miles across at its widest point. It is a little bit less than 400 feet deep. It has all the attributes one would want in a lake. There are islands and inlets and bays that demand exploration. It has clear water that gets warm in the summer. It has beautiful timbered hillsides along its shores, along with sloping acres of cherry orchards and beautiful rolling foothills of wild grasslands that get dry and golden in color before the spring is even over.

It has grizzly bears and snowcapped peaks. Some of these peaks, visible off in the distance to the north, are the summits of Glacier

National Park. To the east, the lower section of the Mission Mountain Range drops right down to the shore. South of the lake, down the Mission Valley, the same range towers high into the air with breathtaking stone edifices.

That year, we got a wonderful tour of the north end of the lake by riding the coattails of my mother-in-law. Oftentimes men don't get along with their mother-in-law, but mine is a wonderful lady who was once described by a coworker as being "a treasure." I guess it's no surprise that, even though she lived 600 miles away from Flathead, she had two close friends, unrelated to each other, who owned homes at either end of the lake. She has friends everywhere.

While we were staying at one of her friends' house in Polson Bay, we got to visit her other friend at the north end of the lake. He was a doctor who had retired there a few years earlier. He was kind enough to take us out on a boat tour of the islands and bays in this area.

While we were out on the water, I mentioned to him that I was writing a book about how Lake Chelan was the greatest lake in the world. He nearly choked on his soda. He looked around at Flathead Lake, and then he looked at me. He made a skeptical expression, as if I just told him that chocolate-covered moose turds made for a delicious snack.

Looking around the lake, I could understand his skepticism. He was a wonderful host, but I think in that brief moment, he may have been considering having me swim back to the dock.

I couldn't live with myself if I were to find fault with Flathead Lake in the interest of proving some other lake was better. Flathead is a jewel in the crown of the Rocky Mountains. It is nearly impossible to criticize.

The same could be said of another famous lake of the West, Lake Tahoe. The hauntingly beautiful deep blue water set inside the dazzling peaks of the Sierra Nevada range is as gorgeous a sight as any on the planet. It also has a breadth and a diversity of visages that make it a compelling contender.

Both these lakes illustrated to me the point that, in a quest to compare Lake Chelan to the greatest lakes in the world, one didn't necessarily need to go to the far corners of the earth. I felt I had now whittled my list down to the top dozen contenders for the title of greatest lake in the world. Two of them, it seemed, were right in the neighborhood. It would take a mighty lake indeed to be able to claim dominance in this talented field. I still felt Chelan had as good a chance as any.

Back in the south end of Flathead Lake, I pulled out my dog-eared old notebook and skimmed my list of lakes. I felt I was now ready to assemble my top-ten list. It took over an hour, and it was tough to do, but in the end I felt I had the correct lakes.

Spoiler alert—the Greatest Lake in the World is one of the lakes from the list below. These were lakes that I had narrowed it down to, in no particular order:

Lake Chelan, Flathead Lake, Lake Como, Lago de Atitlán, Lake Tahoe, Lake Königssee, Lake Zell am See, Lake Baikal, Lake O'Higgins/San Martin, and Lake Wakatipu. As it turned out, I would stumble on to one more contender in the days to come, but at the time, it was a lake I was not yet aware of. It was fascinating to see how many fantastic and famous lakes were not in the final list, but I checked and rechecked my criteria, and I felt comfortable with the finalists.

Lake Mile 25 to Lake Mile 55

The section of lake beyond Emerson Acres on the north shore and Twenty-Five Mile Creek on the south shore is the most pristine area in the Chelan Valley. Only a small number of cabins dot the shoreline, all of them accessible only by boat or seaplane. Most of these are wilderness cabin retreats.

A trail once made its way up the south shore from Twenty-Five Mile Creek to Box Canyon. It was put in place by the Civilian Conservation Corps in the 1930s. The trail was presumably going to go all the way up to Lucerne, or possibly Stehekin, but the deep gash of Box Canyon proved to be insurmountable.

The remnants of the trail are still visible in spots. On occasions when I catch a glimpse of it, I always wonder about the small army of young men who joined the corps and ended up stationed at Lake Chelan. Many of them came from the eastern part of the country and by chance drew Lake Chelan as their assignment. While other members of the CCC were hanging over ledges in the hot canyons of the desert southwest, toiling to build dams, these lucky few were assigned to live right near the lake, next to the beautiful Twenty-Five Mile Creek.

Their days were spent clearing brush and building trails, all the while gazing out at the inviting blue water below them. They must have spent long evenings, during their free time, jumping off docks and cliffs into the lake and exploring the mountains and streams of the area.

Initially eyed with suspicion by the townsfolk of Chelan, they were called in one summer day to help form a search crew and locate a young girl who had gone missing. Their discovery of the girl endeared them to the people of Chelan and they began attending social affairs in town. This gave them the opportunity to meet and mingle with the local young women. At that point, for those young men, many of whom had grown up in the depression-plagued regions of the East

Coast and Midwest, Lake Chelan must have seemed like an especially wonderful kind of paradise.

Seeing the remnants of the trail, I often ponder the twists of fate that brought many of them to the lake. I imagine they, perhaps more than many, found a particular love and passion for the area.

The lake continues past Box Canyon, its shores untouched and unscarred. The Chelan Sawtooth Mountain Range towers ever higher to the north. The depth of the lake increases further, as the water snakes its way over the deepest part of the Lucerne Basin. To the south, visible mountain summits in the Glacier Peak Wilderness loom well over 8,000 feet in elevation.

The most prominent waterfall that spills directly into the lake is Domke Falls. Henry Domke first sighted the falls on his rather ill-fated first trip with William Sanders. After deciding to settle in Lake Chelan, he took to the notion of starting a sawmill and using the water in the falls to power it. He later built the sawmill at the falls, but the business was ultimately doomed to fail. It's not clear if the mill ever actually worked.

The beautiful falls retain his name, as do the creek, the lake from which it flows, and the mountain that sits above it. A climb to the top of Domke Mountain reveals the head of the lake in all of her splendor. The summit is just a little over 4,000 feet, but the sweeping views take in perhaps the most scenic section of the whole lake.

From the summit, the North Cascades National Park complex is laid out in a stunning array. Peaks visible in this area now tower well above 9,000 feet. The lake nestles into the mountains and takes in the never-ending flow of cold glacier fed waters from the Stehekin River. The high, often snowcapped peak of McGregor Mountain forms a mighty wall of distant purple rock, the perfect backdrop for the head of the lake. The small town of Stehekin is perched on the shore near these headwaters. It is civilization's last toehold before the high Cascades, the gateway to the rugged backcountry.

The Lake Monster

No lake could possibly be a contender for the greatest lake in the world if it didn't have a lake monster. It is a fun, mysterious, and slightly creepy necessity. Fortunately, Lake Chelan is home to at least one, and possibly more.

Accounts of the lake monster exist all the way back in Native American mythology. In one of their early creation stories, they speak of Lake Chelan being dug by the Great Spirit to imprison the monster who had been ravaging the land and tormenting the people. The Native Americans were said to have great respect for the monster and at times they would avoid being out on the lake for fear of it.

Accounts of the lake monster began to surface almost immediately after settlers arrived. Over the following decades the monster's notoriety grew. It was usually described as a serpent-like creature that moved in a fashion similar to an eel. There were a few accounts that described it more like a dinosaur with a long neck and fins, like a plesiosaur.

Tales of a monster in Scotland's Loch Ness date back to the seventh century, but a resurgence of fame began when prominent sightings were reported in 1933. Loch Ness became a worldwide sensation shortly after that, and with it, more sightings began to be reported in lakes around the world, including Lake Chelan and Okanogan Lake to the north. This may have been a phenomenon related to popular culture, or perhaps people were simply able to classify whatever it was they were seeing.

In places like Loch Ness, and Lake Champlain, and Okanogan Lake, the lake monsters are local celebrities, with names like Nessie, Champ, and Ogopogo. The monster in Chelan is a bit more of a shadowy secret. It is something that is whispered about from time to time. Stories are told, but not always publicized.

While trying to learn more about the monster, I kept hoping to get in contact with someone who had a firsthand account. I would get secondhand accounts from people, and they would refer me to the person who witnessed it, but I always hit a dead end. A typical telephone conversation would go something like this:

> "I'm writing a book about Lake Chelan, and I was wondering if I could ask you about your lake monster encounter."
>
> "*Click.*"

It wasn't until the very late stages of my Lake Project that I was able to finally talk to someone who had witnessed a creature at Lake Chelan. I don't want her to experience any repercussions for being so bold as to tell me her story, so, for her protection, let's just call her Roberta Giffin. I don't want to give any clues to her actual identity so we'll say, hypothetically, she may have moved to Lake Chelan from Leavenworth in 1958 and she may have spent a few years up in Stehekin where she managed the lodge, and Roberta Giffin may be her real name. Beyond that, I really wouldn't feel comfortable giving any more information.

Her story begins on a calm, clear day in the Mill Bay area not so many years ago. Along with witnesses who will corroborate her story, she saw a creature, which they first mistook to be a seal, break the surface of the water. It was definitely a living animal and it was definitely moving.

They tried to figure out exactly what a seal would be doing in a freshwater lake, and Roberta was reminded of a story she was told as a child that suggested there was an underground cave stretching from the bottom of Lake Chelan under the mountains to an outlet at Deception Pass in saltwater Puget Sound.

After a few moments, however, they realized that what they were seeing was more than just a seal. The "seal" was the front portion of what everyone agreed was a "snake-like" creature that was at least 20 feet long and perhaps longer. She and other witnesses watched this creature appear and swim intermittently for a period of about 20 minutes. Then it dipped below the water and was gone.

This account was intriguing in that it was not a brief glimpse, but a prolonged encounter in which a group of people had time to assess what they were seeing. What she reported sounds suspiciously like a lake monster.

This is one of literally several dozen accounts that have occurred over the years. When a creature is spotted, it is not uncommon for it to spend a prolonged period of time in view. It frequently swims about, disappears, and then reappears. Often, people have no misgivings about what they saw, even if they're not jumping up and down to have their story documented in a book.

Is there a lake monster? If so, how could it have made it into the lake? There is a plausible explanation. Recall that, at one time, the lake level was much higher, and water drained out of the Navarre Coulee and then eventually Knapps Coulee. This happened for a prolonged period of time, probably thousands of years, long enough to carve deep river canyons through the mountains, now high and dry above the lake. This would indicate that an ice dam was backing water up, and it is certainly conceivable that, if the Columbia drainage was blocked as well, then Lake Chelan might have been a finger of a vast lake that stretched up the Columbia Valley, into the big bend area of the Columbia River. At that time, Okanogan Lake, other lakes of British Columbia, and all of the backwaters flooding the land could have been one single connected waterway.

Likewise, the Missoula floods would have swept everything in the waters of ancient Lake Missoula toward the west. This would include ice, fish, logs, and lake monsters alike. When a lake begins to dry up, the aquatic animals that survive always end up in the deep remaining pockets of water. Lake Chelan and Okanogan Lake would be those remaining deep pools.

We don't really know all of the extraordinary geologic and hydrologic events that have occurred on the land over the millennia. We know there are fish in the lake that probably didn't swim up through the Chelan Gorge, at least not while it was flowing the way it does now. If fish found their way in, why not a lake monster?

As to why we don't see the monster more—if there is a monster, or presumably, many of them—there is an explanation. The monsters might prefer the deep Lucerne Basin. The Lucerne Basin is largely unpopulated. Even on the busiest weekends of summer, there are long stretches where you won't see a single boat. For nine months out of the year, the upper basin is a very lonely place.

If a lake monster lived in this area, and very rarely came to the surface, and if it only very rarely ventured down to the more popular Wapato Basin, what you would expect is sporadic sightings, on very infrequent occasions, and usually by boat captains who consistently traveled the upper basin. This pretty much sums up the accounts of the lake monster.

The monster has never really had a name, like Nessie or Ogopogo. The Native Americans (First Nations people) of modern-day British Columbia referred to Ogopogo as Naitaka, which means "lake demon," and it's possible that the same name was used for the Chelan monster. There is also an account of local Native Americans around Chelan calling the monster Geiza, or possibly Geizla but I couldn't confirm that or find a good interpretation.

Attempts had been made in the past to name the monster, and many people had pet names, but like the crazy uncle who still lives with your grandparents and thinks aliens run the government, a lot of people preferred to just not talk about it. The modern-day monster just never developed a consistent moniker. To remedy this situation, a contest was sponsored by the Chelan Chamber of Commerce, some local vendors, and a brilliant and insightful local author.

A big concern, voiced by many, was that naming and publicizing the monster would scare the children and keep them from enjoying the lake. I have made it clear how I feel about scaring children, but since modern science is skeptical about the existence of lake monsters, I suppose it's a valid point. They have enough real-world proven things to be worried about. Anyone who doubts that should watch C-SPAN for an hour. Those people are in charge of our nation.

I was less worried about frightening children. Growing up, I always thought the legend of the lake monster was thrilling and fun rather than scary.

During the contest, the community responded with hundreds of submissions. Then the community voted and, in the end, the name they picked was: Tsilly, pronounced like the word "chilly." This name was overwhelmingly the winner, and it seemed like a great name because:

1) The spelling was a nod to the Native American heritage around the lake.

2) The pronunciation had a nice assonance when paired with the word Chelan.

3) The water temperature in the depths of the lake where the monster resides is very chilly.
4) The name Tsilly is just kind of cool, like a good nickname for a high school kid.
5) It was a name that was not scary for kids. Nobody is going to get eaten by a monster named Tsilly. It's certainly better than "Water Demon from Hell," which was one of the submissions.

Who knows if the name will catch on. "Lake Monster" is also a pretty good name for a lake monster. Besides, people around Chelan may always just continue to murmur about the monster generically and in hushed tones. It may always remain a guarded local "Tsecret."

As for the children, I would like to say that there has never been a recorded case of a lake monster attack in Lake Chelan. Unfortunately, that would be incorrect. One of the earliest non-Native American accounts of the lake monster took place in 1892, when a group of campers reported being attacked right on the shore of the lake at a place they referred to as Devil's Slide.

According to their story, which was documented in *The Daily Picayune*, a lake monster clamped its alligator-like jaws on the victim while he was rinsing off his feet on the lakeshore. Despite the best efforts of his traveling companions, they could not free the man from the jaws of the beast, and the monster eventually sprang into the air and then disappeared into the water, taking its hapless victim down into the depths.

For the sake of the children, I will make a critical assessment of this account. First of all, the story was written in a newspaper in New Orleans. In 1892, the Cascade Mountains were still a frontier wilderness at the farthest reaches of the realm. They were very much unexplored and certainly not conquered. In a country that was hungry for tall tales, this is precisely the kind of terrain that would have lent itself to such a story.

A cryptozoologist is someone who studies creatures whose existence has been suggested, but not recognized by scientific consensus. These creatures are known as cryptids.

I solicited information from two cryptozoologists. One, whose name I won't mention, was not particularly helpful because he wasn't well versed on lake monsters and also because he was crazier than a fat rat in a biffy.

The other's name I will mention, because he was quite the opposite. A British zoologist, Dr. Karl Shukar is a noted author who has been called one of the leading cryptozoologists in the English-speaking world.

He pointed out that the monster described in the story is somewhat famous due to its bizarre nature. It was described as "a winged crocodile." It is unique to any other sightings on the lake either before or since. He felt the report may have been a "nonsense story invented to cover up an accidental death or murder." (Cue sinister music.)

In the two decades that followed that story, however, other accounts from credible people began to surface. These tended to be focused up near the head of the lake by Stehekin Landing. They were of the more traditional serpent variety. I could find no accounts of this version of the monster attacking anyone.

For those who are concerned about the lake monster scaring children and preventing them from enjoying swimming in the lake, I suggest you use the method that I have employed over the years to ease the concerns of my young nieces and nephews. Tell them that there is no "credible" source of any lake monster attacking a person. In fact, they should know that a lake monster is the least of their worries. They should be much more concerned about the "rogue grizzly bear who, just last week, was seen drinking from the lake in broad daylight a little ways up shore. I'm sure he's gone by now. Okay kids, enjoy your swim."

The Stunning Mountains at the Head of the Lake

I knew there were some spectacular mountain climbs in the peaks around Lake Chelan, but I didn't get a chance to explore any of them until a few years after college. My first ascent in the area was to the summit of 8,136-foot-tall McGregor Mountain. This was the location above Stehekin where Kenneth Rexroth helped build the fire lookout in the 1920s. The tower is no longer there, but thanks to a triumph of conservation the view remains almost identical to what it would have been in 1924.

In terms of mountain climbing, this could better be described as a walk-up. I could talk about the treacherous narrow catwalk ledge near the summit. I could extol its scary "death drop" exposure. I believe I actually did on many occasions in the past. Then, while reading the book *The Stehekin We Remember*, I came across pictures of the authors, the Buckner sisters, up on the ledge, leaning back casually and smiling for a picture. I was inclined to tone back my rhetoric about the intrepid nature of the climb after that.

This is not to say that death didn't lurk around every corner during the hike. Quite to the contrary, it did. I encountered my first wild grizzly bear on that climb. With my climbing buddies—two brothers, Matt and Tyson—we were hiking our way happily up the switchbacks that carved into never-ending berry bushes when we came across the bear. We had purposely been making a lot of noise, but this bear didn't seem to care.

He appeared to be a strange anomaly, a bizarre genetic throwback to the Arctodus simus, a huge prehistoric bear that weighed 2,500 pounds and stood 12 feet tall. My understanding was that the Arctodus simus went extinct 12,500 years ago, but from our very close vantage point, it appeared this information was incorrect.

What bothered me the most about this bear was that he didn't give way. I've encountered my fair share of black bears in the woods, including some pretty good-sized ones. My experience was that they always made a concerted effort to quickly move along. This fellow in front of us was of a different temperament. With his color, his size, and his manner, a single word flashed through my head: "grizzly."

Running was not an option. Most bear experts will tell you not to run, because it can trigger a prey response in the bear. I'd like to say that this occurred to me and prevented me from running, but the truth is, I was more or less paralyzed with fear. I was trying to detect whether or not he had the distinctive scooped forehead or the signature large hump between the shoulder blades, but he was standing half behind a tree staring straight at me. There was no way to really tell.

Without turning to look away I whispered, "Is that a grizzly?"

Neither of the two brothers responded.

"I think that's a grizzly," I hissed.

There was still no response. I turned slowly, just in time to see the two of them disappearing at a full sprint around a corner back down the trail. The punch line of an old joke flashed through my head. "You don't have to be faster than the bear. You just have to be faster than your friend."

Apparently someone had made the "every man for himself" declaration without actually verbalizing it out loud. I began backing slowly away, and to my relief, the bear seemed content to sit still and watch as I moved down the trail. I found Matt and Tyson a quarter mile back, still out of breath.

There was no discussion about heading back up the trail. None of us even considered it. Instead, we made a long backcountry arc through the dense berry bushes and thickets, up and away from the bear, finally reconnecting with a higher switchback. We continued on at a rapid pace before getting out of the berry patch and up above the timberline.

About a hundred yards above the bushes, there was a perfect camp spot, with a broad flat rock, a gentle trickle of water for cooking, and a huge boulder to shelter us from the wind. It had been a long day and a hard hike with heavy packs. I was exhausted and could barely walk. I glanced down at the nearby berry patch. I could almost feel the bloodshot eyes of the starving grizzly gazing up at me from the thicket.

"I'm feeling pretty fresh," I said. "I wouldn't mind pushing further upward."

"Me too," said Matt and Tyson in near unison, both of them with eyes glued to the berry patch.

We wandered 500 feet higher. If the spot we had passed by earlier was a perfect camp spot, then this camp redefined the word "perfect." It had natural stone benches that appeared placed there by the almighty himself to rest and rejuvenate weary climbers.

"Boy I'd love to knock off a little more elevation tonight to make our summit trip easier tomorrow," Matt said.

There was no argument. Upward we pushed, through lovely glens and perfect duff-covered meadows, as soft and inviting as a four star hotel. If we had passed by an outdoor Hooters restaurant, full of lonely waitresses offering free beer and hot wings, I still think we would have pushed onward to put some distance between ourselves and the berry patch of death. Finally, with the light fading, and running out of mountain, we set up camp on an uneven, thin, boulder-strewn ledge and scooted back into an overhanging slime-filled muck hole to avoid rolling over the edge and killing ourselves in the night.

The following day, we made the short push up and to the summit of McGregor Mountain. It was my first top of the world look at the Stehekin Valley. What I saw was an alpine wonderland. Dominating the view were the 9,000-foot peaks of Mount Buckner, Mount Logan, and Goode Mountain. There was also another fantastic surprise.

One fortunate attribute of Lake Chelan comes compliments of Buckner Mountain and its neighbor Booker Mountain. Although Lake Chelan carves right into the dramatic mountains of the North Cascades, by late summer a large percentage of the winter snowfields have melted off the surrounding peaks. Only sporadic pockets of snow remain visible. This is more surprising than it might seem. It's surprising because although you can't see them from the west end of the lake, there are a lot of glaciers that are very close.

Standing at the top of McGregor Mountain, we were staring right down at the town of Stehekin and the head of the lake. We were also standing right at the top of the Sandalee Glacier. McGregor Mountain is heavily glaciated. It's simply glaciated on the wrong side of the mountain to be viewed from the lake. The orientation of the lake makes it such that, although there are many glaciers right there, they all face away from the lake.

The only real exception to this is the beautiful glaciers on Booker and Buckner Mountains. These glaciers can be seen from the lake, right at Stehekin Landing.

I have always been extremely grateful that nature provided these two mountains and their year-round snow. They sit in the distance, framed perfectly by the Stehekin Valley. They are a beautiful backdrop when viewed from the lake, but they also represent much more. They are the evidence of the incredible glacier-strewn peaks that surround the lake. They are the token glaciers, representative of the 519 ice caps that are nestled in the North Cascades.

Just adjacent, but obscured from view by other mountains, is Boston Peak, which sits at the top of the Boston Glacier, the largest glacier in all of the North Cascades. It is not visible from the lake. For someone like me, who has on occasion wished that a few more of the glaciers could be viewed from the lake, it is important to be careful what you wish for.

There is a massive complex of glaciers right on the north side of the ridge of peaks that separates the Skagit drainage from the Chelan drainage. The Klawati, Inspiration, Boston, Fremont, Douglas, McAllister, El Dorado, Neve, and Colonial Glaciers all grind their incredible mass across the nearby peaks. The melt water of these ice giants flows away from Lake Chelan and into Diablo Lake to the north. The result is all of the thick milky-green water that flows down the Skagit Valley.

Were Lake Chelan situated in another fashion amongst the mountains, it might appear very different than it does. The crystal blue clear water might be greatly changed in terms of color, clarity, and temperature. As pretty as the turquoise water of glacier melt can be, I much prefer the beautiful clear blue of Lake Chelan. I like the picture-perfect peek-a-boo look up at the glaciers on Buckner Mountain and Booker Mountain because they symbolize everything that is, and is not, a component of creating the splendor of Lake Chelan.

As for the grizzly bear, I filed the encounter under inconclusive. A bear biologist told me that 95 percent of grizzly bear sightings are really black bears in the cinnamon or brown color phase that are misidentified. I would note that after our encounter there was a confirmed grizzly bear sighting just ten miles away.

When we returned to Stehekin and mentioned our encounter to the ranger, he seemed skeptical that we had really seen a grizzly bear. He also seemed very uninterested. This surprised me, because the North Cascades National Park website is adamant that all grizzly bear sightings be reported to a ranger.

I would find out during later research, however, that the North Cascades National Park website is not always to be trusted. As an example, if you surf through the pages of the site, you are rewarded with interesting little factoids about the park that pop up on your screen with a pretty picture and say, "Did you know....?" One of these factoids says, "Did you know that the North Cascades is named after the many waterfalls that cascade through the park? A wonderful example is Ladder Falls near Nespelem."

What a wonderful bit of information, I thought. How much more wonderful it would be if it were true. The North Cascades are actually named after the Cascades on the Columbia River that Lewis and Clark documented on their journey across the continent to the Pacific Ocean. They encountered the rapids near The Dalles in Oregon.

The rapids are now buried under Bonneville Reservoir, which was created with the completion of Bonneville Dam in 1937. Prior to the dam, the river made a tumultuous descent over the carved basalt, creating a dangerous un-navigable stretch of water. This area became known as the Cascade Rapids, or, in some later accounts, the Cascades of the Columbia. The snowy peaks surrounding this portion of the river became known as "The Mountains near the Cascades."

Later, this would evolve into the term "Cascade Mountains," the first reference of this being in the journals of David Douglas, a Scottish biologist who journeyed through the Pacific Northwest in the early nineteenth century. Incidentally, the Douglas fir gets its name from David Douglas who discovered them in mass quantity here, catalogued them, and even returned many specimens of them back to England. A totally unrelated factoid is that David Douglas died in Hawaii at the age of 35 when he fell into a pit trap and was trampled by a wild bull. You will find none of this information on the North Cascades National Park website.

Because I am one of those people who:

1) believes that history needs to be properly preserved

2) feels that the actual origin of the name is quite interesting

3) has way too much time on my hands

I wrote to the North Cascades National Park Service and mentioned to them that they had made an error and might want to correct it.

I received a response that they would not be able to make a correction without the appropriate documentation. I can only imagine the exhausting research that went into their original statement of fact, which was, "Did you know the Cascade Mountains are named after all the pretty waterfalls?" I imagine they have the minutes of the meeting where the US Department of Place Names debated whether to call them the Tree Mountains, because of all the pretty trees, or the Rock Mountains, because of all the pretty rocks, or the Dirt Mountains, or the Insect Mountains before someone finally stood up and said, "But what about all the pretty waterfalls?"

However, with the patience of someone who has nothing better to do, I provided them with the appropriate documentation. Two years later, the change has yet to be made.

The other day while skimming the site I was rewarded with another factoid. "Did you know that many of the names within the park come from the early Spanish explorers to the region? A good example of this is Diablo Lake and Mount El Dorado."

Wrong!

The Spanish explorers did move extensively through the inland coastal waters of the Pacific Northwest well into the nineteenth century, even meeting up and comparing notes with Captain Vancouver on one occasion. They did name such things as the Strait of Juan De Fuca, and the San Juan Islands. Somehow they failed to wander 50 miles up the Skagit River to name a lake that didn't actually exist at the time. Diablo Lake is really a reservoir created by the construction of Diablo Dam, which wasn't completed until 1930. The name was actually given to the canyon below the dam by early miners and prospectors because of the extreme difficulty of passing through the canyon, and possibly in reference to another canyon of that name located in New Mexico which bore a resemblance. These miners didn't arrive until the late nineteenth century.[17]

Nor, by the way, did they head an additional 20 miles up the Cascade River to give the name El Dorado to a beautiful but not prominent peak in a sea of other large peaks. As it happens, the name came from the El Dorado Mining claim in the region, an obvious and common name for a mine that, it was hoped, would produce lots of gold.[18]

Another Spanish name appears near Mount El Dorado on the face of Boston Peak. There, in a giant cirque, is a large glacier called the Quien Sabe Glacier. Who knows where they came up with that name?

If this book were a website right now, you would get a pop-up that would read, "Did you know that the factoids in the National Park website were written by a fifteen-year-old high schooler who just made them all up?"

Despite playing a little loose with the facts, I have nothing but genuine respect for the parks department, and, in particular, their management of the North Cascades National Park complex. Over the years, numerous pushes have been made to develop the backcountry of the park more extensively and provide better access and more roads. The administrators of the national park have consistently opted to keep the backcountry wild and accessible only through good old-fashioned hiking. This speaks to the passion and dedication of the people who have, for decades, acted as stewards of the park. It is one of the major reasons the park has remained such an extraordinary place.

Lake Chelan carves right into the southern end of this beautiful national park complex. Like a red carpet rolled out, or if you like, a blue carpet, the lake provides the perfect access to this stunning wilderness area. H.L. Moremen and Lucille Kercheval published sheet music for a song in 1936 called "Lake Chelan, You've Won My Heart." On the cover, they called the lake "the water gateway to the Switzerland of America." It seems an apt description. Until someone has come up Lake Chelan and passed through Stehekin on their way into the North Cascades National Park, I don't feel they've really experienced the North Cascades. This is one scenario where getting there truly is half the fun.

Lakes of Bavaria and Zell am See

My project was now nearly two years old. With my newly refined list of top ten contenders, it was time to go out and visit some more lakes. From my discussions with people and my research, two lakes in Europe seemed to be rising up the list as formidable challengers.

One was called Königssee, a lake located in Bavaria about two hours from Munich. Königssee is one of Germany's most popular national parks. It is situated very near the storied town of Berchtesgaden.

The other lake was Zeller See, a lake named after the town of Zell am See which sits on its shore. This is located in the Alps in Austria, but not in the Salzkammergut region. It is located further south, closer to Tyrolea. Consequently, we had missed it on our first trip.

If you're familiar with the book *Band of Brothers*, or perhaps the twelve-part miniseries made from the book, you might recall Zell am See. If you're not familiar, I'll mention that the book, written by Stephen Ambrose, details the World War II travails of Easy Company, United States soldiers attached to the 2nd Battalion, 506th Parachute Infantry Regiment of the 101st Airborne Division. They parachuted behind enemy lines on D-day, and then traveled across Europe, through Germany, and eventually into Austria at the end of the war.

They are credited with taking control of the Obersalzberg in the German Alps. The Obersalzberg was the fallback command center of the Nazi party in the event that Berlin was overrun. Easy Company is also credited with taking the Eagle's Nest, Hitler's own mountain vacation retreat, which was perched high on the Kehlstein Mountain above the Obersalzberg.

During the time the Easy Company was conquering the Eagle's Nest, Hitler committed suicide in a bunker in Berlin and the war in Europe came to an official end. Easy Company continued on to Zell am See, and the beautiful Zeller See Lake in Austria. They were stationed there for months as they waited to see if they would be reassigned to the Pacific Theater, where the war continued.

Many of the members of Easy Company described the lake as the most beautiful place in the world. In the movie, the images of this lake certainly seemed to have an incredible appeal, and in my questioning of people I frequently heard the name Zell am See. It seemed like this town and the lake were probably in need of some investigation.

"We have to go to Germany and then back to Austria," I told Amy.

"When?"

"Soon."

En route to Austria, we arrived in Munich, Germany just in time for Oktoberfest.

With Mark and Meggan, we headed to the beer tents of the Oktoberfest Fairgrounds. My mission was to ascertain, on a world stage, what was the most beautiful lake in the world. A three-week-long festival, Oktoberfest is a crossroads of the world, where people come from the four corners of the globe. I felt this was my best opportunity to get input from a truly diverse and international subset of people.

The task was a bit challenging. The biggest challenge related to the fact that Mark and I had to be on constant vigil to guard our wives against the unceasing advances of tall, dark, suave, Italian and Spanish men. They seemed to be drawn to our American wives much the way moths are drawn to a bright porch light. Our vigilance tended to be less about protecting the girls from the men, and more about keeping an eye on our wives to make sure they didn't do anything spontaneous and rash, like, perhaps, disappearing and running away to live out their lives in some exciting foreign city such as Rome or Madrid.

Further complicating my mission to investigate lakes of the world was the reality that it was often difficult to communicate with the many people from other countries. Most of them spoke English, and spoke it quite well. The problem was, after four giant steins of beer, I found I could no longer speak English very well. It turns out that the beer in Bavaria is a little stronger than our local watered-down versions. The Germans often mix in half a stein of lemonade with their beer to cut down on the potency. This was a neat trick that was never properly conveyed to me until much later.

Still, I was able to get a lot of feedback from people, and I discovered there were many diverse and varying opinions on the world stage. Some of the lake names that came up repeatedly were Königssee, Lake Michigan, Lake Como, Lake Bled in Slovenia, Lake Winnipesauke, Lake Tahoe, Lake O'Higgins/San Martin in the Andes, Loch Ness, Flathead Lake in Montana, and there was one delightful young British soccer fan who thought I should definitely visit Lake Gosodyourself.

When I mentioned Lake Zell am See, one of my reasons for coming, I heard a lot of "yes" and "ja" and "sí" and "oui." This, I felt, was very promising.

Not one person mentioned Lake Chelan. When questioned, not one person had ever heard of Lake Chelan. I found this to be a positive attribute for Lake Chelan, rather than a detriment.

After two days in Munich, we headed to Germany's Lake Königssee first. I mentioned earlier the Obersalzberg, which was the second seat of the Third Reich. This sits on the side of the Kehlstein, a prominent rock massif that forms the border between Germany and Austria. On a high prow of the Kehlstein sits the Eagle's Nest, a small castle-like structure that was built for Hitler by his Nazi cronies as a gift for his fiftieth birthday. The tea house, as it is referred to, has historical significance in that it was used by Hitler to entertain heads of state prior to the outbreak of World War II.

We made the trip up the Kehlstein on an impossibly narrow road, which is often described as the most beautiful drive in Europe. The views did not disappoint. The German Alps stretched out as a grand front. To the north we could see as far as Salzburg, and to the south, on the valley floor, tucked in a steep-walled glacier-cut basin, was the beautiful gem called Königssee, a shimmering crystal blue lake.

We sat at a restaurant in the courtyard of the Eagle's Nest, pilsners in hand, gazing at the water far below. Next to our table was a low rock wall, and beyond that, an empty void. The mountain plunged straight down 1,500 feet to the valley. It was spectacular.

We were laughing and smiling and taking pictures, and chatting with our fellow patrons from around the world. It seemed strange to be enjoying ourselves so much in Hitler's own vacation retreat. Our eyes were constantly drawn back to the astounding valley and lake below. We sat riveted to our chairs, even after lunch was done, gazing outward. I couldn't stop thinking about the significance of the place we were sitting.

"You look lost in thought," Amy said.

"I am."

"What are you thinking about?"

I turned my head back from the wide expanse of empty sky below us.

"I was thinking about the most evil form of government the world has ever known."

"A homeowners association?"

"No," I said. "The Third Reich."

I couldn't help but think that, for a while, during that horrible war, the Nazis had controlled almost the whole of the European continent and beyond. With so many places to choose from, this was the location they picked for their vacation oasis. They opted for this beautiful valley, which had been here at least since the last ice age. It was as breathtaking long before the Nazis arrived as it was now, decades after they were vanquished. It was easy to see why this was their choice.

When I visited the lake itself, I was impressed. Königssee has the prerequisite clear blue water. It is billed as Germany's cleanest lake. The mountains that leap up on either side are beautiful, especially the Watzmann, a gorgeous massif consisting of three peaks. It is the third highest mountain in Germany. A boat tour cruises you down the lake to view Saint Barthalomȧ, an 800-year-old Catholic pilgrimage church with beautiful Baroque style onion domes.

This was a beautiful lake. There was no question about that. Was the lake better than Lake Chelan? I had to give the lake extra points for the storybook church. The mountains were impressive to be sure. They were dusted with snow when I visited, but there were no visible glaciers. When viewed from high above at the Eagle's Nest, it was a stunning sight to behold, but I couldn't help thinking about my hike up McGregor Mountain above Stehekin.

From the summit of McGregor Mountain, the North Cascades extended in every direction. A blanket of evergreens swaddled the Stehekin Valley, and Lake Chelan was every bit the jewel that Königssee was as it nestled down amongst the peaks of the Chelan Sawtooth Wilderness Area. The view from McGregor Mountain was just as spectacular, perhaps more so. Glaciers perched in every cirque. The

Sandalee Glacier came right up the north face of McGregor Mountain. Even Glacier Peak, the impressive volcano cone, decorated the southern horizon. And this was just the west end of the lake. Forty-five more spectacular miles of Lake Chelan loomed out of sight to the east.

Königssee and the Obersalzberg Alps were amazing things to see. The whole area is worthy of its designation as a world heritage site. At just five miles long, however, the lake could not supplant the awesome impound of Lake Chelan. Lake Chelan had not yet, in my mind, been bested. We still had more lakes to see on this trip though. The next day, we headed on to southern Austria.

I had seen a lot of footage of Zell am See. There were many scenes of it in the *Band of Brothers* series that had captivated my imagination. One shot showed a stately old hotel with a large elevated courtyard that had a giant waterfall spilling down the mountainside right next to it. From this vantage point, the Austrian Alps looked incredible. I couldn't wait to get there and see them.

When we arrived at Zell am See, however, the valley was socked in. A thick fog hung 500 feet above the lake. The mountains were out of sight, and the lake appeared to be a pencil lead shade of gray. It was a chilly day.

Undiscouraged, we parked in town and wandered down to the Hotel Zentrum Zell am See. We found a table at the restaurant, situated right on the edge of the lake, just three feet from the lapping water. Up close, the lake displayed a beautiful blue-green shade. Zeller See had met the crystal blue water criteria.

The hotel was fancy. It was truly one of the grand old hotels of Europe, with a classic structure and gardens that would be fittingly cast as the setting for a movie. A lakefront promenade extended out from the shore, and tour boats ambled in and out at a lazy pace. The town, with its winding streets, rolled right up from the water and then ended at the base of a large mountain that extended up and into the low clouds. I was yearning to see just how high the mountains went.

We sat at our table and enjoyed the light bustle of lake living, Austrian style. Small sailboats darted around the lake, somehow finding a breeze that we couldn't feel on shore. After about an hour, two brilliant white swans paddled by. These swans, we had learned, are obligatory residents of every lake in Austria. As it happened, they were also a harbinger of good things to come. As if on cue, the sun cut through the clouds and the lake lit up, ripples sparkling in the late morning sun. Within ten minutes, the haze was burned away and Zeller See was on display.

The hills around the lake were a brilliant green combination of grass meadows and light timber. It looked as if we were there in the middle of spring, even though it was early October. Behind the town, the mountains that had been hidden were suddenly revealed, displaying massive ski slopes that dropped down from thousands of feet above.

As the clouds continued to dissipate, the crown jewel of the area came into view. To the east, the sharp pointed massif of the Grossglockner emerged. Ice and snow draped from its grand pyramid-shaped visage. It was an awesome spectacle.

In an instant we had gone from being slightly cold on a gloomy day to sitting next to water and drinking beer in the sun, our favorite pastime. Things were suddenly looking up. Our spirits were soaring.

Mark wandered off to check out the hotel. Secretly Mark wants to be a spy so he's always exploring by ghosting through doors that are off limits and sneaking into closed restaurants. Either that or he is a spy. I'm not really sure which.

Amy, now being warmed by the sun, was sitting with a big smile on her face. She began making plans in an excited tone accompanied by wildly animated gestures. She does this whenever we find ourselves in a place that captures her imagination. Within five minutes, she had an itinerary list that would take no less than ten days to complete. As is her custom, she smacked me on the shoulder with the back of her hand and said, "See, I told you we should have scheduled more time here."

She says this every time we stumble into a remarkable place.

Meggan was engaged in her own similar quirky behavior. She was alternating between statements of disbelief, superlatives, and future trip planning.

"Can you believe this place? We have to come back here. This is extraordinary. We should go to Spain. Look at this lake. Let's move to Rome. Can you believe this place? Let's buy a house here. Can you believe this?"

She can usually get eight to ten short sentences out without taking a breath.

"And we can rent a boat and tour the lake," said Amy.

"We should spend a week in Prague," said Meggan.

"And we can drive to the top of the Grossglockner," said Amy.

"Can you believe this?" said Meggan.

Mark returned to the table.

"There's a nightclub in the basement. It's really cool. I slipped the lock open. You guys have to come check it out."

"And we can take the ski lift up to the top of the mountain behind town," said Amy.

"I bet the fjords look like this," said Meggan. "We have to go to Norway."

"And there's a giant glass atrium at the top of the hotel that's some kind of fancy restaurant. The elevator's locked off, but I found a back stairway," said Mark.

Amy's arms were gesturing like a person swatting at mosquitoes.

"I knew we should have scheduled more time here."

She hit my shoulder again, for punctuation.

"Those mountains are amazing," said Meggan. "How far a drive is it to Slovenia?"

"Let's sneak into the swimming pool," said Mark.

"Can you believe this place?" said Meggan.

Amy hit me again on the shoulder. "I knew we should have spent more time here," she said.

Meanwhile I was quietly looking out at the lake. The water was beautiful. The peaks around the Grossglockner were now reflecting off the surface. The Grossglockner itself was towering in all its glory. It is the highest peak in Austria, and the second most prominent mountain in the Alps behind Mount Blanc. The flanks of the mountain are blanketed by the Pasterze, the largest glacier in Austria. It was hard to imagine a better backdrop. Zeller See and the Austrian Alps were putting on an epic show, to be sure.

My thoughts kept drifting back to Lake Chelan. Although Zeller See was spectacular, it seemed, in a way, sort of one-dimensional. It was a gorgeous lake set in a lush mountain enclave. It was rimmed on all sides by high peaks, but I realized, as I was looking out at the lake, that I was seeing the whole lake from shore to shore. Every part of it was much like the other, altered only by a change in vantage point.

I thought with fondness of the wandering curves of Lake Chelan, each bend revealing something new and different. A trip around Chelan could reveal a low hillside covered in brilliant wildflowers right down to the water. Around the next bend could be a dense forested mountain and high rock crags, maybe even a thundering waterfall. Around the next bend, beautiful dry desert scenery, or lush irrigated orchards, or any number of things to see. The long stretch of Lake Chelan encompassed so much diversity. The small oval shaped Zeller See, though beautiful in every way, clearly lacked what I might call a dynamic personality.

Gazing across the lake, I also realized that something was troubling me. Having seen the *Band of Brothers* miniseries no less than 20 times, I was immediately suspicious that something was amiss. Zell am See was a beautiful place. It was just as astounding as the actual soldiers from Easy Company proclaimed it to be. The problem was, it looked distinctly different than the lake I had seen depicted on screen. We didn't appear to be at the same lake where they had filmed.

My suspicions proved correct. I found out later that, after logging 22 hours of travel time and spending many thousands of dollars, I was in the wrong place. They actually filmed the Zell am See scenes in Brienz in the Bernese Oberland of Switzerland. That's where the Grand Hotel Griess with its waterfall, which featured so prominently in the miniseries, was located. That lake was almost 200 miles away. Through the trickery of Hollywood, I had been lead astray.

I should have known better. A few years back, they filmed the movie *Sleepless in Seattle* on a houseboat on Lake Union, directly across from my own house. In this movie, the character portrayed by Tom Hanks takes his son in a little motorized rowboat out onto the lake while Meg Ryan follows him in her car. Moments later, he arrives at Alki Beach in his boat and she watches as he plays with his son in the sand. Never mind that he would have spent two hours heading through the Hiram M. Chittenden Locks, which separate the freshwater lake from the salt waters of Puget Sound. Never mind that, after leaving the lake, he would have had to drive seven miles around Magnolia and across the wide expanse of Elliott Bay in a six-foot dinghy, with an outboard that probably lacked the gas to get there. I remembered that Tom Hanks, the star of *Sleepless in Seattle*, was also the producer of the *Band of Brothers* miniseries. My conclusion, of course: Tom Hanks is evil.

Even though Zell am See was not the lake featured in the film, it was still the lake at which the actual Easy Company had been stationed. It was everything they described it to be. It was certainly one of the prettiest lakes in the world, but was it the greatest lake in the world?

It didn't take me too long to conclude that Zeller See was not going to win the title. The biggest shortcoming was simply the size of the lake. Zeller See was only two and a half miles long and a mile and a half wide. We actually circumnavigated the whole lake in about 15 minutes. If the competition were only about scenery, then Zeller See could be a frontrunner. As the greatest lake in the world, however, it simply wasn't a contender.

We left the town of Zell am See reluctantly, the day having been better than anyone could have foretold. We all agreed we would return. If Amy's to-do list was any indication, we would likely need to stay for two weeks. Although we hadn't discovered the greatest lake in the world, or maybe because we hadn't discovered the greatest lake in the world, I deemed the trip to be a complete success.

I was left with some unfinished business, however. I would now need to determine whether Lake Brienz was the greatest lake in the world. Amy and I were returning to the United States the following day. It seemed another trip in the future, this one to Switzerland, would be necessary. In my notebook, I added a new lake to the list.

On Shaky Ground

I am not the greatest fan of earthquakes. Unlike tornados, hurricanes, grizzly bears, tidal waves, or undead mummies, there is nowhere to run when an earthquake attacks. That's because it is the earth that is actually attacking. I discovered this distaste for earthquakes when I went through my first tremor in Tacoma on January 28, 1995. This was the Maury Island quake. At approximately 7:11 p.m. and 23 seconds, a 5.0 magnitude earthquake unleashed its unholy fury upon the south Puget Sound region. The epicenter was located just off Vashon Island, 10.9 miles from where we were sitting. It was a very shallow quake, just 11 miles deep.

At first there was the horrible noise, followed by the massive shaking of the ground. I, unlike others in the room, was quick to assess the situation and to determine that we were experiencing an earthquake of notable magnitude. I quickly rose and proceeded to the large doorframe while clearly informing everyone that we were experiencing an earthquake, and that they should join me under the reinforced doorway. Because of the extremely disorienting effect an earthquake has on people, no one else in the room was even able to respond, and they all remained exactly in the same position until the trembling subsided.

I find it regrettable that such a traumatic experience can cause shock and absolute confusion bordering on hallucination. It's regrettable because both my wife and my mother-in-law later described my quick, calm and decisive response to the catastrophe in a completely inaccurate manner. If one were to hear their version, they would be treated to an utterly farcical story in which I sprung from my chair, yelling unintelligibly, and moved in a spasmodic blur toward the kitchen before colliding into the doorframe. Even more regrettable is that, as the years have gone on and the story has been told and retold, there is now a new iteration of the event in which I was actually throwing women and small children out of my way. This is, of course, absurd. There weren't even any small children there.

It is unfortunate what shock can do to the memory. As further evidence, I would submit that both my wife and my mother-in-law recall the earthquake as the sound of a loud truck rumbling down the road, followed by the rattling of a few dishes and some windows. Obviously, the event was so terrifying that they have simply forced it out of their memory, a common defense mechanism, as any psychologist will tell you. I know this to be true because, in actuality, there was a rending screeching roaring rumbling noise that could only be matched if the very gates of hell were thrown open, and every demon within howled out in horrendous depravity. Also, the house was thrown about, much like a small boat on the waves of an angry sea. It's amazing nothing was broken.

That was the Maury Island quake of 1995. I can't even bring myself to talk about the horrors of the Nisqually quake in February 2002. That tremor had a 6.5 magnitude and resulted in building facades in downtown Seattle collapsing and general terror in the streets.

I concluded, after that event, that I had reached my quota for earthquake encounters. Earthquakes are not fun. I will be perfectly happy never to experience one again.

I mention this because, as it happens, Chelan appears to be in what one might call a seismically active zone. We experienced this firsthand just a few years back. On a wet September morning, the weekend of Labor Day, I was sitting at my parents' lake house when I felt a strange jolt. This left the chandelier swinging in the kitchen. I stepped out in the yard where Amy was playing with my son Cooper.

"Did you feel that?"

"Feel what?" she said.

"Nothing," I told her, and went back inside.

The following evening, two blocks away at our farmhouse, we were sitting around a fire with my siblings and cousins. I was about to go get my fishing pole and fake bat to do some quick research into the SHABAM, when we were all startled by a second seismic jolt. This one everyone heard and felt. It was as if a car had run into the house and rocked the whole patio.

I looked into this the following day and discovered that there had indeed been two quakes. They were of relatively small magnitude. The first measured 1.9 and the second measured 2.5. What made them significant to me was that the USGS pinpoint map indicated the epicenter as being directly under the Mill Bay Casino, about a block and a half away. I was rather displeased by this bit of information.

With the rareness of earthquakes, it is probably a concern that should rank far to the rear of my list of worries, somewhere between killer bee infestation and bizarre knife attack by a deranged clown. Because Chelan has a history of earthquakes, however, the threat of a tremor gets a little boost toward the top of the concern meter.

Chelan was right in the middle of, and greatly affected by, the largest earthquake in recorded Pacific Northwest history, on December 15, 1872.

Geologists have pieced together evidence of massive earthquakes that strike the Pacific Northwest every 300–400 years, accompanied by tsunamis on the coast. These quakes, of which one is now overdue, are grand continental plate events that affect the entire region. They predate written history in the region.

The quake of 1872 was not this type of event. It is the largest recorded quake in the region because, by 1872, there were a host of trappers, miners, and missionaries in the area who were able to both record their personal experiences and record firsthand accounts of what had transpired from the Native American tribes of the area.

By all accounts, this was an enormous quake. It was strongly felt from Oregon well up north into British Columbia. One account claims it was felt from Sitka, Alaska to Los Angeles.

The US Geological Service, using a construct of historical data and a process called Modified Mercalli Intensity, reached the following conclusions: "[The quake's] epicentral region was east of the Cascade Mountains near Lake Chelan, Washington, and most probably near the south end of Lake Chelan. The intensity magnitude, M_I, is 6.8 and moment magnitude, **M**, is 6.5–7.0 at the 95% confidence level."

Although it is impossible to tell exactly where the epicenter may have been, some key events that took place in specific locations were cataclysmic. An entire mountaintop in the Skagit River Valley, for example, is said to have fallen off, damming the south fork of the river.

Sketchy reports of a mountainside peeling away and tipping across the Columbia River up in British Columbia exist as well. Most notably, in the Chelan area, just above the outlet of the Entiat River, at a place now called Ribbon Cliffs, the entire side of the mountain above the Columbia River gave way in a massive landslide that completely dammed the Columbia River.

The people of Wenatchee awoke to find the river bed had gone dry. It remained dry for hours, until the backwater behind the landslide reached sufficient pressure to breach the debris and set loose a raging torrent of water down the river.

Where the slide occurred, a massive cliff was exposed that had ribbons of colored rock weaving through it. These ribbons were the result of ancient fissures in the rock that had been filled by hot flowing magma. The sight of the new ribboned cliff face was so striking just after the slide that thought was given to promoting it as a natural wonder for tourists to visit, much like the Grand Canyon. Below the cliff, new tumultuous rapids clogged the Columbia River.

Directly below Lake Chelan, on the west side of the Columbia River, the ground was fractured, and a giant geyser of water erupted upwards and sprayed, by some accounts, as high as 25 to 30 feet into the air. This "geyser"—really just a very high-powered artesian well—was said to spout for many months, gradually decreasing in height and pressure. People believed a fissure had ruptured underground that was draining Lake Chelan itself.

The fountain eventually decayed down to the point where it was just a naturally flowing stream, and is reported to be the same spring that was the source of irrigation for the Beebe apple orchard along the river for many years.

The spring still flows today with a high volume of water, and because the spring water emerges at such a cool temperature, it is used as the source of water for the state fish hatchery along the Columbia River. It also serves as the water source for a rehabilitated wildlife wetland preserve that has reclaimed some of the shore of the river just up from the Beebe Bridge.

The earthquake also created a massive upwelling of water in Lake Chelan with an accompanying hydrological event, a surge of water that rolled down the lake much like a tidal wave. Such events, when they occur in freshwater lakes, are known as seiches.

Two to three foot wide fissures were reported to have opened up in the earth in the Native American encampments along the lake, near the current downtown of the city of Chelan. From these cracks, sulphurous water emerged that flooded the area and ruined cached food stores. The water in the lake was fouled with an acrid taste for a great portion of that year. Fish in the water were killed off in large quantities.

So large was this earthquake that turmoil and aftershocks rocked the entire region almost every day for over a year, and intermittently for three or four years. The results of the quake and the aftershocks were far-reaching, and they had a rather profound effect on human history that is still relevant today. The earthquakes greatly disturbed the Native Americans of the region, many of whom believed it was a harbinger of the end of the world, or perhaps an expression of wrath from the great spirits of nature. Their extreme concern and unease from this event happened to coincide with the arrival of many of the missionaries, who were attempting to spread the Christian faith in the region.

The Native people, who believed strongly in the power of the supernatural, were eager to find some comfort in the face of these terrifying events, and the missionaries were there with a ready solution. This was instrumental in helping to integrate these two very diverse cultures as they were suddenly finding themselves in close contact with each other. At a time when hostilities and outright violence occurred throughout the region, the quake may have been a key event that helped defuse these tensions.

Another historical consequence of the quake relates to the Wapato family. Wapato John was living in the hill just adjacent to Earthquake Point along the Columbia River at the time of the event. He and his family were awoken by the horrendous cataclysm of the mountain pulling away and sliding into the river. Their log home was torn apart, and they were lucky to survive. He thought it was "a bad Ta-man-na-was." This is reported to be one of the factors that inspired him to move up to Lake Chelan where he and his family resettled. It was the reason why he and his family were in residence on the north shore of the lake at the time that the Native Americans were given the right to claim their 640-acre parcels.

Wapato John, who had never been averse to the ways of the new settlers, became a rather devout Catholic and even constructed a church on his land near current-day Manson. St. John the Baptist Catholic Church was completed in 1888 and Wapato John, although not an ordained priest, was given authorization to lead services himself.

His family would later build a racetrack and pavilion on Wapato Point, which was a meeting and gathering place for both recent settlers and members of various local tribes. Gradually, in this way, two cultures with strong reasons to mistrust each other and a history of mutual aggression and conflict began to integrate. All of this was, in part, a result of the quake of 1872.

That the earthquake and landslide happened at that precise time may have, in the end, been fortuitous. Some may cite it as an example of God working in mysterious ways. The Pacific Northwest, however, is no stranger to massive and dramatic upheavals in the earth. Giant displacements of terra firma are actually, in a sense, the norm for this area. Geologic evidence and historical accounts speak to this. Mountains have been collapsing in the region since there have been mountains.

A giant swath of the lower Puget Sound Valley lays across the Osceola mudslide, a so-called electron flow of volcanic debris that slid off the side of Mount Rainier about 5,600 years ago. A slice of earth in the Columbia Gorge near The Dalles, Oregon dammed the river briefly, and then eventually was undermined, leaving a natural land bridge over the drainage that the Native Americans referred to as the Bridge of the Gods.

During the quake of 1872, a large section of Mount Cheam in British Columbia is said to have broken off, and big house-size rocks were observed crashing down off the side of Dirty Face Mountain above Lake Wenatchee. More recently, the largest ever recorded landslide in the world was witnessed, the collapse of the northern flank of Mount Saint Helens during the eruption of 1980.

All of this speaks to the incredibly complex geology that underlies the entire Cascade Range. The oldest portion of the mountains consists of extrusions of metamorphic rock such as granite and schist. These are believed to be some 60 million years old, and the product of a small tectonic plate thrusting upward. Prominent theories now postulate that this occurred somewhere south of Baja, California and that the range itself migrated up north on the shifting plates.

A second, more recent mountain building event began 40 million years ago with the collision of the Juan De Fuca tectonic plate and the North American continental plate. The subduction of the Juan De Fuca plate caused a new and very different form of mountain building punctuated copiously by volcanic activity.

Within the past million years, the volcanic cones such as Mount Baker and Glacier Peak have risen up off the ancient base mountains that anchor them to the continent. Volcanic mountain building has coated the range with lava and debris that has then been partially stripped away in a successive and still ongoing process.

The Cascade Mountains are a truly complex stew of ancient and new rocks strewn together by a vast array of geologic events. Few places in the world are the result of such a complicated history. If the motions of tectonic plates are like a river, then the Cascade Mountains represent the tumultuous rapids. This tumult is what gives rise to such extraordinary features as the Lake Chelan glacier basin and the towering walls that surround it. It is the key component that allowed Lake Chelan to come into existence.

Switzerland

On a warm rainy night, with lightning crashing into the high Alps, Amy and I rolled into the town of Interlaken, Switzerland by train. Interlaken sits on a narrow isthmus of land, next to the Aare River, that connects Lake Brienz to the east and Lake Thun to the west. Lake Brienz was the location where the scenes in the *Band of Brothers* miniseries were actually filmed. This is the heart of the Bernese Oberland.

To the south, the Lauterbrunnen Valley carves up into the towering Alps. It is a classic glacier-cut valley, with a flat bottom and sheer thousand-plus-foot walls of bare rock that stretch unbroken for almost five miles. It is the deepest gorge in the Alps, made more impressive by its narrowness. From rim to rim, it is rarely wider than a half mile.

The fabled troika of alpine mountains, the Eiger, the Jungfrau, and the Munch, rise up to form the eastern rim. The Eiger is one of the holy grails for mountain climbers, and stories of its conquest are the stuff of legend. I was as excited to see it as I was about seeing the lake.

If one cannot analyze Lake Chelan without considering the North Cascades, then one cannot analyze Lake Brienz without getting a closer look at the Swiss Alps. Amy and I made our way up the Lauterbrunnen Valley and spent two nights in the town of Murren. Murren sits on the western side, almost 2,000 feet above the valley floor. It is reached via cable car from the tram station in Stechelberg. It is a small hamlet without cars, perched on the mountainside. From almost anywhere in town, the three summits across the valley are on display.

In our two days there, Amy and I tried to take these mountains in from every angle. We took another cable car up to the Schilthorn, a summit nearly 10,000 feet high, directly above Murren. It hosts an incredible revolving restaurant. The restaurant is yet another structure made famous by the James Bond movies, having been featured in *Her Majesty's Secret Service*. It sits on a motorized revolving platform.

From the Schilthorn, the Alps stretch out in every direction. Mont Blanc, the highest peak wholly in Europe, is clearly visible, as it towers 15,781 feet into the sky. Sitting in the spinning restaurant, eating germknödel and sipping beers, we watched the mountains parade by, with views stretching into Italy, Germany, and France.

The next day, we took paraglider flights from a field just outside our hotel and soared straight across the valley, toward the looming face of the Eiger. The entire length of the Lauterbrunnen Valley wall was ribboned with cascading horsetail waterfalls that plunged in full freefall for 900 vertical feet. These are the highest unbroken waterfalls in Switzerland.

The mountains were awesome. Deep green fields, kept mowed by copious grazing cows, stretched up to spine-tingling teeth of exposed rock. Ice fields crept down every wrinkle in the rocks, terminating in more waterfalls than a person could count. A constant gentle clanging sound resonated through the fields, emanating from the decorative bells that adorned every cow.

One of the highlights was getting to soar off the mountainside. I remember seeing Amy launch on her paraglider and watching her sail out over the massive void of the valley. Left alone, waiting for my opportunity to launch, I heard the low mourn of alpenhorns being played somewhere in the distance. They made a haunting and beautiful melody. The bright colors of Amy's glider were almost lost in a backdrop blend of forests and cliffs and rocks and ice. I felt that being in the mountains couldn't get much more spectacular than this.

As for the lake, nestled below near Interlaken, it lived up to its reputation. If this lake looked beautiful on the TV screen, it was even more impressive in person. Brilliant clear turquoise water was framed by glowing green hillsides. The immediate mountains surrounding the lake were not as high as those above the Lauterbrunnen Valley, but from the town of Interlaken, the Jungfrau was framed in the distance, dressed in snowy white apparel. Interlaken is one of the most popular tourist destinations in Switzerland, and it was not hard to see why.

Was this the most beautiful lake in the world? Was it prettier than Lake Chelan? Were the mountains more stunning than our own North Cascades? Well, what can I say? It's the Swiss Alps for crying out loud. Let's face it: No one is running around the Swiss Alps saying, "These are the North Cascades of Europe." The mountains were extraordinary, and the lake was incredible. Add to the list Switzerland's other incredible bodies of water—Lake Lucerne, Lake Zurich, Lake Constance, and a host of other lakes—and a person could be almost overwhelmed.

Still, I couldn't hand the Swiss Alps the outright title of most beautiful mountains. Though people don't talk about the Alps as being "The North Cascades of Europe," there are, in my opinion, many times when perhaps they should. There are categories of mountain beauty in which the North Cascades simply reign supreme.

The North Cascades National Park is home to a prominent mountain known as Mount Shuksan. This sits next to the shimmering volcanic cone of Mount Baker and rises 9,172 feet. Although not the highest mountain in the North Cascades, Shuksan has a few distinctions. On the face of the mountain is the Sulphide Glacier, one of the largest glaciers in the North Cascades National Park. This feeds the Sulphide waterfall, which is one of the highest cascading waterfalls in North America, tumbling down nearly 2,200 vertical feet.

Mount Shuksan is a mountain of extremes. Most famously, however, is the fact that it is one of the most photographed mountains in the world. From a small lake near the Mount Baker ski area, Mount Shuksan presents a truly classic alpine vista.

The perfect lines of the mountain rise up from either side and combine with a fierce-looking glacier that terminates on a sheer cliff, exposing a giant wall of wrinkled ice, where the glacier calves and tumbles away to the floor below. The mountain has a perfect pyramid-shaped summit that leaps up from behind this glacier.

The coup de grâce is the foreground. In any season, the heather meadows are spectacular, but the autumn, in particular, lends a stunning amount of color. The vine maples blaze red at the base of vibrant evergreens. From the small alpine tarn known as Picture Lake, these colors frame the mountain, and the lake displays a mirror-like reflection of the summit. It is this image, from this spot, that dominates so much film space and so many digital memory cards.

I first noticed this mountain as a child on the cover of a Rand McNally road atlas of the United States. This was long before I knew where it was. It is instantly recognizable. I have seen it since in dozens, maybe even hundreds of places around the world.

While walking in Athens, Greece near the Plaka, we rounded a corner only to see an eight-foot-wide by eight-foot-tall poster of Mount Shuksan in a display window for an athletic store. Even more stunning, we were in downtown Innsbruck in Tyrol wandering the streets when we came across a 12-foot-tall mural of Mount Shuksan adorning the wall of a hotel. Tyrolean Austria is famous for its murals, many of them of alpine scenes, but to see the Austrians post a picture of one of our North Cascade peaks so prominently in a town that sits in the heart of the Alps was a shock to me.

To further emphasize this shock, that same photograph was on the main web page for the official tourist site promoting visits to the country of Austria. When I saw that they had purloined our mountain to promote their own country, which is itself buried in stunning mountains, I realized that Mount Shuksan was truly a special piece of nature.

Someone must have drawn attention to the ruse, because after nearly a year, the picture was replaced with an Austrian mountain on the website, but it had played so prominently on the internet that the most popular search engine continued to pull up a picture of Mount Shuksan as the first image when a search was done for the country of Austria.

With dozens of puzzles, hundreds of postcards, and innumerable brochures, pamphlets, and magazines all brandishing this image of Mount Shuksan, it is clear that this mountain resides in the upper echelon of alpine scenery. I love the mountain myself, but I also feel compelled to note that an important reason why it has risen to such prominence is because, combined with its beauty, there is a paved road that takes thousands of people, every year, right up to Picture Lake. It is the perfect photo opportunity for the tailgate photographer.

Although it would be hard to say that other mountains in the North Cascades surpass Shuksan in beauty, I have always felt there are many in and around the head of Lake Chelan that rival it. Dome Peak, cloaked in the Chickamin and Dana Glaciers, comes to mind.

After careful contemplation about this, I felt justified in saying that, although the Swiss Alps are spectacular, and perhaps from certain aspects more dramatic, the North Cascades cannot be dismissed as lesser in impact. I truly believe that a person born with artistic talent and aesthetic appreciation might opt for the North Cascades as a more fitting setting to capture alpine beauty at its finest. The Alps are in many ways more impressive than the North Cascades, but likewise, the North Cascades are in some ways more beautiful than the Swiss Alps.

Beyond that, the North Cascades remain wonderfully, exquisitely, ruggedly wild. The flanks of the Alps, though verdant and green, have been notably altered by centuries of deforestation and grazing. This doesn't make them less beautiful, but if one appreciates true wilderness, then one is apt to hold a special regard for the incredible triumph of conservation that has protected our rugged mountains.

There is an intangible romance to wandering between berry-clustered piles of bear scat on the side of a remote Cascade mountain. That romance is lost when the mountains are completely devoid of bears and the scat is replaced by never-ending disks of cow patties. The Alps are no less beautiful from a distance, but, perhaps, just slightly less enchanting up close.

As for Lake Brienz at the base of the Alps, it probably couldn't be much more enchanting. I imagine there are moments, in the right light and at the right angle, when Lake Chelan can compete visually with Lake Brienz, but this is a gorgeous lake. It shines, and shimmers, and sits in such perfect harmony with the surrounding hillsides that it captivates a viewer, like a supermodel among lakes.

As beautiful as Lake Brienz is, the contest for Greatest Lake in the World was more than about sheer beauty. In a beauty pageant, Lake Brienz would surely be a finalist, but as the greatest lake in the world, she simply couldn't compete. At just 11 miles long and a half mile wide, she too lacked enough diversity to warrant further consideration.

The lake was just too uniform of a trough in the earth. If one were to go on a boat ride, there was no place on the lake they could drive to and be out of sight from their original departure point. The greatest lake in the world needed to be more than that. It needed to be something that could be explored, voyaged along or across. A trip along the greatest lake in the world needed to tell a rich story in scenery and geography.

Compared to many lakes, Brienz was a beautiful postcard, where others are intricate masterpieces. She was an elegant haiku, where other lakes are multifaceted epic poems.

I felt sure we would return to Lake Brienz and her near equally beautiful sister Lake Thun, but I knew she was not to be the champion. Lake Chelan was still a frontrunner.

Lake Project

Late Year 2

The project on the south shore was now in full swing, and with it came a hiatus from traveling to other lakes. It did create a new opportunity to spend time on the shores of Lake Chelan. In the early summer, the first two cabins at Mountainside were nearly finished. Amy and I were once again full-time residents of Lake Chelan as we worked through the weeks to get the house ready for the summer rental season. Although we had lived permanently at the lake on several other occasions in several other spots, we had never lived on the south shore, and never so far uplake.

Perched on the rocks above the water, the cabins at Mountainside had a panoramic view of the entire lower half of the lake from the town of Chelan up past Twenty-Five Mile Creek. Directly below the cabins, the cliff plunged straight down to the water, and then farther still into the deepest section of the Wapato Glacier Basin. The depth and nearly straight down angle on the water gave the lake the same rich blue color that one might find in the circle at the end of a peacock feather.

After a long day of cleaning, assembling furniture, and landscaping, I would scramble down the trail and then leap from the rocks into the gently lapping water. Then I would float on my back and stare at the forested hillside that vaulted up above the cabins to the very top of Slide Ridge. I reveled in the realization that I was floating 30 feet off the side of a mountain whose base stretched hundreds and hundreds of feet down below me, in a nearly vertical underwater dropoff.

When Amy made a run to Seattle to order more furniture, I snuck away on a drive uplake, past Twenty-Five Mile Creek and into the hills to the very top of Slide Ridge. From there, the lake carved a straight line and then curved in a giant arc around the low plateau above Manson, so that it seemed to form a mammoth azure question mark.

I knew what the question was. It was a question I had, so far, failed to answer. Was Lake Chelan the greatest lake in the world? I continued to ponder this as I headed further out the forest service road, higher up into the hills to the trailhead of Stormy Mountain.

I had planned to take a one-hour road trip and get back to the cabins for more work, but I was alone, high up the slopes of the Chelan Valley, at the head of an empty trailhead. It was two hours before dusk on one of the most beautiful evenings of the year. I really had no choice in the matter. I parked the car and set off up the trail. There were large pockets of snow still covering the trail as I worked my way up the ridge, but the evening was warm. The view of the lake below opened up more and more expansively with each step, as did the sweeping vista of the surrounding mountains.

Stormy Mountain was the proposed location for a ski area. Originally conceived in the mid 1960s, the idea was revisited in the late 70s, and again in 2003. From an importance ranking, for me, skiing falls just below breathing, and slightly ahead of eating. I have always lamented that there wasn't a major ski area right near the lake. I would love nothing more than to spend the bulk of my winters in Chelan, sneaking away daily to a nearby world-class ski resort.

Stormy Mountain, at just over 7,000 feet high, could scarcely be more perfect for skiing. The mountain draws plenty of snow, but because of its location on the eastern side of the mountains, the snow tends to be drier and more powder-like than the snow on the western slopes. Also, the terrain on the mountainside lends itself perfectly to wide open runs and mixed glade skiing.

The only downfall is the name. The group that was contemplating the resort noted that naming a ski resort "Stormy Mountain" was akin to naming an oceanside resort "Shark Beach." Still, the idea has come to the forefront on several occasions, as skiing enthusiasts have attempted to garner community support for the project.

Alas, it was not to be. I was able to find quite a few details about the proposed area, including a site design plan that was purchased by the developers in contemplation of the resort. It was an extraordinary plan, to my way of thinking. Still the idea never came to fruition.

Breaking ground on a new ski area is a difficult endeavor. Just a few months earlier, I had informed Amy that our investment in the ski area in Romania probably wasn't going to pan out. The look she gave me could best be described as the opposite of surprise. It was as if I had just told her it was possible to buy bread at a bakery.

Probably hundreds of times, I had stared up at Stormy Mountain from lake level, and dreamed of where the runs would go. As I worked my way up the ridge, although I still longed for a world-class resort, I had to admit it was wonderful to have untarnished wilderness and unblemished solitude on the lonely mountain.

From the summit, the chaos of the North Cascades was everywhere. The Chelan Sawtooth Range, the Cashmere Crags, Bonanza Peak and its siblings fanned out like an ocean of white-capped waves glistening in the evening light. Every volcano in the state was in view, from the nearby Glacier Peak to the distant Mount Adams. Even the lower crater walls of Mount Saint Helens could be seen peeking over the jagged fronts of the closer mountains. All of them were reflecting the most subtle salmon pink color of alpenglow as the sun dropped low to the west, high on the globe because the solstice had just passed.

Tiny white slices on the lake indicated boats cruising across the water below. The evening was so still, I felt as if I should be able to hear them. The lake at this hour looked distinctly purple, like the color of a ripe plum, as it nestled between golden wheat-colored hills. It was the unchallenged focal point of a staggeringly beautiful panorama. The question begged again. Was this the greatest lake in the world?

Even at the epicenter of this grand vista, I knew I couldn't yet make an unequivocal answer. With my cabin project drawing to a close, it was time to review the final contenders for the title of the world's greatest lake and hone in on my final conclusion.

The Way Through

On the north shore, about a mile uplake from the town of Chelan, is the house of Mike and Mary Sherer. They have a rambler that sits on a wide expanse of waterfront. Mike is a retired US Navy submarine boat captain. His first submarines were hunter killer types, in charge of deterring enemy subs from threatening our coastlines or our ships and holdings abroad. He was later put in charge of a boomer, a boat armed with intercontinental ballistic nuclear missiles.

"The difference," he told me, "is when a hunter killer hears another sub, he heads toward it as fast as he can. When a boomer hears another sub, he heads away from it as fast as he can."

One of my first thoughts about Mike when I met him was, if there's someone you want to take on the awesome and frightening task of being in charge of an arsenal of ballistic missiles, each armed with multiple nuclear warheads, this is the guy.

His wife Mary could probably handle the task with equal calm and precision. I contrast them to a married couple like Amy and myself, where I would probably misplace the launch codes under a pile of magazine clippings, and Amy would probably back the submarine into a rock.

Mary is very active in the museum run by the Chelan Historical Society. She has a wealth of knowledge about the Chelan area both past and present. She and Mike run a number of businesses in the Chelan Valley.

They met in Hawaii, and when Mike retired from the navy they moved to Stehekin. They still own a cabin and some property there near the schoolhouse. They are in the process of building a retreat center on the property. They hope it will be a "ministry of enabling," which will allow large groups to spend time in Stehekin and experience the peace and tranquility of a remote mountain village.

One ambition Mike told me about was to have groups of troubled kids come to the new center from time to time. When I heard that I asked, "How are the people of Stehekin going to feel about troubled kids descending on their peaceful town?"

His answer was a surprise. He told me that they were used to it. In the past, families have moved to Stehekin specifically because their children were having problems in the city. When they fell prey to a seedier element, or got mixed up in the wrong crowd, many parents, over the years, had opted to uproot from the city and move to Stehekin. Perhaps some people weren't always thrilled by this, but Stehekin is a place where people generally go about their business.

Mike told me that the kids spend a while trying to cause problems and create havoc before they find out there are very few opportunities to cause problems or create havoc. Then they get down to the business of swimming, fishing, hiking, and generally having a great time. Many kids have been straightened out in the remote town. Their motto: "Stehekin is what America was."

The town is unique. There are few if any other year-round towns in the lower 48 states that are so isolated. Although fully in touch with the modern age, the people of Stehekin still exhibit the rugged pioneer spirit that their ancestors had when they settled this valley. It is a prerequisite for anyone who intends to endure the harsh winters of the North Cascades. There is need for skill and improvisation in a town where everything must be brought in by boat.

The word "Stehekin" is an Indian word which means "the way through." This is in reference to a Native American trading route that went up Lake Chelan, up the Stehekin Valley, over Cascade Pass, and down the Cascade River Valley to the Skagit Valley. This was a long and daunting trip, to be sure, but in an area of formidable mountains, it was one of the few "ways through."

There is now a hiking trail that follows this same route through the high mountains of North Cascades National Park. When I first heard about this as a young teenager, I knew I had to make that trip. I planned it on several occasions, but the logistics being what they were, I was never able to pull the trip together. Unless one is planning to do the whole 40-mile route and then return, or possibly turn it into an 80-mile loop trip back around Park Creek Pass, the trip requires two cars—one in or near Chelan, and another parked at the trailhead at the top of the Cascade River Valley on the west side of the mountains.

No matter which way you go, the trip requires a bus ride to or from Stehekin and the trailhead, and it also requires a boat trip or floatplane trip up or down Lake Chelan. My personal plan was always to come from the west side, hike through, and culminate on the east side with a climactic plunge into Lake Chelan.

For many years, the trip eluded me. I made other treks and mountain climbs out of the Stehekin Valley, and I made treks and mountain climbs out of the Cascade River Valley, but stringing the two together was an undertaking that kept dangling like a carrot in front of me.

It wasn't until after I began my Lake Project that I was finally able to get the trip scheduled. I assembled a crack team of experienced drinking buddies and a foolproof plan, and on an early September weekend, we made good our departure from Seattle, bound for North Cascades National Park.

We met at the ranger station in Marblemount to get our backcountry permits.

"Are there any spaces available in the Pelton Basin?" I asked the ranger.

"We're loving our wilderness to death," she said.

In a slight deviation from the itinerary, we got camping spots up at the high camp on Mount Sahalee. This would involve an extra 2,500 vertical feet of climbing with our full packs, but I was excited because I knew we would have far more spectacular views, and also because I wanted to take a stab at getting to the top of Sahalee Peak. I hadn't packed any glacier travel gear, but the route to the summit across the Sahalee Glacier can be relatively safe late in the year. I intended to question other climbers on their way down and see what the conditions were. If reports came in of a safe traverse, I planned to make a climb up to the top.

The added and unintended elevation gain was not daunting to me. I am an extremely light packer. I learned the merits of light packing very early in my mountaineering endeavors.

Years earlier, shortly after college, I had made my first attempt to climb a volcano. This was a mountain I had dreamed of climbing all of my life. I was finally going to get my chance to climb Mount Rainier.

The centerpiece of my gear was an old hand-me-down backpack. My friends had asked me why I was so loyal to this pack, as it was older and heavier than the newer packs and lacked most, if not all of the modern backpack advances that have been developed since the Civil War.

"I'm sort of a purist," I told them. "I refuse to get caught up in all the commercialism that seems to have overrun the sport of mountaineering. In the end, it's really just about getting out and being in the wilderness."

"So you're broke."

"Yes," I said. "Basically penniless."

Prior to heading up Mount Rainier, I assembled my outdoor stuff in my retro pack, such that it was of reasonable weight and had just the right amount of gear for a comfortable trip. I did this over a month before the trip. I had done a lot of hiking and scrambling and training, and I had backpacked deep into the woods and camped out on many occasions, but prior to that, I had never done any glacier travel or technical mountaineering. I had carried a heavy pack for many miles before as well, but never straight up a mountain. To prepare, I wore the pack fully loaded and climbed flight after flight of stairs on Capitol Hill in Seattle. I was comfortable with the belief that I could haul it to the top. I even added a few things as I started feeling stronger, thinking the more comfortable I was up on the mountain, the more fun I would have.

My friend Matt and his climbing buddy Eric were going to lead the trip. They were both extremely experienced in the mountains. Among dozens of high climbs, they had summited Mount McKinley in Alaska, as well as a 20,000-foot-high peak in the Himalayas. Eric had been up Aconcagua, the highest peak in South America, and Matt had done most of the Cascade volcanoes as a kid. I had never met Eric before, but Matt told me he was a veteran climber who had been scaling peaks while we were still in diapers, and that he knew his way around the hills.

On the day of our departure, Matt picked me up in the pitch black pre-dawn of a spring morning. We continued on and we picked up Eric. Then we drove up into the Cascades to the trailhead. This is where things went horribly awry.

We pulled our packs out and set them down in the parking lot, and then from the back compartment of the car, Matt and Eric started pulling out ropes, and wands, and carabiners and runners and pulleys and more ropes and more wands, and gadgets, and whosits and whatsits, and sniglets and widgets, and more, until a small mountain of gear had risen behind the tailgate of the car.

"Okay," said Matt, "let's divvy up the stuff."

Then they both got their first look at my small, neatly organized antique backpack. They stared at it with disdain, as if I had shown up for our intrepid adventure with all my gear packed in a ladies French designer purse.

"Not much room in that thing," said Eric.

"We did mention we're going mountain climbing this weekend, right?" said Matt.

Eric walked around my backpack with an appraising eye. He looked like a cowboy who was about to head off with a mailbag across the wild west, only someone had brought him an ostrich to ride instead of a horse. He turned and looked at me with an appraising eye. His expression was about the same. Then he looked back at my backpack.

"Okay," he said, "here's what we're going to do. We'll just use all the carabiners to clip all the wickets onto the outside of that little back...uh...packy...thing, and then Matt and I will carry the rest."

Wickets are two-foot-long ridged aluminum beams with holes that are used to set protection in the snow in hazardous places, or if needed, during a crevasse rescue. Individually they are pretty light. Collected together and attached with a full assortment of carabiners, they start to add a fair amount of heft. When the repacking was done, my perfectly organized and well-thought-out backpack looked like it had been dipped in crazy glue and dropped into the remains of a discarded old Erector set. Wickets stuck out oddly at every angle. My crampons were actually duct-taped to the pack in two very non-symmetrical locations. My ice axe was tied strangely to the wickets because my backpack lacked a critical loop which, I learned on that trip, plays a key roll in storing gear. When I put on the pack, I looked like a malfunctioning cyber-organic robot from a very low budget sci-fi movie.

"There," said Eric, "you're all set. You look like a real mountain climber now." He did a very poor job of hiding his smirk as he turned away. I looked at the two of them, and the host of other climbers who were gearing up in the parking lot, and felt I looked decidedly different than a real mountain climber.

None of that mattered. I was about to make my first real mountain climb, and I was extremely excited. I can still remember fondly the warm sun coming down as we wandered out of the parking lot and through a field of outrageously colored mountain meadow flowers. This is the only thing about the trip I would remember fondly. We were almost immediately socked in by fog. The rest of the climb, at least that which I haven't repressed from memory, was a bitter cold, exhausting ascent into an unfettered hell I had never previously experienced or even imagined possible.

One highlight, I recall, was being pinned down at 12,000 feet on a glacier, near a rubble heap of volcanic rocks, as 90-mile-per-hour winds drove ice pellets and pumice into us and tried to rend us from the side of the hill. I remember Eric saying, "It looks like we missed the weather window. Probably need to hunker down here for a bit, hope for a break, and then turn back."

I remember the ridiculous amount of effort I put into trying to look and sound disappointed, even though I really wanted to start laughing with joy. I remember not having the slightest interest in getting to the top of Mount Rainier on that trip, or any other trip, ever.

Mountain climbing is a strange hobby, however. I have been up dozens of peaks since then and there is, for me, a moment on every climb when I'm camped on the side of a chilling windblown mountainside wondering why I'm not at home in a comfortable bed snug against a warm wife. There is frequently a point when I'm marching zombie-like through loose shale, or knee-deep snow, or skulking in the mud through driving rain trying to navigate windfallen trees, when I vow never to climb another mountain.

The allure of climbing is that intermixed in the struggle of a climb are moments that resonate as epic events. Watching the sun come up over a serac-strewn glacier field that's glowing pink in the morning light is an example. Achieving the summit of a long-dreamed-about peak is another. These moments on any climb are frequent, fantastic, and addictive. The planning and training for a difficult climb, in and of itself, can be half the fun of any outing.

These are the memories that linger after a descent and somehow overwhelm the recollections of the harsh and exhausting miseries that constitute a good portion of any climb. I, and other climbers I've known, have huddled on the side of storm-wracked peaks and made blood oaths that we would never climb again, only to find ourselves, ten hours later, sitting in the comfort of a roadside diner eating scrambled eggs and planning our next trip. The misery is long forgotten, and remains forgotten, until the climber commits the idiotic act of climbing back up a desolate mountain again and remembering just how cold and uncomfortable it can be. The oath to never return is sworn again, and the cycle continues.

So it was, after my descent of Mount Rainier the first time, that I found myself in the town of Ashford, at the base of the volcano, planning my next excursion. I had already identified what had gone wrong on the recent failed attempt. I had made four critical errors.

At 24 years of age, I thought I was in good shape. I wasn't.

I thought I had trained pretty hard. I hadn't.

I thought I had packed well. I had packed extremely poorly.

My first Cascade climb shouldn't have been up the highest mountain in the range.

I vowed never to make those mistakes again.

For this reason, I have developed what some might consider to be a manic tendency to pack lightly. Toothpaste is removed from tubes. The handle of my toothbrush is sawed off. Labels are cut from every piece of clothing. Food is removed from packaging. The stick is removed from the chapstick, leaving just a button of lip balm. Sunscreen is removed from tubes. Superfluous straps, zippers, and buttons are cut from backpacks, climbing pants and parkas, and I have perfected the art of packing food with maximum calories at minimum weight, with a total disregard for anything like flavor or palatability.

Tents, in my opinion, are an unnecessary luxury. My preferred defense against the elements is a 20-ounce bivouac sack, with the bug netting removed and no internal structure poles.

That was why, on the morning I found out we were going an extra 2,500 feet up Sahalee Mountain to camp, I was not particularly concerned. My friends, all of whom were experienced in being outdoors, may have failed to take note of this additional little wrinkle. Having studied the route for years as I longed for this particular outing, I was intimately familiar with every possible camp, how far it was, and how much altitude was involved. I may have failed to communicate that this was going to make the trip tough and that we should jettison some gear.

These were all pretty experienced outdoorsmen, and some may have gathered, from the brief discussion with the ranger, that our trip had gotten a bit more difficult. But with the packs already loaded, and fresh legs and fresh minds, a scant 2,500 feet more of elevation just didn't seem daunting enough to warrant sacrificing anything.

For this reason, the trip up was pretty grueling. I was feeling the vice-like twangs of burning thighs myself, and I was wearing a pack that might have blown away in a slight breeze if I left it unattended. Some of the other packs were monumental in weight. People were joking about what they had packed.

"I brought 10 cans of chili," said Mark. Everyone laughed.

"I brought a boom box," said Zach. Everyone laughed.

"I brought some big rocks to stack up, in case we need to build a wind shelter," said Scott. Everyone laughed.

"I brought a two-gallon box of wine," said my friend John. Everyone laughed.

If this all sounds distinctly unfunny now, bear in mind that the brain grasps for the slightest amount of merriment when a person is set to a grueling task. At the time, it seemed to us like it was such hysterical commentary that it might have been suitable for its own cable comedy show. This is further evidence, I believe, that mountain climbing is a strange sport full of wonderfully strange people who get even weirder when they are out on the trail.

Strange or not, we were a hearty group. We arrived pretty tired, but in good spirits at the Sahalee high camp. This is when the trip took an unexpected turn in a rather favorable direction.

It turns out, of all the not-so-funny jokes murmured on our way up the hill, one was not a joke at all. My friend John actually had brought two gallons of wine almost 5,000 feet up the mountain. He pulled it out of his backpack, still in the box. Two gallons of wine weigh almost 17 pounds, probably more than the weight of my entire fully loaded pack. This was, in my opinion, a true display of human selflessness. After an incredibly scenic if slightly tiring hike up Sahalee Arm, we started what would be one of the most enjoyable nights I've ever spent in the mountains.

The wine flowed. A flask of whisky made the rounds. A bunch of us hiked high on the Sahalee Glacier above camp to peer into the Quien Sabe Glacier basin. We then made an incredible glissading descent back down to the Sahalee Glacier terminus. We laughed, and marveled, and told stories about the glory days. Like all men who are out on a "guys weekend," we spent a tremendous amount of time talking about how wonderful our wives are.

As the sun set, we watched the sky turn red and the entire mountain range turn brilliant pink. Ridge after ridge of glacier-covered mountains glowed in the evening light, with high volcanoes peeking out in the distance. We could even catch a glimpse of the waters of Puget Sound, which looked as if they were blazing with fire. If someone told me there was a more stunningly beautiful place on the planet at that moment, I would have been hard pressed to believe it.

I have always felt that, at any given instant, there is one spot that is the best place on the earth to be. Sometimes it might be at a concert in China. Other times it might be on a beach in Brazil. That spot is always moving, and the instant is fleeting as the earth rolls ever forward, but in that moment, I was certain that we were the lucky ones to be in that one best spot in the world, during that brilliant September evening.

My friend Zach was the most experienced wilderness traveler on our trip. He is a veteran of the Appalachian Trail, or the "AT" as those who have been on the trail are fond of calling it. This famous hiking route covers 2,100 miles from Springer Mountain in Georgia to Mount Katahdin in Maine. One of the real nuisances of this particular trail is the black bear. Because hikers have had so many problems with marauding bears, many of the campsites actually consist of steel cages. Travelers spend the night, along with all of their gear, inside these cages, to thwart any pesky bears that might arrive in search of hikers' food.

Careful camp maintenance is critical on the Appalachian Trail, just as it is critical throughout the North Cascades, and particularly in the Stehekin Valley. Zach was extremely mindful of this on our trip. Zach, it seems, grew rather fond of the bear cages on his voyage up the AT. He is not a big fan of bear encounters.

"Let's be very careful not to leave any food or crumbs around the camp," he said when we left our car. He mentioned it again as we were hiking. Then he mentioned it again when we set up camp near the top of Sahalee. He mentioned it frequently throughout the evening. By my count, he may have brought it up as many as 27 times on the first day.

The trail was covered in bear scat. We knew there were lots of bears around. Also, we passed right by where the grizzly bear was recently photographed. We even encountered a group of biologists studying mountain goats, and they pointed out a large bear on the mountainside across Doubtful Lake which they were convinced was a grizzly. Looking through their binoculars, it was hard to disagree.

For these reasons, I shared Zach's concerns. As a precaution, we cooked our food away from the tents and then brought it back to camp.

He mentioned clean camp etiquette for the final time as we sat in camp on the second day, now down in the woods of the Stehekin Valley. We were preparing to eat our meal just before sundown.

"We probably shouldn't even be eating in camp. We should be eating over where we cooked it."

"I agree," I said, "especially now that we're down here off the mountain and in the trees. Let's just all be careful not to spill anything."

With that said, I set my soup down on a rock and stood up to get my zip-lock garbage bag. I turned and took my first step, and in so doing accidentally kicked the same rock and sent the full pan of soup spiraling up into space. The entire camp froze in place and all eyes fixated on the soaring pan in horror. It paused at the apex of its flight, without a drop of soup spilling out. Then it headed back toward the earth. When it hit the ground, the soup exploded. A broth geyser shot up six feet in the air, only to rain down on the entire camp, including the tents, and perhaps more significantly, the hikers, myself included. Everything was covered in drops of soup stock and micro chunks of chicken and noodles.

It's hard to explain the look on Zach's face. It was as if we were in the middle of a vast shark-infested ocean on an inflatable life raft, and I had just shot a flare gun into the rubber by mistake and exploded the air bladder. It was as if we were freezing to death in wet clothes in the snow-covered arctic woods, and I just dropped the only book of matches into the creek. It was as if I just severed the tether that was holding us to a spacecraft, and we were now all drifting, in our astronaut suits, out into the cold dizzying void of space.

That's the look Zach gave me. The look was clear. We were all going to die now, and it was my fault.

I had, of course, not packed a tent, and had planned on taking my 20-ounce bivouac sack far away from camp to sleep on a large rock by the river, so I was noticeably less concerned. I did do my best to clean up the mess, but knowing that the typical bear could smell a milligram of chicken from the adjacent county, I doubted that it would do much good.

Still, I've done my fair share of backcountry camping, and as Amy will be happy to tell you, I've spilled my fair share of savory dinners into the campfire. We've been harassed by raccoons, chipmunks, and ravens, but this was not Appalachia. I had never really known a bear to come into camp, or even heard a firsthand account from someone who had. We had already placed all of our food and garbage in a bear-proof box provided by the National Park Service far from camp. At the very worst, I thought, a bear might venture to the food cache box, sniff around, and then wander off in frustration.

I bid everyone good night and headed to my chosen sleeping site, 300 yards from camp. I slept like a rock, on my giant rock. It was a perfect night in the woods.

Back in camp, it was more like a living horror movie. With eyes the size of river stones, Zach stayed up all night, ears attuned to every breath of wind, rustle of leaf, and fart of mouse. Zach was a light packer as well, and he had brought a tarp to sleep under rather than a tent. He felt like a tasty bear treat in a thin wrapper. He nearly wore out the power switch on his flashlight, cutting arcs of light at every sinister shadow that reared up in the nearby bushes to attack. He knew the bear would come, and he would be ready.

At some point hours after sunset, he surrendered to the inevitability of his impending demise. Like a man on death row, he made peace with his fate and finally got near the point where he could drift off to a shallow nightmare-riddled sleep. He may have even closed his eyes. That's when the bear arrived.

I was not there, but witnesses to the event tell a story of a wild-eyed Zach appearing in their tent looking, for all the world, like a man tormented by demons. He was hissing about a bear in camp. Those same witnesses further report that they were kept awake for the rest of the night, as Zach and a reluctantly recruited John ran about the camp making strange loud gobbling noises and throwing rocks into every bush, fern, bramble and crevice to drive the vicious man-eater away from camp.

Apparently it was only the light of dawn that brought a cessation to this desperate life or death struggle between man and beast. Some testimony surfaced indicating that the bear in question was just slightly larger than a common house cat, but others take issue with this statement.

I returned to camp the next day, refreshed and relaxed, to find a crazy-haired, red-eyed Zach sitting on a rock with a rather tight-lipped expression. He was staring at the spot where most of the soup had fallen on the ground the night before.

"So how did you sleep?" he said without looking up. His tone indicated he wasn't really all that concerned with how I slept.

"Great," I said. I didn't know what had transpired in the night, and I was unaware until too late that this was not the best answer. A slight twitch played out near his left eye.

"That's wonderful," he said. "Just wonderful."

I could hear him muttering as we began disassembling camp.

"Let's all be careful we don't spill anything. Oh, we'll be careful we don't spill anything. I agree, let's be careful not to spill anything."

If Zach was not a fan of bear encounters prior to the trip, his experience that night did little to alleviate his disdain. He is, however, a person who is perpetually in a good mood. He's the guy you want with you on a long and arduous trudge because he has boundless energy and the ability to keep everybody laughing and in good spirits.

He says things like, "Come on, let's go crush this hike."

This was invaluable, because a long arduous trudge was exactly what we had ahead of us.

Despite very little sleep, by breakfast my accidental bear baiting antics were completely forgiven, though, I would find in years to come, not forgotten. Even while suffering from a notable lack of sleep, it was impossible for anyone not to be in a good mood, nestled as we were in the middle of the upper Stehekin Valley.

This area is a large, classically shaped glacier trough. The walls slope up steeply on both sides and are covered with a dense green carpet of fir trees. As we made our way down toward Lake Chelan, we moved in and out of timber stands and over crystal clear mountain streams. We wandered through meadows cleared by recent forest fires and erupting in a mosaic of flowers.

We passed by Bridge Creek, with its deep indigo pools and stark white rapids. If someone had realistically painted the scene, an art critic would have found the image too pretty to be believed. All the while, huge glacier-capped mountains peeked at us from the head of intersecting valleys.

It was on this portion of the hike that Zach made a comment that struck a chord with me. As we were moving through a wide-open glade with expansive views, he said, "You guys would love the White Mountains. They were the most beautiful part of the AT."

"As beautiful as this?" I said, gesturing with a sweeping arm.

He appeared thoughtful for a moment, and then said, "Yes."

I was stunned.

"Do they have glaciers there? Do they have sapphire blue rivers and streams?"

"No," he said, "it's a lot different than this, but it's still stunning. It's just beautiful in a different way. You have to see it to understand."

This was something that I pondered in silence for a long time as we headed down the trail. There were a lot of lakes in the world that I had dismissed outright, sight unseen. Perhaps they too were surrounded by scenery that was beautiful, just beautiful in a different way.

People around the world have such a wide variety of tastes and preferences. People in Scandinavia, for example, actually enjoy the taste of pickled herring. In my quest to find the world's greatest lake, I had been through Scandinavia. I had eaten pickled herring. The experience was so disagreeable I actually thought I might throw up. I sort of wanted to throw up, thinking the vomit might somehow get the taste of pickled herring out of my mouth. The memory of that experience still makes me queasy, yet somehow the people in Scandinavia eat that fishy, oily, sour muck like it's ice cream. As we wandered down the trail, I worried about just how subjective my conclusions about the greatest lake in the world would ultimately be.

We had to hustle through 14 miles of wilderness to make it in time to meet the shuttle bus that would ferry us back to Stehekin. I was sad not to be able to linger. The trip entailed many miles of not-so-perfectly maintained trails. We had to ford swampy backwaters of the Stehekin River, negotiate washouts and deadfalls, and we happened into another close encounter with the local wildlife.

Despite the copious use of a whistle to alert the resident creatures to our presence, my friend John turned a corner and basically tripped right on top of a pretty good-sized black bear. I was second in line, and when I turned the corner, the two of them were so close that it appeared John was hunched over the poor critter and engaging in an inappropriate act. He dismounted from this impromptu dalliance and careened back toward me at Olympic sprinter speed. He was able to yell the word "Bear!" no less than seven times in under a single second. The bear wandered off into the woods, clearly feeling violated by the encounter, and probably in need of therapy.

Four hours later, we arrived at the High Bridge Campground, where the shuttle bus was scheduled to pick us up. We even had time to dip in the river and wash away three days of dust and dirt before the bus arrived.

We caught the bus at the appointed hour and swapped tales with other hikers who had taken different routes in and around the Stehekin Valley. It was apparent that everyone was awestruck by the things they had seen. People were describing waterfalls and vistas they had encountered in a tone that a young child might use to describe a coveted Christmas present they had just received the morning before. I confess to being one of those people. I was totally swept up by the trip we had just taken.

We stopped at the Stehekin Bakery, and I bought enough food to last a week. It didn't last an hour. We made a second stop at Rainbow Falls, where we had a 20-minute break to walk out to the base of the thundering freefall of cold water and thick white mist. The 312-foot tumult that dropped from the gap between towering blocks of granite was actually causing the ground to vibrate, and the percussion seemed to resonate inside my ribcage.

Three layers of rainbows blazed in the dense spray. One of them made a complete circle, forming a glowing prismatic halo. I stared at the waterfall and thought to myself, not for the first time, that whenever I felt the Chelan region had shown its best profile, a new wonder presented itself that could steal your breath away.

We continued on to Stehekin and, at last, the welcome shores of Lake Chelan. We sat with our feet dangling in the lake and watched as tourists wandered about the Golden West Resort and National Park Complex. These weren't the throngs of tourists who mob the lodge at Old Faithful, or jockey for position at the bottom of Yosemite's waterfalls. These were sparse groups of scenery hunters and hikers, lounging next to the lake and enjoying the warm sunshine in one of the most remote towns in the lower 48 states. The communal sense of happiness was tangible, as if we were all sharing in a secret about which no one else knew.

I sat there with the cool lake water swirling around my legs and the bright sun warming my face, and I conjured up the images from what had been the highlight of my trip through the mountains. On the morning of our second day, when we awoke at sunrise high on the flanks of Sahalee Peak, my friend Scott and I had decided to make our bid for the summit. Just 2,000 feet above where we were camped, it seemed close enough to hit with a rock. We set out early and made our ascent up the glacier. We traversed through erratic crevasses to a large sweep of rock shale and, within an hour, we were at the base of the fin-like tower that was the summit proper.

The rock portion of Sahalee is not a technical climb, but it sits in the gray area of near-vertical scrambles where a person ought to put on a harness and rope, but most people don't. The actual straight-up portion of the climb is fairly short, maybe 40 feet, but the exposure is extreme, such that a slip would take a climber a thousand feet or more down to his death. Sadly, Sahalee has been the site of at least one climbing fatality.

We hit the ledge just below this section where a few climbers were opting to forgo the last section out of a healthy respect for gravity. Another group down-climbed, and then the summit was left alone, empty and beckoning. A few hair-raising moments later, I was reaching my hand up over the lip of the summit tower.

This was the penultimate moment for me. Having climbed a fair amount of peaks by that point, some of which I could see nearby in the clear blue morning, I really felt that this particular summit was special. I had probably dreamed of it almost every day that I had ever spent at Lake Chelan. When I would look uplake, I would fixate on the bend where the valley twists behind Slide Ridge and in front of the Navarre Peaks.

I knew this was a gateway of sorts to the high Cascades, a route to "the way through." Although Sahalee is not the highest mountain that drains into Chelan, and not even the highest peak above the Stehekin Valley, it had always, for me, represented the apex of the Stehekin Valley. If a snowflake falls on the top of Sahalee and then starts to slide toward Doubtful Lake, it will eventually melt and find its way down to Lake Chelan. This spot, at the very summit, represented the farthest distance from Lake Chelan that such a snowflake could fall and still drain back into the giant freshwater fjord.

If Chelan Butte is the guardian of the end of the lake, then Sahalee Peak and the Sahalee Glacier are the keepers of the headwaters. From my vantage point on top, I could take in nearly all the peaks that fanned out to the east capturing and then doling out the snows that feed Lake Chelan.

To the south, near eye level, were the purple-gray peaks that line the Ptarmigan traverse. This weeklong climber's trek that moves through the high rocks and glaciers is a world-renowned excursion for alpinists. It spans a remote section of mountains from Cascade Pass to the Suiattle River in the west while never straying far from the crest of the range. This is the main route to classic climbs up mountains like Dome Peak, Sinister Peak, the beautiful blue-hued Gunsight Peak, Spire Mountain, and more. I took them all in with a covetous eye, and dreamed of a day when I would attempt the traverse. Beyond them, the never-ending sea of mountains gleamed in the morning light.

In the other direction, stunning rock teeth jutted up toward the heavens. I could see the enormous Boston Glacier and the deep waterfall-drizzled scoop of the Horseshoe Basin. The peaks near Ross Lake in which the Beat Poets had held vigil so many years ago stretched all the way to Canada. The giant peaks that hemmed in Lake Chelan seemed to go on forever.

Picture a man standing on the top of a 3' x 3' rock with two- and three-thousand-foot cliffs dropping away on all sides. Now picture his head tilted upward toward the sky and both his arms stretched out to form a large *Y*. Next, picture this all filmed from a helicopter doing circles around this man so that the background of the most beautiful snowcapped mountain scenery in the world is rotating by behind him. Now set all of this to a triumphant symphony, maybe something like Aaron Copland's "Fanfare for the Common Man."

Finally, have the helicopter move away and have the camera pan out to show the vastness of the North Cascades, the gaping maw of the Stehekin River Valley and the reflective cobalt waters at the head of Lake Chelan. If you can do a good job of picturing this, and if you can conjure up the music loudly enough in your head, then you will have some idea how I felt standing atop Sahalee, my long-coveted summit in the Lake Chelan catchment. It was a moment I'll never forget.

When the boat arrived at the Stehekin landing, we boarded and began our trip home. Moving out to the middle of the lake, I looked at the broad valley of the upper lake basin. I was gazing across water and forest and snowcapped mountains.

I read once that Michelangelo was the first person to realize that distant mountains appear to have a blue color. He was one of the pioneering Renaissance painters who captured this in his paintings, his predecessors tending to paint the brown and gray colors that they believed to be true depictions rather than what they actually saw. Sitting on the back deck of the *Lady of the Lake II*, I was reminded of this as I took in the huge coliseum of mountains surrounding us. The entire picture was a study in varying shades of blue. The lake beyond the aft was a color that seemed impossible to exist in nature, something akin to a blue raspberry slushee, almost neon in its intensity.

Looking across the bay, it transformed across every hue of the blue spectrum. It was as if someone took the cover of a Tina Brooks jazz album and then attached all the individual squares together in a parade across the surface of the water. Finally, at the far side of the lake, a deep navy blue turned abruptly to jade green near the trees of the shoreline. Myriad evergreens, like myrtle green brush strokes, rose up the steep slopes. Higher still, they gave way to the barren rocks that were colored slate blue, just as Michelangelo would have depicted them. The more distant the mountains, the more purplish blue they appeared, until they gave way to the deep cerulean sphere of a near cloudless sky.

To add an exclamation point, brilliant white glaciers gleamed in the distance, and the thin whispering white tail of a waterfall tumbled straight down the cliff that rose up to the summit of Castle Peak. Already the larches were changing so that brilliant yellow and gold patches punctuated the mountainside. One word came to mind, and I couldn't help but say it out loud.

"Perfect."

The mountains along the shore moved slowly by as we headed downlake, past Purple Point and Domke Mountain. We cruised past Domke Falls as it spilled white plumes directly into the lake. We slowed at a natural mineral salt lick to watch mountain goats as they perched with ease on the steep cliffs of the lake.

We passed by Railroad Creek, the gateway to Bonanza Peak and the Glacier Peak Wilderness waiting to be explored. We floated down the empty shorelines of the wilderness for over an hour. We passed out of the Lucerne Basin and into the Wapato Basin and watched the rugged mountains melt into low rolling hills of dry grass, sparse pines, and finally the hypnotic straight lines of well tended agriculture. We watched the Columbia Plateau come into focus above and beyond the town of Chelan, with Chelan Butte proudly rising to the south. Then we docked at the landing.

My dad was waiting at the gangway and drove us back to his place, where we finished the day with running leaps off the end of the dock to soak our weary bones in the warm Indian-summer waters of Lake Chelan. I drifted there and stared back uplake toward the gap between Slide Ridge and the Navarre Peaks. I dreamed of the many more adventures that were waiting up beyond the narrows, on the long sweeping lake and in the high alpine terrain that surrounded it. I couldn't wait to go back.

The Greatest Lake in the World

My trip through the mountains from the west side through to Stehekin represented the culmination of my quest to determine what the greatest lake in the world was. When I returned to Chelan, I pulled out my notebook, which by this time was really three notebooks, and reviewed what I had learned.

In a perfect narrative, I would have visited every lake on my top ten list. I would also have found the perfect unassailable reasons why each one could not possibly be the greatest lake in the world. Without indicting any lakes, I can say that some of the great ones were fairly polluted, and some were plagued by very high humidity and haze during the best summer months. Some were too crowded, and some didn't have lake monsters. Others were too small, or too cold, or not quite as scenic as accounts had led us to believe.

It would be tedious to tell every story about every lake, large or small, that we did visit, but after nearly three years we had seen a staggering amount.

On the 200-year-old advice of Percy Bysshe Shelley, we had visited the lakes of Ireland and the Arbutus Islands and got lost in the back roads of Killarney.

We had an epic battle to protect our lunch from howler monkeys on the shores of a jungle lake near the border of Belize and Guatemala. We tried to go explore a lake deeper in Guatemala, but the road was shut down by bandits, honest to goodness bandits who were targeting American travelers, so we never made it to our destination. Sitting in the thick oppressive 400-degree heat and humidity of the jungle, fighting mutant mosquitoes, I was confident that we were probably not missing the greatest lake in the world, no matter how beautiful Aldous Huxley declared it to be.

We chartered a seaplane and loaded up collapsible kayaks and headed to Friel Lake in a remote part of British Columbia. We stayed two nights there and spent hours battling floating logjams trying to get to the top of a waterfall that spilled 1,200 feet down out of the lake into a fjord. When we finally got there, Amy nearly fell off the dang thing.

We returned to Lake Como again and gave it a second review along with some of the other Italian lakes in the region. Mark and I did a 1,600-foot vertical wall climb to visit a lake in the Dolomites.

We toured up and down the western United States and visited lakes in Glacier National Park and Yellowstone National Park. We went to Crater Lake and Lake Tahoe. To see an endorheic basin lake, we went to the Great Salt Lakes. We visited lakes in the United Kingdom, but due to a scheduling conflict, I never made it to Loch Ness.

We reviewed lakes in South America and discarded them. I wanted to see Lake Wakatipu in New Zealand, but my parents got there first and reported back that it would not unseat Lake Chelan. I considered them a trusted source.

One of my great failings was that I never made it to see Lake Baikal. It is a truly extraordinary lake of the planet, but the more I refined my criteria, and the more I considered the romance of a lake that I was trying to capture, the less likely I felt that what I was looking for would be found in Siberia.

Lake Baikal can often be partially covered in ice until May. It is not uncommon for large chunks of ice to be floating in the lake all the way into July. In some years, the lake can get up to 68 degrees at the southern end, but that happens only in the shallow parts of some bays. In some years it does not get that warm. The season for frolicking in the lake is very short, and not really ideal. I felt this fact by itself was enough to disqualify the mighty lake from being a contender for the greatest lake in the world. I still intend to go there, and if it turns out I'm wrong, I will write a retraction and wear a Russian fox fur hat for a full summer at the lake.

Likewise, Lake O'Higgins/San Martin in the Andes was just too cold. With a high temperature of only 60 degrees, it simply was not a lake that could vie for the title. I discarded it from afar as well.

Along with our various friends, we had now traveled over 100,000 miles to look at different lakes. The things we had seen and done were experiences I will never forget. The question remained, however. Had I determined the greatest lake in the world?

It would be a crime against nature to come up with a list of shortcomings for such beautiful lakes as Lake Como, or Flathead Lake, or Lake Tahoe, or Lago de Atitlán, or the lakes of Patagonia. It also seems like a sure way to invite death threats or endure physical violence. If I learned anything on my trip, it's that people are passionate about their favorite lakes. Also, as my friend Zach had said, lots of places can be beautiful, just beautiful in a different way.

What I can say is that back home I felt more enchanted by Lake Chelan than ever. She was a gem among gems. Lake Chelan was, without question, a world-class lake. After all of my observations, what I felt was the most seductive aspect of this particular body of water—and what I failed to find in any other part of the world—was the marriage of so many diverse attributes.

Within the Wapato glacier basin was a crystal blue warm-water lake that nestled into a mosaic of fruit-laden hillsides. It was a region that exemplified a Rockwellian vignette of American small town life. Lower Lake Chelan was a lake lover's utopia set in a quiet picturesque corner of the country. Taken as a whole, the area could best be described as idyllic, encompassing everything one would want in a lake retreat or a country getaway, or perhaps a quieter slower life than can be afforded in the cities.

This was just the tail end of the lake. The mighty Lucerne Basin represented a more awesome depiction of nature's power. It was the incredible grandeur of the great outdoors, dressed to the nines, stretching through rugged untouched mountains with beauty rivaling any location in the world. The lake, I felt, was the amalgamation of still glassy reflections, powerful storms, waterfalls, and shifting shades of color in deep clear water. It was everything that a lake could hope to be.

Borrowing words from early pioneer Mrs. Ben F Smith, it was like "an oasis in the desert." Borrowing words from Gary Snyder, it was "a chaos of perfection." Borrowing words from my youngest sister Kim, it was "heaven on earth."

Amy and I sat on the patio of Tsillan Cellars winery. It was one of those perfect late fall afternoons where the light angled below brilliant skies, bathing the mountains in subtle pink pastels. The water shuffled every color of radiant blue around the surface with the rolling of calm gentle waves. The bright red-orange gash of Slide Ridge towered above the lake, and billowy rose-colored clouds erupted from summit to sky like the background of a Maxfield Parrish painting.

It was a warm day, and the air was thick with the sweet earthy smell of the newly crushed grapes. On the nearby hillsides, a cherry orchard was adorned in blazing red leaves. Above it, in the distance, Stormy Mountain had a dusting of snow on the summit.

"Winter is almost here," I said to Amy.

"Yes," she said.

"This year Mark and I are going to go helicopter skiing on Stormy Mountain."

"That's a great idea," she said. "Let me know if you want me to help schedule it."

I studied her profile, looking for the slightest hint of sarcasm. There was none.

She glanced down at my notebook sitting on the table.

"Did you succeed?"

"In what?"

"Were you able to prove that Lake Chelan is the best lake in the world?"

I took a sip of pale, sweet wine and gazed out at the lake. I reflected on my endeavor. I had conducted dozens of interviews, and explored myriad places. I had dropped myself, voyeur-like, into the lives of the first settlers and read every account of theirs that I was able to put my hands on, trying to get to the heart and soul of Lake Chelan, and yet, it escaped me. The lake and the valley that holds it meant such different things to different people. Still, I had so thoroughly enjoyed doing the research and trying to establish Chelan as the paragon of all lakes that, in the end, it really didn't matter if I succeeded. I wondered why I ever thought that it had. The effort had been an end unto itself.

I turned to Amy. "You know, I think I might write a book about the Cascade Mountains."

She looked at me with her incredible poker face. How she masks her excitement so well, I may never understand.

"We'll probably need to go to Tibet," I said.

Without a word, she sipped her wine and gazed out across the vines. I opened up my notebook. "Mountain Project—Day One," I wrote, and then started making notes. I paused every once in a while to watch as the late evening sun sparkled on the surface of the greatest lake in the world.

Afterword

In the middle of the book, I took a dig at the Great Slave Lake, and that is unfair, particularly since I never actually went there. When I started sharing the manuscript, the feedback from some of my Canadian friends regarding the Great Slave Lake was very passionate. It seems you can't judge a lake only from the air.

Growing up in western Washington and going to high school in Seattle, it was not uncommon for me and my friends to make the trip up north across the border. From my excursions up there, I learned Canadians can fight.

I never had much experience with hockey, so I was 18, outside a bar in White Rock, when I had my first encounter with a brawling technique called "shirting." This is an effective way to immobilize your opponent during a scuffle. In that instance, I was the opponent.

That's not to say I didn't get a few punches in, but no one could say that I won that fight. As I recall, none of my friends did say I won that fight. Those kids raised on the rink can brawl. So, with that in mind, in the interest of not offending any Canadians: the Great Slave Lake is by most accounts pretty spectacular. I have made it a point to go visit there some day.

A few technical notes: There is a slight disagreement about the actual meaning of the word Chelan. Almost all accounts indicate that it means "deep water," but some sources also indicate that it could mean deep notch, or deep fast moving water, or even just rushing water, or bubbling water. This could possibly be in reference to the Chelan River, which moves so quickly through the gorge that it is a seething bubbling froth at Chelan Falls. To further add credence to this claim, there is a reference to the geyser that erupted below Chelan after the earthquake of 1872, and in this reference the local Native Americans referred to the geyser as a Tsillane.

By the majority of accounts, Chelan means deep water. Even if this is not assuredly accurate, it has become the accepted and favored interpretation. Perhaps the words for both deep water and for bubbling water were similar and therein lies the discrepancy, but we may never know. Most people I spoke to, including Native Americans of the region, seem to prefer the translation "deep water."

Likewise, the word Stehekin is said to mean "the way through." There are some accounts that say it might actually mean rough water. Again, the way through seems to be the preferred translation, particularly among those who live there. It may be a simple case of the word Stehekin originally meaning rough water, but over time, as it was the name of the major route through the mountains, it became synonymous with the meaning of the way through. It is very difficult to trace word origins and word evolutions without the luxury of written records of the language. Translations are sometimes as much art as science.

In the book, I credit William Sanders and Henry Domke with being the first European settlers in the valley. There are some accounts that indicate Ignatius Navarre and his wife were the first to settle there. In all events, it appears that the timing of all of their settlement was almost concurrent, possibly sometime in the spring of the same year.

The geology referenced in the book comes from a number of sources and from discussions with geologists. Geology is, however, largely based on theory, and today's theory can frequently become tomorrow's archaic belief. As such, there are some variations in opinion about the formation of the mountains and the lake itself. In writing this book, I tried to rely on generally accepted ideas. Where opinions differed, I opted for the more popular versions of events. There is hard science to back up most of these theories, but there will always remain an element of conjecture.

I regret not being able to discuss more of the history of the families in the valley, and to incorporate more information on some of the longstanding businesses in the region. I selected a few because I was familiar with them, oftentimes by happenstance. There are so many interesting families and incredible histories that it would simply be impossible to detail all of them. Perhaps there is a whole other book about that, yet to be written.

I made a quip about the Quien Sabe glacier in this book. Later, while doing further research, I found the identical quip was penned by Ira Spring in his fantastic book *High Rocks and Glaciers*. Mr. Spring "beat me to the punch," as the saying goes. He and his brother Ben were pioneers in photographing the mountains of the Cascades. The creation of the North Cascades National Park is due, in no small part, to their efforts to document in pictures and demonstrate to the world the magnificent nature of the wilderness that was to be preserved.

I would highly recommend to anyone with a passion or even an interest in the Cascade Mountains that they procure a copy of this book. If a picture is worth a thousand words, then the book can be equated to many volumes of any expository that could be written about this incredible mountain range.

Also, with regard to the North Cascades, the extraordinary book *Range of Glaciers* by Fred Beckey is an invaluable read to anyone interested in the history of the area. Fred Beckey is a legend to all who love climbing, and all those who love the North Cascades. He pioneered so many routes up the mountains that he is, himself, a major character in the historical accounts of the region. His book is a must read, as is another of his books, *The Challenge of the North Cascades.*

Additional recommended reading is *The Stehekin We Remember* by the Buckner sisters, *Mountain Air* by Sandy K. Nelson Bryant, and *Stehekin: A Valley in Time*, by Grant McConnell. I also highly recommend a fantastic and meticulously researched book by John Suiter entitled

Poets on the Peaks.

A great historical summary of the area is found in the book *Images of America: Lake Chelan Valley,* written by Kristen J. Gregg and the Lake Chelan Historical Society. Another fantastic read is the publication *North Cascades: The Story Behind the Scenery*, by Saul Weisberg.

Acknowledgments

Acknowledgments must be made to the Chelan Historical Society. It was with great foresight that James Lindston began the process of preserving artifacts, stories, and accounts of the history of the Chelan Valley. He and his wife, along with a host of other civic-minded supporters, began the process of creating the Chelan Museum and the Historical Society in 1969. The museum, the society, and the fascinating volumes of historical notes are a priceless link to the past and represent an amazing treasure for all those who hold the Chelan area dear. Great thanks are owed to the current members of the society who hold all these treasures in safekeeping.

I have to express appreciation to Mike and Mary Sherer for support and insight with this book and my other various schemes and projects in the Chelan Valley.

Thanks are also due to Erin Baebler. She was a white knight who swooped in with invaluable editing assistance. Her help was very much appreciated.

Also thanks to Marcus Corder and the folks at Gray Dog Press. I had no idea how collaborative the book-making process is, and they were a wonderful group of collaborators.

Special thanks are due to my Uncle John and Aunt Barb who put up with me on my childhood summer outings to Wallace Lake. They acquainted me with the joys of lake living at an early age. For that I am forever grateful.

Also, a special thanks to my parents, Pat and Barb. They made Lake Chelan a part of the lives of all their six children and their double-digit (and still growing) number of grandchildren. This has been, and continues to be, the catalyst for many of our fondest memories.

To Amy, for whom this book is dedicated, thanks for your patience and your sense of humor.

Finally, to my crew of quirky characters, friends and family alike, who are chronicled in this book, thanks for letting me draw upon our adventures together. I look forward to many more in the future. Beware! You never know when I'm taking notes.

Glossary

biffy: A Canadian term for an outhouse. On hot days, the smell from a typical biffy could make a maggot wretch.

Bonanza Peak: The highest non-volcanic mountain in the Cascades, and the highest mountain that drains into Lake Chelan.

Cascade Mountains: Possibly the greatest mountains in the world.

Chelan: *See* pages 1 through this page.

cliff jumping: A dangerous act of flinging oneself off of a high precipice, preferably over water. Cliff jumping should never be attempted by anyone unless they have taken proper steps to ensure that they are not jumping from my property, because I have very crappy insurance.

Deep Water Extreme: Possible working title for the screenplay adaptation of this book. The film rights are still available. Call me, we'll talk.

ECLIPS: Extremely Complicated Life-altering Impending Project Scale. Any large project that, from the onset, seems to be manageable and maybe even fun. In reality, it totally overwhelms your life and crushes your soul, leaving you a worn-out, wasted, mere shell of your former self. The scale runs from 1 to 5. A 1 could be doing your taxes, especially if you have to calculate original issue discount. A 5 usually involves working with government agencies and procuring permits, hence the crushed soul.

Hot Bikini Babes on a Lake: Another possible working title for the screen adaptation of this book. Seriously, call me.

Lake Chelan: Arguably the greatest lake in the world.

Lake Titicaca: I can't even write the name without giggling.

Lake Union: A small lake in downtown Seattle that is not the greatest lake in the world, but it might be one of the coolest lakes. I'm including it here in the glossary of terms, really more as just a shout out: "Yo, Lake Union—we love ya!"

leeches: Mindless parasitic worms with no real function other than to bleed you dry.

Manson: A small unincorporated town about eight miles uplake on the north shore of Lake Chelan. It bills itself as the village on the bay and might possibly be the greatest undiscovered gem of a town in all of America.

Sahalee Peak: A prominent, glaciated peak, part of the Boston Massif, that is at the extreme end of the Chelan drainage system. The peak looks over the Pelton Basin and the Stehekin River Valley on one side, and the Boston Basin on the other.

septic system: An extremely complicated waste deposal mechanism that also acts as a wormhole in space that can somehow cause random things like balloons, small toys, and kite string to materialize out of nowhere and lodge in the grinder pump. This is the only explanation, because signs at every toilet clearly state not to flush anything down except for toilet paper. Anything means anything, people. Show some mercy.

SHABAM: Simulated Human Automatic Bat Avoidance Maneuver. The effect of a fake bat dangling from a fishing pole, used expressly to deceive a person into believing they are under attack by a bat. Possibly the greatest scientific tool invented in the 21st century.

Stehekin: An Indian word that means "the way through" or possibly "rough water." It is the name of the town at the head of the lake, accessible only by hiking, boating, or by floatplane. The town has about 80 year-round residents. Also the name of the largest river that flows into Lake Chelan at the top of the lake.

technology: Any cool gadget or gizmo that is invented exactly two years after it would have been useful for me.

toilet: A convenient indoor plumbing fixture that makes life wonderful and only clogs or breaks down twice a year. This would not be much of a problem, unless you happen to own 27 of them.

US Congress: *See* leeches.

vacation rental business: A non-profit organization that allows people to take up residence for a short period of time in a fun place that is not their home. Unfortunately, it is not non-profit by choice.

Zell am See: I wanted the glossary to be a little longer and this started with the letter z. You can read more about Zell am See in the book if you want. Better yet, your friends and family can read all about it, because this book makes a wonderful gift!

Notes and References

1. Lake Chelan Historical Society. *History Notes* 1(1).

2. Ruby, Robert H., and John A. Brown. 1996. *Indians of the Pacific Northwest.* Norman, OK: University of Oklahoma Press.

3. Giles, Harry F. *The Beauties of the State of Washington, A Book for Tourists.* [Reprinted as part of the licensing agreement of Project Gutenberg. Ebook #30139.]

4. Laws, Edward A. 2000. *Aquatic Pollution: An Introductory Text, 3rd edition.* New York: Wiley.

5. Washington State Department of Ecology. "Lake Chelan—Chelan County." http://www.ecy.wa.gov/programs/eap/lakes/wq/docs/chelan.pdf. [Keith S. Marney volunteered his time to monitor the lake in 1990.]

6. Kendra, Will, and Lynn Singleton. January 1987. *Morphometry of Lake Chelan.* http://www.ecy.wa.gov/biblio/871.html.

7. Nasmith, Hugh. 1962. *Late glacial history and surficial deposits of the Okanagan Valley, British Columbia, Victoria, BC.* Canada: BC Ministry of Energy, Mines and Petroleum Resources.

8. There are at least three theories related to the glaciers in Lake Chelan. One involves a collision of the glaciers somewhere up the lake from Wapato Point. Another theory states that the two glaciers never met, and that the alpine glacier stopped further uplake near the narrows. A final theory is that, at some point, the alpine glacier pushed all the way to the Columbia River Valley where it impacted against the Columbia Lobe and the sediment it brought down actually became the earthen dam that suspends Lake Chelan above the Columbia Valley.

9. DeGrey, Laura, and Paul K. Link. "Lake Missoula Floods." http://geology.isu.edu/Digital_Geology_Idaho/Module13/mod13.htm.

10. Lake Chelan Historical Society. 1974. *History Notes* 2(1).

11. Lake Chelan Historical Society. 1982. *History Notes* 7(1) (Spring).

12. Twelve species of bats are thought to inhabit the North Cascades. Eight were documented during a study by National Park Service Biologists. http://www.nps.gov/noca/naturescience/mammals.htm.

13. Luxenberg, Gretchen A. 1986. *Historic Resource Study: North Cascade National Park.* Seattle: National Park Service.

14. Casan, Daniel Jack. 1995. *The Smithsonian Guides to Natural America: The Pacific Northwest.* New York: Random House.

15. McPhee, John. 1980. *Encounters with the Archdruid.* New York: Farrrar, Strauss and Giroux.

16. Kerouac, Jack. 1965. *Desolation Angels.* New York: Coward-McCann.

17. Information from the Tacoma Public Library Washington Place Names database. http://search.tacomapubliclibrary.org/wanames/wpnv2.asp.

18. Beckey, Fred. 2003. *Range of Glaciers.* Portland, OR: Oregon Historical Society Press.

Author John Fahey

Like many people from the Pacific Northwest, John Fahey fell in love with Lake Chelan from an early age. He has spent hundreds of hours exploring the mountains, streams, rivers and valleys of the Chelan Basin. It is from these adventures that he came up with the notion that Lake Chelan might be the greatest lake in the world. In a moment of questionable sanity, he set out to prove it.

He is currently working on his next book, in which Lake Chelan also features prominently. He divides his time between Lake Chelan, where he and his wife own and operate a vacation rental business, and Lake Union in Seattle, where he works in the financial industry managing a bond portfolio.

Visit his website at: greatestlakeintheworld.com